THE
FRENCH OCCUPATION
OF THE
CHAMPLAIN VALLEY
FROM 1609 TO 1759

PHOTOGRAPH OF A SCALE-MODEL OF FORT ST. FREDERIC, MADE FROM THE ORIGINAL PLANS BY MR. A. S. HOPKINS, STATE CONSERVATION DEPARTMENT, ALBANY, N. Y.

The French Occupation of the Champlain Valley from 1609 to 1759

by

Guy Omeron Coolidge

Biographical Index Included

PURPLE MOUNTAIN PRESS
Fleischmanns, New York

The French Occupation of the Champlain Valley from 1609 to 1759
by Guy Omeron Coolidge

First paperback edition 1999

The first edition of this title (1979) was reprinted from the
Proceedings of the Vermont Historical Society
New Series, Vol. VI, No. 3, 1938

This reprint is based on the second edition (1989) to which a
biographical index was added. The index was completed by the
author in 1940 but was not included in the first edition.

Published by Purple Mountain Press, Ltd.
1060 Main Street, P.O. Box E3
Fleischmanns, New York 12430-0378 USA

914-254-4062
914-254-4476 (fax)
Purple@catskill.net
http://www.catskill.net/purple

Library of Congress Cataloging-in-Publication Data

Coolidge, Guy Omeron.
    The French occupation of the Champlain Valley from 1609 to 1759 /
by Guy Omeron Coolidge. -- 1st paperback ed.
        p.   cm.
    Originally published : 2nd ed. Mamaroneck, N.Y. : Harbor Hill
Books, 1989.
    Includes bibliographical references and index.
    ISBN 0-916346-68-4 (acid-free paper)
    1. Champlain Valley- -History.   2. French- -Champlain Valley-
-History.   I. Title.
F127.C6C725   1999
973.2- -dc21   99-18316
                                                                                        CIP

On the cover:
Detail of a romanticized painting of Samuel de Champlain's 1609 voy-
age to the Lake that would bear his name.
(National Archives of Canada, Neg. no. C6163)

Manufactured in the United States of America.

Printed on acid-free paper.

TABLE OF CONTENTS

THE FRENCH OCCUPATION OF THE CHAMPLAIN VALLEY FROM

1609 to 1759

By Guy Omeron Coolidge

With this study I have attempted to fill a gap in the history of Vermont. For many years the story of the French dominion over lands now forming part of Vermont has remained hidden. Occasionally, a military engagement or a vague discussion of a mist-enshrouded seigniorial grant received a paragraph or two in printed history; but the connected account of the plan, the struggle to realize that plan, the life-stories of the personalities who conceived and executed that plan, and the final tragic moments experienced by the French colonists under that plan, have never been adequately related. From an enormous mass of correspondence, and from a great number of isolated references in published works, I have tried to resurrect the story of one hundred and fifty years of effort—a struggle marked by frequent indifference on the part of the Mother-Country, constant discouragement through the pettiness and self-interest of the official world, but ennobled by deeds of shining glory and unselfish sacrifice, heroic courage in the face of overwhelming odds and sublime examples of whole-hearted devotion to principles and ideals of the highest. It is the story of the attempt by a woefully small group of persevering patriots to establish their civilization in a wilderness, to erect an enduring structure representative of French culture in the New World.

I wish to thank many friends who have given me valuable aid—the gift of their time, suggestions, and unfailing interest has been a constant source of encouragement. Among them are Mr. Thomas Frederick Longeran of the Crown Point Museum, Captain Lorenzo Frederick Hagglund of Port Washington, Long Island, New York, the Reverend Fathers of St. Edmund of St. Michael's College at Winooski, Vermont, Mr. A. S. Hopkins of the New York Conservation Department of Albany, and Miss Mary E. McKeogh of Rutland. Miss Leila A. McNeil of the Egbert Starr Library of Middlebury College, Miss Cynthia M. Gorton of the Rutland Free Library, Miss Helen M. Shattuck of the Billings Library of the University of Vermont, and Miss Agnes K. Lawson of the Vermont Historical Library at Montpelier have been very helpful in arranging for material to be placed at my service. The officials of the New York State Library at Albany, the Municipal Library at Montreal, the Bibliothèque Nationale, the Archives de la Marine and the Bibliothèque Mazarine at Paris, the Archives de Québec and the Archives Bureau of the Secretary of State at Ottawa have been very kind in offering the use of their facilities.

I should make special mention of my indebtedness to the Honorable Millard F. Barnes of Chimney Point, Vermont, and also to one who prefers to remain unnamed, but whose constant aid and inspiring confidence have brought this study into its present form.

G. O. C.

CHAPTER I. *The Beginning*

ON July 4, 1609, Samuel de Champlain saw for the first time the great lake which bears his name to-day. He was the first man of the white race known to have seen the waters of this great "lost sea" and its shores.

The lake region of which Champlain became the first explorer was a wilderness. Seventy-four years before, Jacques Cartier of St. Malo had climbed the heights of Mount Royal (thus he named it) at Hochelaga with Donnacona, the friendly Algonquin chief, who pointed out to him the country toward the south, speaking of rivers, "seas," lakes, and the route by which one could penetrate as far as the lands of the Iroquois, sworn enemies of the Algonquin race.[1] Although Cartier was the first to see the mountains of Vermont, it was from such a distance that he could have had no conception of the importance and beauty of the region. It was the arrival of Champlain which raised the veil of mystery covering this "wilderness" between the country of the Iroquois and New France.

Samuel de Champlain was then forty-two years old; he had already made many voyages of exploration to the borderlands of civilization and journeys into the wilderness beyond—in Mexico, in Panama between 1599 and 1601 (he had then been the first to conceive the advantages of a canal between the two oceans), and with the Sieur de Monts in Acadia in 1604 at the founding of Port Royal. From 1604 to 1606 he explored the Atlantic coast from Port Royal to Cape Cod. A born explorer and cartographer, from all his voyages he brought back maps (unusually accurate for the period) of the regions which he had visited as well as detailed journals of his experiences.

Upheld by an unshakable faith in the mission which he wished to accomplish, that of extending the frontiers of New France, Champlain listened to the plans of the Algonquin chiefs who proposed to him an expedition into the Iroquois country. As early as 1608, the citadel of Quebec was taking form before the eyes of the Indians. They began to realize that the French had come to stay and that their aid was necessary in carrying on the struggle against the Iroquois.

In the course of preceding centuries the Iroquois had driven the Algonquins from the region known to-day as Vermont. In 1609, it was a wilderness—virgin forests, rivers and lakes which heard only the gentle swish of the bark canoe of the hunter—with not a single inhabitant in the entire valley except during hunting seasons. Constantly, Algonquin bands met Iroquois hunting parties; the Iroquois, being better fighters, almost always had the upper hand. The Algonquin chiefs came to Quebec to ask the aid of the French against their common enemy, recalling to Champlain's memory the alliance contracted by the French in 1603 with the Algonquins of Tadoussac.[2]

Champlain, convinced that Algonquin friendship would be of invaluable assistance to the new-born colony, gave ear to their plans;

1. Hemenway: *Vermont Gazetteer*, II, p. 89. Article, "Franklin County," by George F. Houghton.
2. Sedgewick: *Samuel de Champlain*, p. 24.

they would go to attack the Iroquois in their own country, dealing the death blow to Iroquois claims to this great hunting-ground which from time immemorial had belonged to the Algonquins. The governor of Quebec could not foresee the effect upon the Iroquois of this little venture with the Algonquins, undertaken through friendship as much as a desire for exploration in the name of the King of France; otherwise, he would have hesitated long before embarking upon an adventure from which incessant warfare was to result. Champlain left Quebec, June 8, 1609, with a party of forty-nine men, including the pilot La Route and Des Marets and accompanied by a few Indians.[3]

At Isle St. Eloi he met 300 Algonquin warriors, curious to know something of the white man's mode of life. These red men bluntly refused to continue the expedition before visiting one of the French villages. Champlain was obliged to postpone his journey and return with them to Quebec in order to show them a French settlement.

The actual beginning of the expedition took place on the eighteenth of June.[4] They took eight days to reach the River of the Iroquois (since called successively the Sorel, the Chambly, and the Richelieu). While awaiting the arrival of a band of his Indian allies, Champlain explored the lands near the mouth of the river. At the first falls, although the Algonquins had assured him that the route was open and that one could go by boat to the lake, he perceived that nothing of the sort was true. When the Indians arrived, quarrels ensued, and three-quarters of them went off to their homes. Champlain, faithful to his promise to see "this great lake full of beautiful islands and a great extent of fine country on the shores of the lake," sent back the French with the exception of two volunteers, Chauvin and Dupont,[5] and continued on his way. On July 3, the little party of three whites and about sixty Indians camped at the outlet and the next day embarked upon the waters of the lake.

Champlain judged from information given by the Algonquins, that the lake was between fifty and sixty leagues in length—a fair estimate since the French league was two and one-half miles. He passed four beautiful islands, Isle La Motte, Long Island, Grand Isle, and Val-

3. *Voyages de Samuel de Champlain*, I, p. 181. Constantin-Weyer, *Champlain*, p. 80.

4. *Voyages de Samuel de Champlain*, I, p. 181.

5. Coolidge and Mansfield: *History and Description of New England;* "Vermont," p. 705.

cour, which had formerly been inhabited by Indians (as were also the banks of the River of the Iroquois) but which had been abandoned since the beginning of the war between the Iroquois and the Algonquins, a century before. In his *Voyages* Champlain speaks of several rivers which empty into the lake, lined with beautiful trees of species known in France; of the great number of wild grape vines, the finest that he had ever seen in New France; of chestnut trees, which he had seen nowhere on this continent except on the shores of this lake; of an abundance of fish and game. Passing along the west shore, he saw the Green Mountain—very high mountains at some fifteen leagues to the east, covered with "snow." (Snow in the month of July? Champlain must have been mistaken; the white spots were doubtless outcroppings of marble similar to the White Rocks near Wallingford.) "And other mountains were soon discovered south upon the west side of the Lake," not less high than the first and without snow. It was in that direction, said the Algonquins, that their enemies were to be found; one would have to "carry" around a waterfall and cross another lake three or four leagues long (Lake St. Sacrement, now Lake George); at the end of this lake there would be a portage of four leagues before reaching a river (the Hudson)—a journey of two full days in boats.

From this moment on, being no more than two or three days' distant from the Iroquois country, Champlain and his warriors rested during the day, traveling only at night. July 29, having embarked at twilight, they rowed along carefully and without noise. At ten o'clock, "at the end of a cape which advances into the lake from the west coast," they met the Iroquois ready to engage in battle. The two parties withdrew in common accord—the Iroquois toward the point, the Algonquins toward the lake—in order to prepare for the battle on the morrow. The Iroquois, with about 200 warriors, barricaded themselves in an entrenched camp; the Algonquins, their three French allies hidden for the moment in the boats, landed before the camp. The Iroquois led by their three chiefs advanced from the camp "slowly and gravely," which action greatly pleased the old soldier in Champlain. The moment of attack arrived. At a signal given by the chief of the Algonquins, Champlain appeared and his Indian allies separated to form a lane through which he advanced. He came forward, his armor gleaming, his arquebus in position, loaded with four bullets. He fired. One Iroquois chief and two warriors standing beside him fell dead. The arrows darkened the air in quick reply, but a shot fired by one of Champlain's companions completed the rout; the Iroquois, disconcerted by this sudden and terrifying destruction, whirled and fled in disorder. Victory remained with Champlain and his allies, but it was disastrous in its results because of the hatred for the French awakened in the breasts of the savage Iroquois.

This battle took place, Champlain states, at a cape whose latitude was forty-three degrees and some minutes, which information locates the position between Ticonderoga and a point just north of Crown Point. One may have faith in the statement of Champlain, for he was an experienced cartographer—author of accurate maps of the regions which he explored. I believe, therefore, that I am justified in accepting the authority of Champlain himself as to the site of the first French battlefield in the valley. In spite of the historians who insistently affirm that Ticonderoga was the location of the battlefield, the statement of Champlain quoted above—"at the end of a cape . . . etc.," a minute study of maps, and a personal survey of the ground convince me that Crown Point is the site of the battlefield.[6]

During the voyage from the foot of the lake to the battlefield, Champlain and his warriors had spent twenty-one or twenty-two days on the lake: what did they do during those three weeks? In his *Voyages* he speaks at length of the shores of the lake. His encampments, it appears, were chosen along the rivers which empty into the lake and at some distance from their mouths, for fear of being surprised by the enemy. It is probable that he followed the west shore as far as Cumberland Head, crossed the lake to the southern point of Grand Isle, and landed on the east shore at Colchester Point ("Windmill Point," on the first English map of this region, drawn up after 1760), a base from which to explore the

6. It is of interest to read on this question: Parkman: *Pioneers of New France.* Article by Thomas H. Canfield in Hemenway: *Vermont Gazetteer,* I, pp. 656-708. "Local History," signed "J.S." in the *Vergennes Citizen,* Dec. 25, 1857. Article by Dr. Bixby, in Reid: *Lake George and Lake Champlain,* pp. 20, *et seq.* The latitude of Ticonderoga being 43 degrees and 50 minutes, and that of Crown Point 43 degrees and 55 minutes, the question can only be settled by following the description of the ground given by Champlain. As for the latitude, Champlain, having only an astrolabe at his disposal and being hurried by the presence of the enemy, did not give us the exact minute. The study of Champlain's narrative and the examination of the ground can lead to no other conclusion than this—Crown Point is the only cape which fits his description.

"Ouynouski" (Winooski to-day). A little to the north was the "Riviere à la Mouette," (meaning sea-gull, written "Mouelle" on a map by Charlevoix in 1744, the engraver forgetting to cross the t's; to-day the name is written "Lamoille"). Cumberland Head, or perhaps Valcour Island, is certainly the limit of his advance along the west shore as he would have avoided surprise attacks by crossing the lake to follow the east shore. He speaks also of the mountains to the west (the Adirondacks) whose cliffs rise abruptly from the water's edge; one can only see them from the east shore. Finally, Champlain mentions great chestnut trees on the shore, the only ones which he has seen since his first voyage to New France.[7] The only spot where chestnut trees have been found which could date from the time of Champlain, is on the left bank of the Winooski River.[8] According to the map drawn up by Champlain, and from a careful study of his *Voyages,* it is evident that he visited and examined, as much as time permitted, the shores of this "grandicime lac" from St. Johns to the battlefield at Crown Point.

After the battle, Champlain, his Algonquin allies and their Iroquois prisoners crossed the lake, only a few hundred yards wide at this place. At Chimney Point, on the shore opposite the battlefield, he gave his name to the "grandicime lac." Later in the day, they started toward the St. Lawrence. Some ten miles from Chimney Point at the mouth of Otter Creek (in my opinion) they stopped to spend the night and to subject the prisoners to excruciating torture. Champlain refused to take part, protested against savage brutality, and even cut short the suffering of one victim by a quick shot from his arquebus. The next day, they resumed the return to Canada by a much swifter voyage than that of the discovery, fearing pursuit by the Iroquois. At the falls of Chambly, the Algonquins went away to their homes; Champlain and his companions, at a speed of thirty leagues a day continued toward Quebec, without the slightest idea of the hatred against the French aroused in the Iroquois by this expedition—an active hatred which was to endure until the conquest of Canada by the English in 1760.

7. *Voyages de Samuel de Champlain,* II, p. 195. Murray: *Lake Champlain and Its Shores,* pp. 204-214.

8. Hemenway: *Vermont Gazetteer,* I, p. 659. Here is given the result of research made on this subject by President Torrey of the University of Vermont and by Mr. Charles Adams who examined the shores of the lake about 1860. They discovered stumps of chestnut trees 300 years old in a clearing at this spot and nowhere else.

Champlain did not realize the importance of his discovery. He noted the fertility of the valley of the lake, especially of the eastern shore; he appreciated the value of direct communication by this route with the country of the Iroquois; perhaps he vaguely foresaw French colonization of this region. Certainly he had no idea of the extent of the territory which France could claim by right of his discovery. For 150 years the French did their best to establish their sovereignty over the valley of Lake Champlain even to the sources of the rivers which mingle their waters with those of the lake. The map above shows quite clearly the limits of the French claims.

At first, New France included within its limits, at least in theory, the whole country of the Iroquois, which placed the southern frontier below the Mohawk River. Later, these claims were given up, and the frontier was established at the Hudson River near Glens Falls, following the river to its sources, thence by the most direct line to the St. Lawrence. This southern frontier always remained rather indefinite; in general, it marked the region where the French and English claims overlapped. The unsettled question of the frontier caused struggles, sometimes diplomatic but more often military, between the two nations. The military value and perhaps the agricultural possibilities of this region were clearly apparent to Champlain; it may be that he foresaw a commercial development of his discovery. Early in the seventeenth century, the French established an important trading-post at the spot where Champlain had fired the first gunshot heard by the Iroquois. In the *Correspondance Officielle* we find many references to this post; the Indians went there to exchange their furs for Dutch or English merchandise, an illicit traffic generally, hidden behind military or colonizing activities. This study is primarily concerned with these activities.

CHAPTER II.   *1609-1664*

FROM the departure of Champlain in 1609 until the visit of Father Jogues in 1642, I find no record of continued exploration nor of French settlement in the valley. The protection of the growing settlements of the St. Lawrence valley, slowly creeping up the river to Montreal (founded in 1642) required all the efforts of the leaders of the colony. However, New France did not cease to occupy the attention of the Mother-Country overseas.

France had employed the same means as England and the Netherlands in developing her colonies, that is, the organization by a group of speculators of a company holding broad powers under royal charter. Thus the Company of One Hundred Associates, headed by Cardinal Richelieu himself, had been formed to develop and exploit New France. Under the provisions of the charter, certain conditions were set down as to settlement of colonists in the new territories and payment of duties to the King. Champlain held his position as governor under an earlier company, whose rights and privileges passed to Cardinal Richelieu and his associates. All the tricks and inspirational methods of the modern realtor in creating a "boom" in connection with New France were employed by the company to little or no avail. Until 1663, the control of New France remained in the hands of this company, but the conditions of the charter had not been fulfilled—colonization lagged and payments to the King were frequently omitted with the plea of indefinite returns from fur-trading, etc. Inefficient and inactive governors soon caused the cancellation of the royal charter and the establishment of New France as a "royal colony," administered directly by the Crown.

Champlain pushed his explorations toward the west in 1615, traveling by Lake Ontario to reach the villages of the Five Nations. It does not appear that he ever saw Lake Champlain again. His most active efforts were devoted to the development of Quebec, besieged and taken by the English in 1628 and recovered by the French in 1632, three years before his death. Interest at court became more and more active in everything concerning New France. Jesuit missionaries, settled for some time in the colony, kept this interest alive by means of their *Relations.* Between 1630 and 1635 they began to penetrate into the region south of the St. Lawrence.[1]

The Iroquois often raided the growing hamlets along the river and frequently came to prowl, if not to attack, in the environs of Three Rivers and Quebec. The governors of the colony, in order to prevent attacks, decided to build a fortified post with the purpose of "discouraging" the Iroquois before their arrival at the French villages. At the mouth of the Richelieu River (the Indians usually came down Lake Champlain and this river to the St. Lawrence), a

1. Hill: *Old Fort Edward*, p. 8. According to Hill, Iroquois expeditions against the French and French expeditions against the Iroquois were passing over the "Great Carrying Place" (between Lake George and the Hudson River at Fort Edward) as early as 1630.

palisaded fort was built and named Fort Richelieu in honor of the founder of the Company of One Hundred Associates, construction being completed in 1641. In the following year, inspired by a "holy faith" and an inexhaustible eagerness to convert the savages, Maisonneuve and his associates founded "Ville-Marie,"—Montreal—and Father Isaac Jogues made his first voyage through Lake Champlain.

In the month of August, 1642, Father Jogues, named missionary to the Hurons, was traveling toward the west, accompanied by two "donnés" (lay brothers) of Quebec, Guillaume Couture and René Goupil. Near the mouth of the Richelieu River, a band of Iroquois warriors suddenly attacked them. Father Jogues could have escaped, being a short distance from his comrades, but faithful to his religious duties, he rushed to aid the wounded and the dying. As the leader of the three, Father Jogues had to undergo horrible torture—fingernails torn out by the roots, fingers terribly mutilated, excruciating pain. With their prisoners the Iroquois began the return journey to their villages along the "Rivière des Agniers."[2] The first stop was at Isle La Motte to spend the night and inflict new suffering upon Father Jogues, Couture and Goupil.[3] On August 8, they met another band of warriors at an encampment on Jogues Island (near Westport). Here the prisoners were forced to amuse their conquerors by undergoing the "salvo, which consists in having the prisoners pass between two rows (of savages), each discharging upon them blows from sticks,"[4] tomahawks, and leather straps—this is what Father Jogues called "the narrow road to Paradise." At each halt the Iroquois invented other amusements of this type. Once, in the

2. This is now called the Mohawk River.

3. It has often been said that a Jesuit mission was established at Isle La Motte in 1642. "The first white settlement on Isle La Motte was a Jesuit mission established in 1642." (Henry Wayland Hill, *The Champlain Tercentenary*, Albany, 1911, p. 4.) The enforced visit of Jogues hardly means the establishment of a mission. The following note may have significance: on a map of 1663, entitled "Acadie" (Massachusetts Archives: *Documents Collected in France*, II, p. 147), a church or Jesuit mission is indicated on the western shore of Lake Champlain, halfway between Ticonderoga and the foot of the lake.

4. *Relation de ce qui s'est passé en la Nouvelle France, ès années 1664 & 1665*. François le Mercier: Kébec, 3 novembre 1665.—"le salve, qui consiste à faire passer les prisonniers, comme entre deux hayes, chacun déchargeant sur eux des coups de bastons."

midst of his suffering, Father Jogues baptized two candidates with drops of dew from the stalk of a plant; often he heard the confessions of the converted as they burned at the stake. On the first or second of September, the party arrived at the head of Lake "Andiatarocte," —to-day Lake George—and by a short portage reached the Hudson to follow the Saratoga Trail.[5] After reaching their homes by the Mohawk, the Iroquois sent Couture back to Three Rivers by way of Lake Champlain.[6] René Goupil was killed September 24.

"For thirteen months he (Father Jogues) will serve as slave to an Indian family."[7] In the month of March, 1643, the Iroquois brought Father Jogues with them for the fishing at Saratoga Lake; in August, they were a few leagues to the south of Fort Orange.[8] Father Jogues returned from this last excursion before the main group. At Schenectady, Arendt van Corlaer, a Dutch merchant, and the Rev. Jan Megapolensis, a Lutheran clergyman, ransomed him, sending him to France by way of Manhattan and England. Receiving a dispensation from the Pope permitting him to celebrate Mass (a necessity because of his terribly mutilated hands, for according to the rules of the Church, the hands of the person administering the Sacraments must be perfect), he returned to New France in 1646, ready to serve again at his mission.[9]

Father Jogues was not the only priest, as prisoner of the Iroquois, to travel through the Champlain valley. In the spring of 1644, Father Bressani, accompanied by a few Algonquins, was seized near Three Rivers and his companions were massacred. Journeying by way of the lake with his captors, he soon reached the Iroquois villages. In September, Mr. William Kieft, "governor of New Belgium," rescued Joseph Bressani from the hands of his "executioners" and had him sent to Holland.[10]

On his return to New France Father Jogues was sent in May, 1646, on a political mission to the Mohawks, with Sieur Bourdon,[11]

5. See *Appendix A*.
6. Hill: *The Champlain Tercentenary*, p. 387.
7. Kerlidou: *Le Fort et la Chapelle de Ste. Anne*, p. 10.
8. Albany.
9. Brandow: *Old Saratoga and Schuylerville*, pp. 3-5. Carpenter: *Summer Paradise in History*, pp. 85-86.
10. Hill: *The Champlain Tercentenary*, p. 387. *Mémoires et Comptes-Rendus de la Société Royale du Canada*, 1897, section 1, p. 74.
11. O'Gallaghan: *Documentary History of New York*, IX, p. 21.

engineer, and two Algonquins. Leaving May 16, traveling by way of Lake Champlain and stopping as usual at Isle La Motte and at Otter Creek, they reached Lake "Andiatarocte" on the eve of Ascension Day. In memory of their visit Father Jogues christened this body of water "Lac du Saint-Sacrement," a name which it kept until 1755.[12] They intended to follow the Kayadrosseras Trail,[13] but near the Hudson the weight of the gifts sent by the French governor to the Iroquois forced a change of route and they continued along the river to Saratoga. There Father Jogues decided to go down to Fort Orange to thank the Dutch friends who had ransomed him in 1643.[14] At length reaching the Iroquois villages on May 28, Father Jogues carried out his mission and started back to Canada, June 16. Retracing his route by way of the two lakes, he reached Canada, June 26, bearing an invitation from his former Mohawk enemies to return and establish a mission in their country. The Superior of the Jesuits gave his approval, and Father Jogues left New France for the last time in August, 1646. "He went away toward death with his friend René-Jean de la Lande." Received at first in a friendly way by the Mohawks, in October the missionaries were accused of sorcery and held captive at Ossernenon (now Auriesville, New York). An epidemic, developing after the celebration of the rites of the Church, and the loss of grain devoured by the caterpillars, were attributed to Father Jogues and La Lande. At first, they underwent cruel torture, strips of flesh being cut from their arms and bodies. While a council was being held to determine their fate, the missionaries were invited to attend a Mohawk feast; as they were approaching the council circle, Father Jogues and La Lande were killed by their treacherous captors, October 18, 1646,[15] and their heads were torn from their bodies and exposed on the palisades of the village.

During an Iroquois attack on Quebec in 1653, Father Antoine Poucet was seized and taken to the Mohawk villages, probably by the Lake Champlain route.[16] There he was tortured and then sent back to Quebec.

12. In 1755, Sir William Johnson, the noted English general, changed the name to Lake George, in honor of the English King.

13. See *Appendix A*.

14. Hill: *Old Fort Edward*, p. 10.

15. Kerlidou: *Le Fort et la Chapelle de Ste. Anne*, p. 11.

16. Kenton: *Jesuit Relations and Allied Documents*, XLI.

Father Simon Le Moyne made a tour of inspection in the Mohawk and Onondaga country from July to September, 1654, with a view to establishing missions among those Iroquois tribes. In 1655, during a four weeks' journey, Father Claude Dablon and Pierre-Marie-Joseph Chaumonot founded the Onondaga mission, while Father Le Moyne undertook to establish the Mohawk mission. Father Dablon went to Quebec in the autumn, returning to Onondaga in the spring of 1656 with Father François Le Mercier (Superior of Canadian Missions), René Menard, two lay brothers and a party of colonists under the leadership of a captain of militia, who made a definite attempt to found a French settlement in the Mohawk country. Father Paul Ragueneau and Joseph-Hubert du Perron went there in July, 1657. The Mohawks did not welcome this effort to colonize their lands. Hearing of Mohawk plans to destroy the French settlement, the entire colony stole away during the night and escaped safely to Montreal in March, 1658. Efforts were not abandoned to preserve some measure of French influence among the Mohawks. Father Le Moyne returned to the mission for the winter of 1660 and 1661 and in the spring brought back some French prisoners to Canada.

Fathers Julien Garnier, Étienne de Carheil, Pierre Millet and Boniface were sent to the Iroquois territory, and by the spring of 1668 a mission had been established among each of the Five Nations. Although the Iroquois missions were given up in 1687, after Marquis de Denonville's expedition of the preceding year, spasmodic efforts were made to keep alive a modicum of French influence over the Five Nations. Father Bruyas returned to the Mohawk post in 1701 where he was joined in 1702 by Fathers Jacques de Lamberville, Julien Garnier and François le Vaillant du Gueslis. Some time later, Fathers Jacques d'Hue and Pierre de Mareuil were added to their numbers. Finally, the Mohawks turned definitely against the French and their influence (probably inspired by English counsels), driving them out of their territory forever in 1708.[17]

The Lake Champlain valley was the favored route for reaching the Mohawk country from New France, although occasional journeys were made by way of the St. Lawrence and Lake Ontario. It seems likely that most, if not all, of the trips back and forth between New France and the Iroquois missions were made by way of Lake

17. Kenton: *Jesuit Relations and Allied Documents*, XLI-XLIII.

Champlain. In nearly every group at least one priest is mentioned whom we know to have been familiar with the lake.

In 1664, frequent rumors of war and the presence of war parties completely destroyed the peace of the Champlain valley. Then it became the scene of military maneuvers; the forests were thronged by men wearing uniforms very different from the cassocks of priests; the wilderness echoed with the drums of war.

CHAPTER III. *The Iroquois War*

KING Louis XVI, in 1663, convinced that the colonization and trade of New France (objectives in view at the time of the organization of the Company of the One Hundred Associates), were making but little progress, decided on a new régime. Under the King's plan, New France would be raised to the dignity of "colonie royale," whose government would be responsible only to the King; the administration would be entrusted to a viceroy or governor and to an "intendant de la justice, de la police, et de la finance," both appointed by the King and responsible directly to him. These two royal representatives, with the vicar-general of the Church at Quebec, would meet in council to regulate the affairs of the colony. The first governor under the new régime, Augustin de Mézy de Saffray (died May 5, 1665), was replaced March 23, 1665, by Daniel de Rémy, Sieur de Courcelles, a veteran of European wars and governor of Thionville, strong and alert in mind although aged and infirm. At the same time the King replaced the first intendant, Louis Robert (who never left France and scarcely concerned himself with his post in America), by one of the most remarkable men who ever came to this continent, Jean-Baptiste Talon, friend of the great minister, Colbert.[1] Talon, born about 1625, in administrative service since 1653, had already won distinction as intendant of Hainault and commissary for war in Flanders. What Canada owes to his efforts should be the subject of a special study.

Louis XIV and his renowned minister, Colbert, were deeply interested in the progress of New France; the marginal notes written by their own hands on official documents show an intelligent comprehension of the needs of the colony and a well-defined plan for de-

1. See *Appendix B* for a list of governors and intendants of New France.

veloping its resources. The King's keen insight will astonish the reader whose only knowledge of him has come from conventional history and extravagant legend.

Beginning in 1665, the detailed reports of the governors and intendants supplemented by the *Relations* of the Jesuits, are an inexhaustible source of exact and authentic information about what was taking place in New France. The *Correspondance Officielle*, deposited in the Archives of the Ministry of Marine (for the colonies were formerly administered by this Department), is filled with details which allow us to reconstruct the life of the colony; the fear of Indian and English attacks, the plans discussed for defense, the heroic deeds, the sublime courage, and the often petty attitude of mind of the colonists who struggled for the foundation and preservation of French civilization in the new world, live again for us.

Fort Richelieu, which had adequately protected the settlements along the St. Lawrence since 1641, had been burned by the Iroquois in 1646. The Mohawks were threatening a renewal of their incursions in 1663, when Baron d'Avaugour, governor of the colony, wrote to the minister to suggest an ambitious and interesting plan— a plan for completing the defenses of New France by the construction of three fortresses, one on the site of Fort Richelieu, a second on "the same river where the Dutch have built a wretched redoubt, which they call Fort Orange," and the third between the two, at the foot of Lake Champlain.[2]

About 1664, Fort Richelieu was rebuilt. This was the first step of Governor de Courcelles in the campaign against the Iroquois, undertaken to secure the peace so much needed by New France in carrying out the aims of Talon and the King.

Colbert wrote to Talon in the spring of 1665: "The King is sending the Sieur de Tracy with four companies of infantry, and the Sieur de Courcelles with 1000 good men of the Carignan regiment; he will join to them three or four hundred colonials who know the manner of fighting the Iroquois."[3] M. de Tracy had been named viceroy of New France, or rather "Lieutenant General of all the Americas," November 19, 1663.[4] The four companies of the

2. Baron d'Avaugour au ministre, Gaspé, le 4 août 1663.

3. "Manner," says M. Benjamin Sulte, "which the French officers unfortunately did not understand." (*Mémoires et Comptes-Rendus de la Société Royale du Canada*, Second Series, 1902, p. 36.)

4. Rameau: *La France aux Colonies*, II, 23. Cf. Sulte, "Le Régiment de

Carignan-Salières regiment landed at Quebec June 19, 1665; M. de Tracy, Father Claude Bardy and François du Perron, with the first-mentioned four companies of infantry arrived June 30.[5]

The four companies, with Father Chaumonot as chaplain, left Quebec July 23, 1665, to rebuild Fort Richelieu on the site of the present city of Sorel; with them marched a company of Canadian volunteers, under command of Jean-Baptiste Le Gardeur de Repentigny. They appeared before Three Rivers just in time to free the city from fear of the Iroquois, who had recently resumed their raids. On August 10, M. de Chambly, at the head of the troops from Three Rivers, started to cross Lake Saint-Pierre; in September, the news came that his barques and sloops had gone up the Richelieu River as far as the falls near the "Basin" (Chambly Basin), each of the forty boats carrying twenty men ready for action.

The Jesuit *Relation of 1665* says; "The second fort, christened Saint-Louis . . . has been built by M. de Sorel." This fort, begun August 25, 1665, was later named Fort Chambly. During this same month of August, M. de Chambly built a temporary fortification at Richelieu; later, M. de Sorel gave his name to the larger permanent fort which he built on this site.

On September 12, M. de Courcelles and Intendant Talon landed at Quebec; a few days later, M. de Salières went to the rapids situated above Fort Saint-Louis and began work on the third fort; it was completed October 15, the festival of St. Theresa, in whose honor it was named Fort Sainte-Thérèse. Late in the fall, a fortified post was established on the site of the present city of St. Johns. All of these forts were strengthened by palisades of logs.

M. de Courcelles, immediately upon his arrival at Quebec, left on a tour of inspection of the posts on the Richelieu River. October 1, four companies went to Three Rivers to await M. de Tracy. October 3, Father Chaumonot returned to Quebec from Saint-Louis de Chambly, where he had gone with the troops sent out in the preceding July. Intendant Talon wrote to Minister Colbert, October 4, saying, "The four companies of the Carignan regiment . . . are to be stationed in winter-quarters in the newly built forts."[6]

On October 28, new developments were announced in Quebec.

Carignan," in *Mémoires et Comptes-Rendus de la Société Royale du Canada*, Second Series, 1902.

5. *Journal des Jésuites*, MS. Laval University Library, Quebec.

6. Faillon: *Histoire de la colonie française au Canada*, III, p. 127.

M. de Salières had ordered a boat built at Fort Sainte-Thérèse for a new project. Under command of M. de Repentigny, eighteen or twenty men had gone by boat to look over the land near the foot of Lake Champlain; they had advanced four leagues up the lake, admiring the beauty of its shores and choosing the sites for new defenses.[7] "This lake, after 60 leagues length, ends finally in the lands of the Mohawk Iroquois. It is there that we plan to build next spring a fourth fort which will dominate this section and from which continual sorties may be made upon our enemies if they do not listen to reason."[8] This was to be Fort Sainte-Anne.

M. de Courcelles returned to Quebec, October 31, from his journey "on high," where he had gone to inspect the work on the forts and to establish winter quarters. M. de Salières arrived at the same time, and "there were some misunderstandings between them," says the Jesuit *Journal*.[9] November 4, M. de Salières went to Montreal to spend the winter.

The Iroquois, during the few years preceding the establishment of the "colonie royale," had grown bold and had often attacked the scattered farms and villages along the St. Lawrence. In 1664 and 1665, their raids spread fear through the whole colony. M. de Courcelles, realizing the effect of these raids on the colonists and wishing to impress the Indians by the power of his troops, planned a sudden and decisive attack on the center of the enemy country; it was to be a mid-winter attack while the enemy rested from fair-weather raids. Against the judgment of competent advisers the enthusiastic governor made his preparations.[10] "M. de Courcelles was aware neither of the rigor of the climate nor of the fearful obstacles which beset such a march with troops not merely foreign to the country but led under European discipline. Except for the aid given by our Canadian militia it would have been a complete disaster."[11]

The departure from Quebec took place January 6, 1666. M. de

7. Kerlidou: *Le Fort et la Chapelle de Ste. Anne*, p. 13.

8. *Relation des Jésuites, 1665*, pp. 10 and 25. We must believe that the erection of Fort Saint-Jean had not been considered at this time, since the fourth fort was to be built on Lake Champlain. However this may be, Fort Saint-Jean dates from the end of the year 1665 and Fort Sainte-Anne, the *fifth* fort, situated on an island at the north end of the lake, was built during the spring and summer of 1666.

9. *Journal des Jésuites.*

10. Cf. Nicholas Perrot, p. 111.

11. *Relation de 1666*, p. 6

Courcelles was in command, accompanied by M. du Gas as lieuten-ant, M. de Salampar, gentleman volunteer, the Jesuit Father Raf-feix, 100 Canadians and 300 men of the Carignan regiment. "This march could not be other than slow, each having snow-shoes upon his feet to which the men were unaccustomed, and all, not excepting the leaders and M. de Courcelles himself, burdened with 25 or 30 pounds of biscuits, blankets and other necessary provisions."[12] As early as the third day, several men had their noses, cheeks, ears, fingers, and knees frozen, and they began to complain of soreness in their shoulders, arms, legs and feet; "snowshoe-sickness" also made its presence distressingly felt. Some of the soldiers, benumbed by cold, would have died in the snow, if they had not been picked up and carried to shelter.

January 16, M. de Courcelles was at Three Rivers, and on the eighteenth continued his way toward Fort Richelieu. January 24, captains de la Fouille, Maximin, and Laubia of the regiment of Carignan arrived at Three Rivers to join the 300 men gathered there; the next day the entire force was in motion, and they marched across frozen Lake Saint-Pierre to Fort Richelieu to join the com-mand of M. de Sorel. Young Chartier de Lotbinière, an officer of the expedition, has left a manuscript in verse which gives us precious details.[13] He gives his impressions of the march "in order to reach Richelieu . . .":

> *But this spot, become sterile,*
> *Furnished us no shelter.*
> *We had to build ramparts*
> *Of snow and scattered ice-blocks.*
> *Under the shelter of the open sky*
> *Build a house of a bit of canvas*
> *And set up hamlets*
> *With saplings and branches.*

Montreal militia, familiarly called the "blue-coats," under command of Charles Le Moyne (later Seigneur de Longueuil), joined the ex-pedition at Fort Richelieu; there were 70 men, among them the Sieur de Hautmesnil, who nearly perished on the march.

12. Sulte: *Le Régiment de Carignan*, p. 41.

13. *Mémoires et Comptes-Rendus de la Société Royale du Canada*, Second Series, VIII, pp. 42-44.

M. de Courcelles left Fort Saint-Louis January 29, with captains Petit and de Rougemont, and Sieur Mignardé, lieutenant of the "Colonel's Own" company, among his officers, and a force of nearly 600 men. The general rendezvous was Fort Sainte-Thérèse, and there they waited the arrival of the Algonquins who were to serve as guides under Louis Godefroy de Normanville; drunkenness of the Indian guides delayed their arrival, and M. de Courcelles was imprudent enough to leave without them.

January 30, the whole army left Fort Sainte-Thérèse and advanced with a thousand handicaps and miseries; a longer and more difficult march cannot be imagined; there is nothing like it in history. The soldiers were provided with snowshoes but did not know how to use them; each one carried at least twenty-five pounds of supplies and provisions; they had 300 leagues to travel over ice and snow, following unknown trails without dependable guides, sleeping in the snow with winter temperature several degrees below that of the most rigorous season of the home-country. Passing over ice-bound Lake Champlain, they reached Bulwagga Bay (Crown Point) and went overland to the Hudson River.[14] Mistaking their way, the Indian guides again being drunk, the troops found themselves on February 14, within two miles of the Dutch village of Schenectady instead of in the neighborhood of the Mohawk villages.[15] Here, on the next day, they learned definitely that the Dutch province had passed into English control.

On Saturday, February 20, the troops attacked "a cabin-full" of Iroquois, killing "more than two savages" and one old woman. In a skirmish a few hours later, four Iroquois fell, but six Frenchmen lay dead upon the field. In spite of his lack of "success," the French governor congratulated himself that his presence and that of his army in this region, at the winter season, had deeply impressed both the Iroquois and the English.

M. de Courcelles left Schenectady February 21, because the Dutch governor, Van Corlaer, assured him that the Mohawks were no longer in their villages, having set out for war with the savages to the west. In the evening, the army broke camp in haste and marched all night and a part of the next day in a blinding snowstorm. On February 22, Louis de Normanville arrived with his

14. Hemenway: *Vermont Gazetteer*, I, p. 2.
15. Brandow: *Old Saratoga and Schuylerville*, pp. 10-11. Cf. Nicholas Perrot, p. 111.

thirty Algonquins bringing the trophies of the hunt, a welcome arrival for famine threatened the troops. Lotbinière sings of it thus:

> Victory would have spoken well
> Of the march and defile
> Which you have accomplished, great Courcelles,
> On horses made of cord,
> But in seeing your harness
> And your bread dryer than walnuts
> She could not have described you
> Without making us burst with laughter.[16]

The Mohawks, returning home at the moment of the French retreat, followed and skilfully harassed the troops, making the situation more critical than before. In a rear-guard skirmish about 60 French were ambushed by 200 Indians; the Sieur d'Aiguesmortes and four soldiers fell and 30 of the Iroquois were killed.[17] Lotbinière, who succeeded M. d'Aiguesmortes, was slightly wounded.

M. de Courcelles had reached Pointe à la Chevelure (Chimney Point) on Lake Champlain when provisions failed. Here he remained two days.[18] The messengers, sent to open a "cache" of provisions which had been prepared for emergency needs of the troops on the return march, found it empty. (This "cache" was located at Colchester Point or Isle La Motte, probably the latter.) Father Raffeix and Charles Boquet, lay-brother, lost effects "worth $80 of our present day money," says Benjamin Sulte. More than sixty

16. "La Victoire aurait bien parlé
    De la démarche et défilé
    Que vous avez fait, grand Courcelle,
    Sur des chevaux faite de ficelle.
    Mais en voyant votre harnois
    Et votre pain plus sec que noix
    Elle n'aurait pu vous décrire
    Sans nous faire pâmer de rire."

17. Sulte: *Le Régiment de Carignan*, pp. 44-45. Crockett: *History of Lake Champlain*, pp. 40-41; also, *History of Vermont*, I, pp. 90-91, says that there were eleven French killed, including one lieutenant, and several wounded; that the Iroquois losses were three dead and six wounded. As far as possible where figures are concerned, I have based my conclusions upon the official reports of French authorities; when English historians are not in agreement, I give their figures in footnotes.

18. Hemenway: *Vermont Gazetteer*, I, p. 2.

soldiers died of hunger because of this unforeseen calamity, but we must forget neither those who had already died in misery during the advance and retreat, nor those who could not endure the hardships of the later march from Chimney Point to Quebec. The Algonquins and Canadians succeeded in relieving the misery of a good number of the soldiers by providing wild game and by giving useful advice to those "poor novices" on how to live under such conditions.[19]

Finally, on March 8, the army returned to Fort Saint-Louis de Chambly in lamentable disorganization. M. de Courcelles now blamed the Jesuits for the failure of his enterprise. He continued to speak of them with bitterness and reproach until he reached Quebec, where he was convinced that his own obstinacy in carrying out a hazardous military operation in the month of February, with European soldiers, had been the real cause of his discomfiture.

The troops, says Lotbinière, went from Chambly overland to Montreal, instead of going down the river to Sorel. About March 12, they began to return to Quebec under a hotly gleaming sun. The soldiers, exhausted by the unending hardships of the campaign, now underwent the cruel experience of snow-blindness. M. de Courcelles arrived in Quebec on March 17, aware of many things whose existence he had not suspected before coming to New France.

CHAPTER IV. *Fort Sainte-Anne*

FIFTY-EIGHT years before the first English settlement within the limits of Vermont, that of Fort Dummer in 1724, the French were at work on the construction of a fort on Isle La Motte. The successive establishment of military posts along the Richelieu River, Forts Richelieu-Sorel, Saint-Louis de Chambly, Sainte-Thérèse, and Saint-Jean, indicate logical development of defenses against Iroquois raids. The completion of the plan required the construction of Fort Sainte-Anne, the outpost furthest advanced toward the enemy country.

Jean-Baptiste Le Gardeur de Repentigny was sent out in October, 1665, with twenty men, to determine the spot most favorably situated for this advanced post. The boat for his use had been built at Fort Sainte-Thérèse. Four leagues from where Lake Champlain

19. It is clear that Fort Sainte-Anne had not been built; otherwise, the expedition could have been revictualed there after the discovery of the pillaged "cache."

flows into the Richelieu River, he chose the sandy point on the north shore of the first island. Winter being near, construction of the fort was postponed until the next spring.

The first island is seven miles long and two miles wide; at the northwest a point projects into the lake, a point covered to-day as formerly, no doubt, with maple, oak and especially pine trees; it is dominated by a hill from which one may see the lake for a great distance to the north and south. The point was a meeting-place for the Algonquins and the Iroquois, who often camped there,[1] and was well known to the missionaries, who had been traveling up and down the lake since the time of Father Jogues; no spot more suitable for an advanced post could be found.

In spite of the disastrous expedition of January-March, 1666, M. de Courcelles and the Sieur de Tracy had not given up their plan of carrying the attack into the heart of the Iroquois country. They were actively urging preparations undertaken for the defense of the colonists, especially the construction of this "fourth fort," on the shores of Lake Champlain; for this purpose they sent out in early spring "a certain number of men with the company of Captain de La Motte of the regiment of Carignan."[2]

Pierre de Saint-Paul, Sieur de la Motte-Lussière, "noble man," was captain in the royal regiment of Carignan-Salières. "About the end of 1668 he replaced Zacharie Dupuis, commandant at Montreal. When he was at this post, 'man of heart and honor, his company was the only one of the regiment remaining in the country,' remarks Nicholas Perrot, who was in Montreal with the Ottawas trading, in the summer of 1669. M. de la Motte left for France early in the summer of 1670, leaving the Sieur de la Fredière in his place. Until then, he had awaited the arrival of François-Marie Perrot, appointed governor of Montreal, but who was delayed a year because of the dangers of navigation. Perrot having landed at Quebec with his relative Talon August 18, 1670, it is supposed that he relieved de la Fredière of his functions about September 1. In any case, Pierre de Saint-Paul, Sieur de la Motte-Lussière, did not return to the colony."[3]

1. *Relation de 1646.*

2. Sulte: *Le Régiment de Carignan*, p. 46.

3. *Ibid.*, pp. 70-71. There is no reason to-day for the frequent confusion of Pierre de Saint-Paul, Sieur de la Motte-Lussière, with any one of the four following persons.

a. Jean Deleau, Sieur de la Motte, who commanded at Chambly in 1677.

b. Dominique de la Motte-Lussière (probably a younger brother of Pierre),

The Sieur de la Motte had in his command during the construction period, about 300 men, including his company of the Carignan regiment. It is not known on what day the construction of the fort actually began, but we know that it was completed on July 20.[4] In Volume III of the *Jesuit Relations* there is a map and model of this fort; it seems to have been similar to Forts Richelieu-Sorel and Sainte-Thérèse. The construction of Fort Sainte-Thérèse required a month and a half; therefore, we assume that construction of the fort on Isle La Motte began late in May or during the first few days of June. At that time, M. Dubois, chaplain of the regiment, celebrated the first Mass, as was the custom, at the moment of the benediction of the site of the fort.[5]

The new fort was dedicated to Sainte-Anne July 26, 1666, in the presence of Captain de la Motte, his company, and the soldiers sent from Quebec, Three Rivers, and Montreal to work on its construction. From the descriptions of Forts Richelieu-Sorel and Sainte-Thérèse we can visualize Fort Sainte-Anne, of which there remain only traces, half effaced toward the northwest by the waters of Lake Champlain. It was 144 feet long by 96 feet wide, and can be measured to-day only in width. The terrain was surmounted by a double log palisade fifteen feet high, with a walk in the interior raised a foot

who came with Cavalier de la Salle in 1678, was married at Montreal in 1680, and died there in 1700.

c. Claude de la Motte, Marquis de Jourdis, who was married at Lachine in 1685, and was killed by the Iroquois in 1687.

d. Louis de la Rue, Chevalier de la Motte, a lieutenant, who was killed by the Iroquois at Saint-du-Lac in 1690.

4. Thwaites: *Jesuit Relations*, L, p. 193 (see note). Cf. *Journal des Jésuites*, III, and Charlevoix: *Histoire de la Colonie française*, III, p. 135. The varying dates for the construction of Fort Sainte-Anne are listed below with the authority for each:

    1642—Hemenway: *Vermont Gazetteer*, I, p. 659.

    Before 1666—S. R. Hall: *Geography and History of Vermont*, p. 101.

    1664—*Americana*, XXVIII, p. 23.

    1665—Palmer: *History of Lake Champlain*, p. 14.

    1665—Reid: *Lake George and Lake Champlain*, p. 28.

    1665—Carpenter: *Summer Paradise in History*, p. 61.

    1666—Sulte: *Le Régiment de Carignan*, p. 46.

    1666—Kerlidou: *Le Fort et la Chapelle de Sainte-Anne*, p. 18.

    1666, summer of—Crockett: *History of Lake Champlain*, p. 39.

5. It is possible that Father Raffeix, the Jesuit priest with the expedition of M. de Courcelles, January-March, 1666, celebrated mass on the journey to or from Schenectady.

and a half above the ground; there were four bastions, one at each corner. In 1868, Mr. David Read described Fort Sainte-Anne: he speaks of fourteen mounds, situated on the north and east sides, made of stone and covered with earth and sod; the largest was at the southeast corner where there were the ruins of a covered door; at the southwest was a forge and near the center, a well. The mounds were inside the palisade and seemed to have served as foundation for the inner walk. To the east of the fort was the parade-ground of several acres of level land.[6] Mr. Walter Crockett speaks of the site of the fort as it appeared in 1896, after careful excavations had been made. The terrain of the fort formed a square or rectangle; the mounds had been opened and in each was found a hearth still covered with ashes; in one there was a brick oven. The foundations of several buildings had been uncovered, some measuring 12 by 16 feet, others 16 by 32 feet. Strewn about almost everywhere there had been found knives, forks, two silver spoons (one engraved with the name "L. Case"), dishes, buttons, kitchen utensils, carpenter's tools, pipes, detached parts of firearms, bullets, arrowheads, tomahawks, Indian pottery, nails, charred beams, and even coins, one piece bearing the date "1656."[7]

The establishment of the fortifications on Isle La Motte did not pass unnoticed in the English colonies. Governor Winthrop of Connecticut sent spies to Lake Champlain to find out what the French were doing there, and an active correspondence between the governors of Fort Orange and M. de Courcelles was carried on at the same time.

During the construction of the fort, life had its gay and adventurous aspects; the officers often organized hunting parties for relaxation from hard work. It was not only recreation, but at the same time furnished a welcome addition to their food; game was abundant especially on the west shore of the lake. Unfortunately, and perhaps this fact added to the zest of the hunt, there was the imminent danger of meeting bands of Iroquois hunters or braves, and then the hunt sometimes turned into tragedy.

One day in May, M. de Chasy, officer in the regiment, cousin of Lieutenant General de Tracy[8] and a relative of Marshal d'Estrées,[9]

6. Hemenway: *Vermont Gazetteer*, II, p. 561, Article by David Read.
7. Crockett: *History of Lake Champlain*, pp. 48-49.
8. Nicholas Perrot: *Mémoires*, p. 112.
9. Sulte: *Le Régiment de Carignan*, p. 47.

left with six companions to hunt along the river[10] which is only a short distance from the fort on the opposite shore of the lake. Among his companions, I have been able to identify five: M. de Montagny and Louis de Leroles (nephew of M. de Tracy), both officers;[11] M. de Traversy[12] and the Sieurs Chamot and Morin.[13] Hardly had they landed when they were attacked without warning by some sixty Mohawks under their chief, Agariata.[14] M. de Chasy and two of his companions, surrounded by savages, resolved to cut their way through or sell their lives dearly. Their courage was of no avail against overwhelming numbers, and they fell mortally wounded. The other Frenchmen would have rushed to their aid, but their hands were bound, and at the slightest movement the tomahawks suspended above their heads threatened them also with death. The Iroquois hastily scalped their victims, stole their weapons and clothing, and started off toward their own country with their prisoners. The bodies of MM. de Chasy, de Traversy, Chamot, and Morin remained on the battlefield; among the prisoners was Louis de Leroles.

It is not known whether one of the prisoners escaped to the fort to tell what had happened or if it was after vainly awaiting their return that M. de la Motte surmised the misfortune that had occurred. It is not known either whether the dead were carried across the lake to be buried in the cemetery at Fort Sainte-Anne, or if the Iroquois left them where they fell, or shared their dismembered bodies "in one of their horrible feasts."[15]

10. The Chazy River, named in memory of M. de Chasy.

11. Louis de Canchy, Sieur de Lerolle: prisoner of the Iroquois; at Quebec, November, 1667; returned later to France. (Sulte: *Le Régiment de Carignan*, p. 67.) Tanguay: *Dictionnaire Généalogique*, III, p. 264, mentions "Elizabeth de Canchy de Lerolle, wife of Jean-Baptiste de Beaumont."

12. Jean Laumonnier, Sieur de Traversy, ensign in the regiment of Orleans, appears in a marriage contract drawn up in Quebec August 12, 1665, in the presence of M. de Tracy, etc. (Tanguay: *ibid.*, I, pp. 87, 494, 571.)

13. M. Talon à MM. de Tracy et de Courcelles, Québec, le 1er septembre 1666; 'La mort de Messers. de Chazy et Traversy, et des sieurs Chamot et Morin . . ." (*Dépôt du Ministère des Affaires Etrangères*).

14. La Potherie: *Mémoires*, II, 85. At the moment of this attack, ambassadors from three tribes of the Five Nations (the Mohawks and the Oneidas held back), were in Quebec to demand peace and to reproach the French for the establishment of Fort Sainte-Anne, a pre-emption of territory claimed by them. Instead of throwing them into prison the French treated them as men of honor.

15. Kerlidou: *Le Fort et la Chapelle de Sainte-Anne*, p. 24.

M. de Sorel, then in command at Fort Richelieu, "made up a party of 300 men whom he led by forced marches into the enemy country."[16] Proceeding by way of Lake Champlain and the Kayadrosseras Trail,[17] he met a few Mohawk chiefs at about twenty miles from their villages; among them he recognized Louis de Leroles. M. de Sorel allowed himself to be persuaded that he must lead the Mohawk chiefs to M. de Tracy for peace negotiations: "the ruse was taken seriously as always."[18] The troops retraced their route and at last reached Quebec about the first of July. Peace was signed July 12, 1666, a peace which lasted but a few days. It was broken in the following manner: M. de Tracy while host at dinner, mentioned at table how deeply the recent loss of his nephew had touched him, but in spite of his personal grief, he had consented, for the public good, to grant peace to Bâtard Flammand who had demanded it. That viewpoint should have been enough to make the proud Agariata understand the grief of M. de Tracy and to force the Mohawk to conceal his pride in the murder. However, far from showing any understanding of the governor's grief, Agariata raised his arm before the governor and the entire company, boasting loudly that this was the arm which had wielded the murderous tomahawk. This outrageous insolence broke the peace which M. de Tracy had granted; with a hasty reply to the foolhardy Mohawk that that arm would never kill another, M. de Tracy had him seized and bound; sending for the executioner, he ordered that Agariata be strangled in the presence of his ambassador, Bâtard Flammand.[19]

M. de Tracy and Governor de Courcelles, who was not proud of his failure of the preceding winter, had not given up the great expedition planned by the King. On September 1, 1666, these gentlemen received a letter from Talon who expressed his opinion that autumn was the best time for undertaking a decisive attack on the Iroquois centers.[20] "September 5, 1666, Sieur Couture arrives with an escort of two Mohawks, of whom one is of the Neutral Nation, chief of the band which killed M. de Chasy." They ask for peace, but "M. de Tracy decides to go, in person, to Annié (the Mohawk village) with 1000 or 1200 men."[21]

16. *Relation de 1666.*   17. See *Appendix A.*
18. Sulte: *Le Régiment de Carignan*, p. 47.
19. Nicholas Perrot: *Mémoires*, p. 113. La Potherie: *Mémoires*, II, p. 85.
20. O'Callaghan: *Doc. Col. Hist. N. Y.*, IX, p. 52.
21. *Journal des Jésuites*, quoted by Benjamin Sulte, p. 48.

M. de Tracy called together the military leaders and arranged a general assemblage of troops at Fort Sainte-Anne for September 28.[22] On the fourteenth, "M. de Tracy and the governor set sail for war with more than 400 colonists, native sons, volunteers, etc. . . ., he asked me for Fathers Albanel and Raffeix; on our own initiative we grant him six men, among others Guillaume Boivin and Charles Boquet."[23] Between September 14 and 28, the army gathered at Fort Sainte-Anne: "A salvo of artillery, such as it was, and joyous huzzas greet their landing."[24] The Carignan regiment, numbering 600 men was quartered in the fort; 600 Canadians and 100 Algonquins were encamped opposite the fort at the mouth of the Chazy River. Among the Canadians were 100 militiamen from Montreal under command of Charles Le Moyne and Picoté de Belestre; those from Quebec were led by their chief, Pierre Le Gardeur de Repentigny. At the fort were M. de Tracy who, in spite of his great age, insisted upon going in person, and M. de Courcelles, eager to start that he might obliterate the memory of his first failure by a dazzling success. Grouped a bit to one side were the officers of the regiment, whose names were to become well known within the next few weeks, Chaumont (aide to M. de Tracy), Salières, Berthier, Chambly, La Motte, Joybert de Marsan, Sorel, Carion du Fresnoy, Morel de la Durantaye, Pécaudy de Contrecoeur, and many others; further on were the men of the Church, M. Dubois (chaplain of the regiment), Dollier de Casson, Albanel, Raffeix, Boivin, and Boquet; "they have brought what is needed to celebrate Mass and the troops attend with devotion."[25] At the foot of the trees confessionals were set up which, says Dollier de Casson, are "besieged" day and night. "We hear news from the army which certainly numbers 1400 men. All these gentlemen are in very good health."[26]

On September 28, some of the troops had not yet arrived at the rendezvous and M. de Tracy wished to wait for them. M. de Courcelles, better acquainted with the country and as eager as ever to advance, started ahead with 400 men, the militia of Montreal leading the way under Charles Le Moyne. On October 3, MM. de Tracy, de Chaumont, and de Salières, began the march with the

22. Kerlidou: *Le Fort et la Chapelle de Sainte-Anne*, p. 25.
23. *Journal des Jésuites*, quoted by Benjamin Sulte, p. 48.
24. Kerlidou: *Le Fort et la Chapelle de Sainte-Anne*, p. 25.
25. Kerlidou: *Le Fort et la Chapelle de Sainte-Anne*, p. 26.
26. *Journal des Jésuites*, p. 48.

main body of the army; the rear guard followed closely on the seventh, commanded by MM. de Chambly and Berthier.[27]

The *Relation of 1666* (p. 811), speaks of the preparations undertaken for this expedition: 300 light boats and "bark canoes of which each carries at the most five or six persons, and two small cannon." As on the first expedition, the preparations showed lack of good judgment; the season alone was favorable. The Iroquois, aware of their danger, had forts well supplied with means of defense, so that for successful attack artillery had to be transported over almost impossible trails.

Advancing by way of Lake Champlain, the French reached the head of Lake Saint-Sacrement where they hid their boats and canoes near the site of Lake George village; thence to the Mohawk villages their route followed the Kayadrosseras Trail,[28] the most difficult route to be chosen, because rivers had to be forded and long marches made over pathways "which were no wider than a plank, and filled with brush, roots and very dangerous holes."[29] On the backs of the soldiers provisions had to be carried, weapons, baggage, and (the straw to break the camel's back) those two "small cannon" which M. de Tracy believed would make a deep impression on the Iroquois. Naturally delays and difficulties resulted; food became so scarce that the soldiers called the commissary officers by the derisive title of "Grand Masters of the Fast." Neither food nor clothing was suited to the needs of the march. The soldiers were on the point of revolt when, before their hungry eyes, appeared a grove of chestnut trees; courage revived and the expedition neared its goal.

At this time the Mohawks could put into the field only 400 warriors armed with tomahawks, bows and arrows and a few arquebuses, furnished, please note, by the English. For fortifications they had only log palisades around their four villages. Think of the terror which the prowess of the Mohawks must have inspired in New France! An army of more than 1300 men was sent to destroy them; 600 "élite" soldiers of the royal regiment of Carignan, 600 Canadian militia, and 100 Algonquins from the Missions, all under the personal leadership of the governor of the colony and the lieutenant general of the King! It must be said that the real enemies of

27. Cf. Crockett: *History of Lake Champlain*, p. 43.
28. See *Appendix A*.
29. *Lettre de Marie de l'Incarnation*, 12 novembre 1666.

the French were the obstacles of nature, forests, rivers, lakes, climate, and ever threatening famine.

The *Journal des Jésuites* gives a concise account of the exploits of this expedition into the enemy country: "On November 5, in the evening, M. de Tracy returns from Annié with his troops, about 1300 men including Indians; nine or ten were drowned in Lake Champlain. The Mohawks having fled at the sound of the drums, he burned their four villages with all their grain; there were in all 100 great cabins."[30] The return journey was even more exhausting and disastrous than the advance; there were incessant rains and the overflowing rivers and the storms on Lake Champlain took their toll of life. Journeying down the lake two boats were overturned and eight persons drowned, the most regrettable loss being that of Lieutenant du Luques, distinguished alike in France and Canada.[31]

M. de Tracy returned to Quebec November 5, and there the people celebrated with joyous ceremonial "the defeat of the Mohawks," which was in no sense a defeat, as time proved; however, the ensuing peace was to endure for twenty years.

The expedition in the fall of 1666 had no more lasting effect than those of the spring and summer. The European feeling of superiority led to the commission of errors in tact if not in action. "The 600 Canadians who merely served as scouts could have accomplished something decisive if permission had been granted them; but no! They were only allowed to accompany the fine soldiers and witness European stupidity."[32] Such criticism is not startling to the student of the history of the English colonies in America; similar criticism is recorded of Braddock's expedition and of Abercrombie's attack on Carillon. We have all read of the scorn expressed by the British regular in referring to the American colonial forces during the Revolution. How often scorn on the part of the European and jealousy on the part of the Colonial led to disaster, through lack of mutual understanding! "The number of soldiers dying from cold, hunger and disease surpasses that of all the garrisons France has sent us since the establishment of the colony; it is true that these garrisons were always deplorably inadequate."[33]

M. de Tracy, marching toward Quebec after his "victory" over

30. Sulte: *Le Régiment de Carignan*, p. 49.
31. Kerlidou: *Le Fort et la Chapelle de Sainte-Anne*, p. 29.
32. Sulte: *Le Régiment de Carignan*, p. 50.
33. Sulte: *Le Régiment de Carignan*, p. 50.

the Mohawks, stopped at Fort Sainte-Anne where, following the well-conceived policy of manning the advanced posts with the experienced troops of the Carignan regiment, he left Captain de la Motte with his company of sixty men. He had, at first, intended to abandon this fort as being too far from the settlements and too near the enemy.[34] M. de la Motte had with him as principal officer, Olivier Morel de la Durantaye, captain also in the Carignan regiment, who had aided in the construction of the fort. Among the officers of his company were Paul de Morel, ensign, and Philippe de Carion du Fresnoy, lieutenant.[35]

It was in the month of November that M. de Tracy left the little garrison at Fort Sainte-Anne, the nearest post to the Mohawks and the most exposed to attack in all New France. The nearest French village, Fort Saint-Louis de Chambly, was twenty leagues away.[36] At the beginning of winter it was evident that there was insufficient food: "M. de Tracy, at first resolved to abandon this fort, did not think of keeping a garrison there until approaching winter had made it impossible for the Intendant Talon to revictual this post."[37] Moreover, the food at their disposal consisted mainly of salted meat and bread made with flour spoiled at sea during the crossing of the troops. "Of 60 soldiers garrisoned at Fort Sainte-Anne, 40 were ill with scurvy, an affliction which always attacked the Europeans because they did not wish to be guided by experience and because they scorned the advice of the Canadians."[38] Without doubt in most epidemics of scurvy, the "mal de terre" of Cartier and Champlain, the cause cited above was the real, and most frequently, the sole reason for this illness. This time the garrison, forsaken so to speak by the intendant, could not remedy the situation without having aid from the settlements, the nearest of which, Fort Saint-Louis de Chambly, was also stricken with the malady.

This horrible disease cast terror and desolation among the soldiers, already worried by rumor of wandering bands of Iroquois warriors in the forest, from day to day fearing an attack without hope of aid, and isolated in a desolate outpost. To plumb the depths of their

34. The nearest enemy settlement was that of the English at Fort Orange, about 72 leagues from Fort Sainte-Anne.

35. Kerlidou: *Le Fort et la Chapelle de Sainte-Anne*, p. 29. Parkman: *The Old Régime in Canada.*

36. Forts Saint-Jean and Sainte-Thérèse had been abandoned.

37. Kerlidou: *Le Fort et la Chapelle de Sainte-Anne*, p. 32.

38. Sulte: *Le Régiment de Carignan*, p. 50.

misery, good Catholics as they were, they were deprived of the offices of the Church, no priest having been assigned to the fort. M. Dubois was at Fort Saint-Louis, doubly distant in winter, and his garrison was also stricken. At last M. de Tracy, "having been informed," wrote to M. Souart, superior of the Sulpicians at Montreal, who told one of his priests to hold himself in readiness to go to Fort Sainte-Anne.[39] This priest was M. Dollier de Casson, assuredly a fortunate choice for chaplain of the troops. Born at the Château de Casson, near Nantes, in 1636, at the age of nineteen he had been captain of cavalry under Marshal de Turenne, before entering the Seminary of Saint-Sulpice in Paris in 1657; a Breton of magnetic and dynamic personality, endowed with physical strength so extraordinary "that he carried two men seated on his two hands";[40] he thoroughly understood the soldier's temperament. Arriving in New France with the troops, he had already proven his courage and good-fellowship during the two campaigns of January and September, 1666; a good soldier, a nobleman, gigantic in stature, intelligent, the soldiers respected and loved him.

Although he was suffering from a painful swelling of the knee, injured during the recent Mohawk campaign, and was at the moment much weakened by too copious bleeding, he wanted to leave for Fort Sainte-Anne without delay. At this juncture, two soldiers from Fort Saint-Louis having arrived at Montreal, he resolved to leave with them, asking a delay of only one day in which to regain his strength. The escort was very small, considering that bands of Mohawks were prowling through the entire region; therefore, three brave colonists, inspired by the ardor of the valiant missionary, wished to share his peril and spontaneously offered themselves as escort; they were Charles Le Moyne, Jean-Baptiste Migeon de Bransac, and Jacques Le Ber.

Dollier de Casson started out with these companions, all on snowshoes and with heavy packs on their shoulders. It was a painful march from Villemarie to Fort Saint-Louis over a half-blazed trail; his knee hurt him, the snow was deep, he was unaccustomed to snowshoes. At Fort Saint-Louis, concealing his weakness, the priest requested additional escort. Fear of the Iroquois had aroused such terror in the officers that for twenty-four hours they absolutely refused to grant his request. This delay was useful to him in affording

39. Kerlidou: *Le Fort et la Chapelle de Sainte-Anne*, p. 29.
40. *Ibid.*, p. 29.

much needed rest, for he could not have continued further that day owing to the condition of his knee; nevertheless, he threatened to proceed alone over the twenty leagues which separated him from Fort Sainte-Anne. Perhaps the officers were somewhat ashamed to show less courage than a priest, for they decided the next day to grant him an escort of ten men commanded by M. Darienne, ensign.

At Fort Sainte-Anne scurvy was raging; forty soldiers were ill, two had just died without the rites of the Church, and several others, at the point of death, were pleading for a priest. The arrival of a missionary was anxiously awaited; therefore, MM. de la Motte, de la Durantaye and the other officers had no sooner sighted M. Dollier in the distance than they rushed eagerly to meet him in transports of joy. The priest, aided by the officers, immediately set about his task of caring for the sick and dying.[41] There was a scarcity of food and wine, especially of the nourishment required in the treatment of scurvy. De la Motte and M. Dollier de Casson sent one poor soldier to the hospital at Villemarie to save his life. M. Souart and Mlle. Mance, profiting by the return of the escort, sent M. Dollier, whom they thought to be in danger of dying from hunger, several sledges loaded with excellent food "which through the gentle and intelligent charity of the missionary, saved the lives of a great number of these soldiers."[42] Among these provisions were salt, purslane, onions, fowl, capons, and a great quantity of prunes. M. Dollier

41. On the journey from Montreal, M. Dollier had occasion "to arouse admiration, not only for the ardent courage, but also for the generosity and saintly audacity of his charity." Kerlidou: *Le Fort et la Chapelle de Sainte-Anne*, p. 30. He and his escort, forced to travel over the frozen Richelieu River and Lake Champlain, frequently fell and suffered serious accidents. One soldier, chancing to step on a spot where the ice was thin, fell through; the entire band thought him lost. Fortunately, he avoided sinking by holding onto his gun laid across the opening; the difficulty was how to climb up onto the ice, his snowshoes preventing his escape from death. Among his comrades no one dared to go to his aid. M. Dollier, making the reverent sign of the Cross, advanced toward the soldier and seized him by the arms in an attempt to draw him from the icy water. This poor fellow, being of great size and weight, M. Dollier could only draw him half out, the snowshoes always catching under the ice and holding him fast. M. Dollier called for the aid of his escort, but no one had the courage to share his danger. M. Darienne, the officer in charge, did not dare order his men to advance, but at the urgent appeal of M. Dollier went to help him himself; uniting their efforts they succeeded in dragging the exhausted soldier from the water. Cf. Parkman: *The Old Régime in Canada*: "La Vie de M. Dollier" (manuscript by Grandet).

42. Kerlidou: *Le Fort et la Chapelle de Sainte-Anne*, p. 32.

took the precaution of storing all this food in his own room and distributed it personally according to the need of the sick. Moreover, as "the air was laden with infection at Lake Champlain, an astonishing thing," says Benjamin Sulte, as soon as a patient had regained sufficient strength to bear the fatigue of transportation to Villemarie, M. Dollier sent him there to the hospital; upon recovery the soldier returned to the fort.

The disease persisted for about three months after the priest's arrival. The active strength of the garrison (about a score of officers and men) had to care for the sick in addition to the ordinary duties of an outpost, the continual round of guard duty, frequent alarms, etc. There was no time to remain with the convalescent, no matter how much the latter desired companionship. Several patients, to get attention from their comrades, had recourse to ingenious devices which the exigencies of their situation render excusable; they made wills in which they appeared to be owners of great property in France which they bequeathed to the comrade willing to care for them. "The reason was that the stench about them was so unbearable that no one dared approach them except M. Dollier and the Sieur Forestier, the surgeon sent from Villemarie."[43]

In the midst of all this misery, according to M. Dollier's *Histoire de Montreal,* if the body were cast down at Fort Sainte-Anne, the mind had great satisfaction because of the holy life which the garrison there began to lead. The soldiers, both sick and well, lived "as if they had taken communion" every day, and they did so very often. Masses and prayers were said at stated times, and each man was "careful to go." The priest officiated at the death of eleven of his flock.[44] If anything were neglected, it was not the well-being of the soldiers.

M. Dollier de Casson, when not in the quarters of the sick or in his own for much needed rest, was forced to avoid contagion and take vigorous exercise by running back and forth between the bastions. One might have thought him mad on seeing him, he tells us, if one had not known how necessary such violent exercise was for warding off this disease. Moreover, his room was a cell so narrow, so low also, that the sun almost never shone into it; one could not stand erect in it.[45]

43. Cf. Faillon: *Histoire de la Colonie française.*
44. Kerlidou: *Le Fort et la Chapelle de Sainte-Anne,* p. 34.
45. *Ibid.,* p. 34.

One day, as M. Dollier was indulging in his habitual racing up and down between the bastions, M. de la Motte watched him from the height of the palisade; realizing his depleted strength in a post so exposed, the captain laughingly said to the missionary, "You see, Sir, I shall never surrender; I shall give you a bastion to defend." The churchman, sensing raillery, replied in kind: "Sir, my company is composed of the sick with the surgeon as lieutenant; give us some stretchers on wheels, we'll take them to whatever bastion you say. They are brave now, they won't run away as they did from your company and Durantaye's when they deserted to join mine!"[46]

Thanks to the good disposition of the priest and to the trust inspired by his activity in their behalf, the officers and soldiers spent the rest of the winter in merriment and good-fellowship. Suddenly, in the spring, a new alarm! The Iroquois were at hand! At the fort great fires were lit in all the cabins, and the doors were closed to hide the fact that the cabins were empty or peopled only by convalescents. The effective garrison rushed to position on the palisade to welcome the savages. Fortunately, they were only Iroquois ambassadors coming to sue for peace, accompanied by a few French prisoners restored to their own country. When the ambassadors entered the fort, they were told that it was a marvel that they were not killed coming to the post, so many soldiers were scouting in the forest on all sides. The Indians believed this statement to be true; on their way to Montreal they had met groups of convalescents numbering fourteen or fifteen coming toward them, muskets covering them as they advanced to point-blank range. The savages would have been killed, had Bâtard Flammand not shouted to a French prisoner to speak quickly, which he did, crying out: "Comrades, do not fire! They come in peace!"[47]

M. Dollier ends his story by saying, "What we still have to note concerning Fort Sainte-Anne and Montreal is that, if the Churchman had not gone there at that time one would not have attempted the trip from Montreal so soon, believing it to be impossible because of the ice; that would have caused many men to die without confession."

When the ravages of disease ceased in the spring of 1667, M. Dollier went back to Villemarie where other enterprises awaited him.[48]

46. Dollier de Casson: *Histoire de Montreal.*
47. Dollier de Casson: *Histoire de Montreal.*
48. He was at Lake Ontario with Galinée, 1669-1671; Superior of the Semi-

The garrison of the fort, free from worry of Indian attack, went hunting and fishing without apprehension, enjoying health-giving exercise and bringing back good food. M. de la Motte remained in command.

The Iroquois ambassadors, after the conclusion of peace, had asked for missionaries. MM. de Tracy and de Courcelles were happy to be able to grant this request. "Our eyes fell on Father Jacques Frémin and Father Jean Peyron [or Pierron] for the Mohawk mission, and Father Jacques Bruyas for that of Oneida. The three Fathers, having received the blessing of Mgr. de Pétrée, always burning with very special zeal for the salvation of the Iroquois, left in the month of last July with the Indian ambassadors, and, reaching Fort Sainte-Anne at the foot of Lake Champlain, they learned that a band of 50 or 60 Mohigans, whom we call Wolves, was in ambush near the lake ready to attack the ambassadors of the Iroquois with whom they are at war."[49]

The Iroquois refused to go farther as long as the presence of the Wolves made the passage of the lake dangerous. The good Fathers were annoyed by this delay as they were eager to settle in the new missions. The garrison profited by the enforced sojourn of the priests to celebrate fittingly the festival of their patroness, Sainte-Anne. The missionaries remained at the fort a month and before leaving conducted a mission for the soldiers.[50] Father Jean Pierron wrote a letter dated at the fort August 12, 1667.[51] Finally, August 23, "at four o'clock in the afternoon," the eve of Saint Bartholomew's Day, they embarked for the Iroquois country. At nightfall they took shelter a league from the fort near the southern extremity of Isle La Motte.

Their report, included in the *Relation of 1668*, traces their route through the lake; ". . . as much by day as night we pursued our way happily, discovering no trace of the enemy. They had taken the southern shore to their country, and we kept the north shore of Lake Champlain. Rowing like poor convicts from morning until evening

nary of Saint-Sulpice at Montreal 1671; Vicar-General of the diocese of Quebec after 1676. He died, Sept. 25, 1701. Faillon: *La Vie de la Soeur Bourgeoys*, gives interesting details of the life of François Dollier de Casson.

49. *Relation de 1667*, p. 28.

50. *Relation de 1668*, p. 4.

51. Original letter in the Bibliothèque Nationale in Paris: copy at the Collège de Sainte-Marie at Montreal.

to spell our companions we gayly crossed this whole great lake already too renowned by the shipwreck of several of our French and quite recently by that of the Sieur Corlart commanding a Dutch hamlet near Agnié, who coming to Quebec to settle several important affairs, was drowned crossing a great bay where he was overtaken by a storm.[52] We arrived at three quarters of a league from the Falls, the outlet of Lake Saint-Sacrement. We all stopped at this place. . . ."[53] Then, traveling over Lake Saint-Sacrement, they discovered five leagues from the lake, a great slate quarry very like that of the Ardennes in France; the color of the stone was a fine blue. Just before reaching their missions they paused to say prayers, out of respect for Father Jogues, at Gandaooague, where he had been killed.

After the departure of the Jesuit Fathers, life at Fort Sainte-Anne continued in a tranquillity which left few traces in the history of the time; apart from the visit of Charles Boquet and François Poisson in 1667,[54] there is nothing noteworthy to record until May, 1668. The winter was not severe or at least the lack of definite information leads to this conclusion; no report of any lack of food nor of an epidemic is to be found. It is probable that M. de la Motte and his company remained in the garrison, that means of communication with the settlements were unhampered by the season, and that life at the fort went on with no extraordinary events to record.

In the spring of 1668, the garrison was agitated by important news: the head of the Church in New France was to visit Fort Sainte-Anne. Having already received the lieutenant general of the King and the governor, M. de la Motte and his soldiers were now honored by the visit of Mgr. de Laval, Titular Bishop of Petraea and Apostolic Vicar of New France.[55]

Bishop de Laval had given his benediction to the soldiers sent to Fort Sainte-Anne in September, 1666. When he learned what trials

52. Arendt van Corlaer is first mentioned in connection with New France when Father Jogues was ransomed. As commandant at Rensselaer, near Fort Orange, he showed himself again friendly to the French in connection with the prisoners taken by the Mohawks during the expedition of Courcelles in 1666.

53. *Relation de 1668*, pp. 4-5.

54. *Champlain Tercentenary Commission Report*, p. 389.

55. He did not receive the title of Bishop of Quebec until October 1, 1667. In Quebec as early as 1658, he was the first Roman Catholic Bishop in North America.

the garrison had undergone during the winter of 1666-1667, he decided to include this post in his Diocesan Visit. Here, according to a biographical note, is the manner in which Mgr. de Laval made his Episcopal rounds: "This man, great in birth and still more so in virtue, visiting his diocese, was transported in a little bark canoe by two peasants without any other suite than one ecclesiastic and carrying only a wooden cross, a very simple mitre and the rest of the vestments by a Bishop . . ." He was forced to travel by water and to make his way through the woods around rapids and falls.

The Jesuit *Relations* thus note the visit of His Eminence to Fort Sainte-Anne: "All the wandering tribes of savages gathered at Tadoussac had the consolation, sometime later, of enjoying the presence of Mgr. the Bishop of Petraea, who after having completed his whole visit by boat, that is to say at the mercy of a frail bark canoe, and after having passed through all our settlements from Quebec to the Fort of Sainte-Anne, which is the most distant of all the forts, at the foot of Lake Champlain, wished to bestow his blessing on our Church at Tadoussac and went there at the end of June."[56] Fort Sainte-Anne is the only mission mentioned which the first Bishop of New France visited in this part of his diocese.

About the end of May then, or perhaps early in June 1668, Mgr. de Laval went to Fort Sainte-Anne. It is not known how long he remained there, not very long in any case, for at the end of June he was at Tadoussac far beyond Quebec. He must have stayed at the fort several days at least, "to offer the sacrifice of Mass and perhaps administer the Sacrament of confirmation to the converted Indians who now liked to remain near the forts in order to see more easily the men of prayer."[57]

Peace now reigned in the whole extent of the Lake Champlain valley. The Iroquois received the Jesuit Fathers with cordial welcome; a permanent mission had even been established among the Mohawks. As we have seen, King Louis XIV, with no apparent lessening of his interest in New France, was now more actively concerned in the tangled affairs of Europe. He recalled to France the regiment of Carignan and the few detached companies, which had followed it to Canada. Four companies of the Carignan regiment, chosen among those whose captains had married in the colony, or who were so disposed, "were left behind to defend the more ex-

56. *Relation de 1668*, pp. 23-24.
57. Kerlidou: *Le Fort et la Chapelle de Sainte-Anne*, p. 41.

posed forts and to protect the inhabitants against enemy raids."[58] It is certain that the company of M. de la Motte remained in New France.

After the visit of Mgr. de Laval in June, and probably rather late in the year, M. de la Motte replaced Zacharie Dupuis as governor of Montreal;[59] and his company followed him there. In my opinion, the fort most open to attack by the Iroquois would not have been left without garrison. It is true that peace was current and that the Iroquois had requested and welcomed missionaries. Nevertheless, so many instances of treachery on the part of the Indians in the past would have significance; the French would not have abandoned such an important post without assurance that peace would endure. Although the Jesuit *Relations* speak no more of Fort Sainte-Anne after 1668, I believe that the governors of New France maintained a garrison in this fort until 1671. Indisputable proof is lacking, but the following documents (I give merely a title résumé), deposited in the Archives of the Ministry of Marine in Paris support the assumption that the important outposts continued to play a part in the defense of the colony:

A. February 12, 1669. Ordinance of the King for the subsistence of four companies of infantry, being in Canada, composed each of 53 men, during the year 1669.

B. March 22, 1669. Ordinance for the pay and maintenance of 25 soldiers in each of the companies left in Canada, during the year 1669.

C. March 22, 1669. Ordinance for the pay and maintenance of the four infantry companies left in Canada, on the footing of 78 men each, during the first six months of the year 1670.

D. March 25, 1669. Promise of Captains Chambly, La Durantaye, De Grandfontaine, Laubia and Berthier[60] to place their companies on the footing of 50 men each, of 20 to 30 years of age, and to furnish them subsistence until their embarkation, in return for 1000 crowns.

E. March 29, 1669. Ordinance for the raising and armament of six companies of infantry and for their subsistence during nine months of 1669 and six months of 1670.

58. Ferland: *Cours d'histoire du Canada*, II, p. 62.
59. See page 165.
60. At one time or another all these officers were at Fort Sainte-Anne.

In 1669, the Intendant Talon visited France and returned in 1670 with six companies of soldiers, 300 men, destined to strengthen the garrison in Canada.[61] I wish to quote also two Vermont historians: "Fort St. Anne was maintained for five years, and destroyed by the French themselves when they left."[62] "The fort was probably deserted in 1670."[63]

There is no question that, after 1671, Fort Sainte-Anne was abandoned, at least as a fortified outpost. Peace had come and the Mohawks no longer sent their warriors against the French settlements. The new governor could devote his efforts to peaceful development of this entire region, French by right of the discovery of Samuel de Champlain. Although the fort may have been allowed to fall in ruin and the chapel, the cabins, and the stockade may have disappeared little by little, the site of the fort became a favorite stopping-place for the numerous travelers going back and forth between Canada and Fort Orange. Often during the years following, there is mention in official documents of "abandoned" Fort Sainte-Anne and of Isle La Motte.

In addition to the military chronicle of Fort Sainte-Anne, the religious developments brought about by the presence of more or less permanent garrisons add to our realization that the French planned a continuing occupation. "Besides the chapels in Maine, there was also for some time another chapel in New England, that of Sainte-Anne on Isle La Motte in Lake Champlain, erected in 1666."[64] It has often been said that a Jesuit mission was established at Isle La Motte in 1642.[65] Contemporary maps show no trace of such a mission, but a map of 1663, entitled "Acadie,"[66] shows a church or Jesuit Mission on the western shore of Lake Champlain, half way between Ticonderoga and the foot of the lake. Possibly this was at Isle La Motte.

"One of the first cares of the French, upon their arrival to found a new settlement or a new fort, when they had the good fortune to be accompanied by a priest, which had always been the case since the

61. Rameau: *La France aux Colonies*, II, p. 30. E. Richard: *Rapport sur les Archives*, 1899, pp. 53 and 238.

62. Stone: *The Vermont of Today*, p. 37.

63. Crockett: *History of Lake Champlain*, p. 47.

64. Shea: *Histoire de l'Eglise Catholique aux Etats-Unis*, p. 507.

65. Hemenway: *Vermont Gazetteer*, I, p. 659. Hill: *Champlain Tercentenary*, p. 4.

66. Massachusetts Archives: *Documents Collected in France*, II, p. 147.

arrival of the Jesuit Fathers and the priests of St. Sulpice, was to prepare everything needed for the dignified celebration of the Holy Mysteries."[67]   The missionaries had portable altars and a suitable place had to be arranged for them; the first chapels in New France were often nothing more than evergreen boughs "and other greenery tastefully arranged."[68]   When time permitted and the necessary wood was available, they replaced the foliage and boughs by wooden buildings, and later by "stone edifices."[69]

At Fort Sainte-Anne the first Mass was probably celebrated in a temporary chapel of boughs and foliage.   When the fort was finished, and perhaps even before, all evidence points to the construction, as at Fort Richelieu,[70] of a chapel of wood.   During the summer season and even at the end of September, when four priests were stationed at Sainte-Anne with M. de Tracy's troops, an open-air chapel would have sufficed.   However, when M. Dollier de Casson spent three months there during the following winter, having, as he says, "numerous communions and acts of piety every day," he needed a solid, warm chapel.   Moreover, he could not celebrate Mass in his quarters since "there was hardly space to turn around."[71]

Dollier de Casson's energy is well known, and had he found no chapel upon his arrival, he would have immediately started to build one.   We may make the same comment regarding the month's sojourn at the fort of Fathers Frémin, Peyron, and Bruyas.   Lacking direct evidence, the personal character of the priests concerned confirm Shea's statement that the chapel was erected during the summer of 1666.[72]

CHAPTER V. *Peace*

THE arrival in 1672 of the new governor and lieutenant general of the King, Count de Frontenac, inaugurated a period of comparative calm under a strong personal government.   Louis de Buade, Count de Frontenac, born in 1620, had distinguished himself from his fifteenth year, in all the European campaigns of the

---

67. Kerlidou: *Le Fort et la Chapelle de Sainte-Anne*, p. 19.

68. *Ibid.*, p. 20.

69. Kerlidou: *Le Fort et la Chapelle de Sainte-Anne*, p. 21.

70. *Relation de 1643*.

71. Dollier de Casson: *Histoire de Montreal*, 1665, 1666, etc. (Manuscript in the Bibliothèque Mazarine at Paris, H, 2706, folio).

72. Crockett: *History of Lake Champlain*, p. 39. *Americana* XXVIII, p. 23.

century. Godson of Louis XIII, relative of Secretary of State Phélypeaux (and consequently of the Talons, Colberts, Beauharnois, *et al.*, who play so great a rôle in the history of New France), M. de Frontenac was chosen by Marshal de Turenne to serve in Candia during the campaign against the Turks in 1669. A polished and gallant courtier on the surface, he concealed with difficulty an untamed nature which often led him into heedless action; it is even said that the King appointed him to the post in New France to remove him from Court, where his difficult disposition made his presence disturbing. Whatever the reason for his appointment, de Frontenac knew how to command obedience and gain admiration from both Iroquois and Algonquins. This was a gift which very few colonial governors could claim. The documents of the time recording negotiations between the French and the Indians often quote the exact words of the Indians; de Frontenac is always honored by the name "Onontio" meaning "father," while the governors of New York are called merely "brother."

The valley of Lake Champlain is rarely mentioned in French documents between 1672 and 1689; the interest of the governors and colonists seems to be directed toward the exploration of the country to the west, the region of the great lakes Ontario, Erie, and beyond. There was, however, a steadily increasing activity along the Richelieu River. The King was granting seigniories to distinguished colonists, generally former officers of the royal troops; thus we note the grant of the seigniories of Sorel, Chambly, Rouville, Longueuil, etc.

Frequently one sees in the documents and histories of these times the name Champlain; one assumes that Lake Champlain is referred to and is often led into error, for, unless other details definitely show that Lake Champlain is meant, "Champlain" refers rather to a small village situated on the St. Lawrence, not far from Three Rivers. Mr. Stevens among others reaches, I believe, an erroneous conclusion when he attributes to the valley of Lake Champlain the following statements: a. ". . . the years after abandoning Fort Sainte-Anne the French seem to have trouble in the Champlain valley"; this sentence is based on the "Mémoire d'un missionaire du Canada sur les conditions dans ces lieux." b. "1674. Protest made to Frontenac by the settlers in the Champlain territory, asking that no powder or shot be sold to the Indians."[1] Charlevoix says, "The people adhering to

1. Stevens: *The French Occupation of the Champlain Valley*, pp. 15 and 42.

the French missions in the Champlain territory in 1683 were 295."[2] Here, again, I believe that the village on the St. Lawrence is meant, rather than the lake.

We know, however, that the French had not abandoned the valley of the lake. In the *Correspondance Officielle* we find reports of frequent journeys from Canada to Fort Orange. The official documents of the State of New York and the histories of the New England colonies give many proofs that the valley swarmed with travelers intent on diplomatic affairs, often on military missions, and occasionally busied with commercial interests.

In 1677, during an attack made by the Algonquins from the Missions on the village of Hatfield in the Connecticut River valley, the wives of Benjamin Wait and of Stephen Jennings were seized and taken to Canada. Their husbands, supplied with letters from the governor of Massachusetts authorizing their journey for the purpose of ransoming their wives, left Hatfield October 24, 1677. In the spring of 1678, they returned from New France with their rescued wives, "and were generously furnished with a guard of French soldiers, by order of the governor."[3] After a sixteen days' journey by way of Lake Champlain and the Hudson River, they reached Fort Orange in early summer.

From the discovery until 1665, the French had been opposed by the Indian tribes composing the Five Nations (especially the Mohawks) in attempts to extend their influence into the Champlain valley. When the English acquired the province of New York from the Dutch by treaty in 1665, the character of the opposition changed. Royal grants to Massachusetts in 1620 and to New York in 1664, confirmed by the treaty of 1665, gave the English shadowy claims to the Lake Champlain territory, which they attempted to enforce against French aggression. Scouts were sent to find out the extent of French operations in 1666, when the construction of Fort Sainte-Anne was under way. Diplomatic objections to French encroachment were frequently made, but this opposition only served to increase French efforts to maintain and strengthen their legitimate claims to the valley, claims justified by right of discovery and priority of occupation.

For some years the English of New York were busily occupied in

2. Charlevoix: *History of New France* (Shea's Translation), I, p. 307.
3. Hill: *Old Fort Edward*, p. 11. Hoyt: *Indian Wars*, p. 148.

developing the province. They cleverly played upon the traditional ill will of the Iroquois toward the French and urged their Indian allies to carry on active opposition to French expansion toward the south. Thus until 1690 the conflict seems to be as before between the French and the Iroquois.

In spite of English claims and Iroquois opposition, the French had no idea of withdrawing from the Lake Champlain valley; on the contrary, they undertook a program of carefully planned expansion, re-enforcing their legitimate rights by the settlement of colonists grouped around military posts. Land grants were made to military leaders of experience, whose fortified homes would serve as defense outposts, manned by the settlers living in the vicinity. Spaced at intervals, the established forts on the Richelieu River (Forts Richelieu-Sorel and Saint-Louis de Chambly) would give necessary protection, and further construction was planned to the south as soon as the need became apparent.

For about fifteen years the English, doubtless under pretext of commercial relations, continued to send "intelligent men" into New France, especially to Montreal, to spy out the French plans and report them to the English authorities at Fort Orange. From 1675 to 1690, Frenchmen, established in trade at Fort Orange, sent exact information concerning the English plans, even the most transitory, to the governors of New France. Travelers often visited the settlements of both colonial powers, bearing letters to and from their governors filled with interesting details concerning events in the two colonies.

November 14, 1679, the Intendant Duchesneau received a letter from M. de Sorel, now living on his seigniory at the mouth of the Richelieu River; he had received news from Fort Orange of the French fleet whose appearance had interfered with English commerce. "Lafleur, an inhabitant of St. Louis, brought them . . . Having gone to Lake Champlain to hunt for Ranontons (beavers), he met Guillaume David, who resided about two years ago in these parts, and who went with a big boy, his son-in-law, his wife and several small children to New Netherland, where he lives at present . . . Lafleur was at Orange . . ."[4]

A short time later, Governor de Frontenac drew up a plan to regulate trade by the establishment of a commandant and garrison

4. *Doc. Col. Hist. N. Y.*, IX, p. 138.

in a post on the Richelieu River. He suggested for this post a former soldier of the Carignan regiment, married and settled in the country, Pierre de Saint-Ours, the well-known owner of a seigniory on that river.[5] Evidently de Frontenac had seriously displeased the King by his incessant struggle with the heads of the Church and the intendants. Louis XIV recalled him in 1682, a great loss to the colony. The new governor, Jean-Antoine Lefebvre, Sieur de la Barre, took up de Frontenac's plan with the addition of a few details of his own invention; instead of one post on the Richelieu River, there would be several, not merely to regulate trade but also (much more important in M. de la Barre's opinion) to give the alarm in case of war which he believed to be inevitable.[6]

Before November 4, 1683, the governor had sent to Fort Orange and to "Manatte" (Manhattan) the Sieur de Salvaye of Sorel, often employed on similar missions by de Frontenac and de la Barre. The latter wrote to M. de Seignelay, June 5, 1684, saying that he had sent an officer to "present his compliments" to Colonel Dongan. In a memorandum on the war against the Five Nations, October 1, he speaks of having sent, about June 15, the Sieur Bourbon to Fort Orange and "Manatte" with reproaches addressed to Colonel Dongan concerning injuries done to the French by the Iroquois of the West. M. de Bourbon had returned August 5. M. de la Barre, not being a de Frontenac, could neither impose his ideas on the Iroquois nor make war upon them with success. The King replaced him after the campaign of 1684 by Jacques-René de Brisay, Marquis de Denonville.

Colonel Dongan, governor of New York, thought it wise to strengthen English claims to the valley of Lake Champlain by the grant, November 4, 1684, to Messrs. Peter Schuyler, David Schuyler, Robert Livingston, and others, of the land situated along the Hudson River north of Fort Orange; this grant is called the "Saratoga Patent," and was the first in a series extending toward New France.[7]

The correspondence of M. de Denonville is filled with plans for continuing and ending the conflicts with the Iroquois. May 8, 1686, he writes to M. de Seignelay telling him that he had sent a lieutenant and eighteen soldiers to Saint-Louis de Chambly with orders to stop all who wished to pass that point. A problem which irritated him at

5. Le Comte de Frontenac au ministre, 2 novembre 1681.
6. Doc. Col. Hist. N. Y., IX, p. 205.
7. Ibid., IX, p. 290.

the same time was the desertion of two sergeants by this route, also that of Sieur de Chailly who, he fears, will have told at Fort Orange all he knew "of our plans."[8]

In a memorandum on the present state of affairs in Canada, November 8, 1686, M. de Denonville asks again for troops to man the outposts, expressing the desire to send a detachment to the Mohawk country by way of Lake Champlain at the same time that he leads a second force by way of Lake Ontario, a further development of de Frontenac's plan. He also mentions the visit of Antoine L'Epinart, long resident among the Dutch and now living among the English, who has come by way of the lake for his daughter whom he left in a convent. November 16, 1686, in a letter to M. de Seignelay, M. de Denonville speaks of the return of an "intelligent man" whom he had sent to "Manatte"; and again, "I received, at the moment of writing this present letter, new communications from Orange." All the information thus secured led M. de Denonville to push actively his plan of attack on the Iroquois; however, the realization of his plan continued to be postponed.

June 8, 1687, M. de Denonville wrote from Villemarie to M. de Seignelay that he had received November 12 of the preceding year, the news that Gédéon Petit of Chambly was going to desert to the English; that the governor of Villemarie, M. de Callières, had arrested the said Petit and had put him in prison; and, finally, that the said Petit had escaped in the month of March, 1687. Why was there at this time such an ardent desire among the inhabitants to desert to the English? There were very different reasons: often, as I have noted before, a change of residence, with the tacit approval of the governor or at his suggestion, as a means of securing exact information about English plans; again, the desire to lead a more comfortable existence, trade being less bound by official regulation among the English; also, the climate of Fort Orange was less severe. Among the deserters there were sometimes traitors, for such is human nature, renegades intent upon selling their knowledge of French plans to the English. Most frequently, however, the Frenchman whose name appears in the *Correspondance Officielle* is of the type of that "Sieur de Salvaye, inhabitant of Saurel," who for many years with honorable devotion, carried to happy conclusion the missions entrusted to him by the governors.

8. Hill: *Old Fort Edward*, p. 12.

Slowly and with extreme caution, M. de Denonville formulated his plans of attack on the Iroquois. At each step he wrote to the minister, discussing the situation and suggesting details of additional defense. March 8, 1688, in his "Projet pour terminer la guerre contre les Iroquois," he spoke of a garrisoned post which he wished to establish at the landing-place on Lake Champlain. In the same memorandum, speaking of the forts needed in New France, he says that a fort *at the end of Lake Champlain toward the Mohawks* will contribute to the safety of the colony. I underline these words, for therein I find the first mention of the site of a fort at Crown Point, where Fort St. Frederic will later stand. The French maps of the time mark the end of the lake at that point; the part to the south, between Crown Point and the Petit Sault (Whitehall) is called either "Grand Marais" or "rivière du Chicot." This point is "the cape which advances into the lake" of Champlain's voyages, the battlefield of July 30, 1609. It is also the point on which developed little by little an important trading post where Indians, French, and English carried on the fur trade.

M. de Denonville, always the negotiator rather than the man of action, sent Father François Vaillant du Gueslis that same spring to confer with Governor Dongan at Fort Orange. The English were working constantly to prevent enduring peace between the French and the Iroquois. M. de Denonville, through his ambassador, reproached Governor Dongan for the secret activity of the English against French interests. It must be remembered that at this time Louis XIV was supporting James II of England against the revolutionary party; open war will not be declared between France and England until after the fall of James II.

M. de Denonville, well-informed of the undercover efforts of the English to turn the Iroquois, especially the Mohawks, away from their neutral position in reference to the French, set to work to define and elaborate his plans. The *Résumé des défenses nécessaires en Canada*, drawn up toward the end of 1688, speaks of fifty or sixty soldiers to be sent to Crown Point (this name appearing for the first time), or its vicinity to protect the two shores of the lake and warn the governor of war-parties coming from Fort Orange and from Lake Saint-Sacrement.

Plans for war multiplied, and the situation became more threatening because of European developments, especially the struggle in England between James II, supported by Louis XIV, and William of Orange. M. de Callières, governor of Villemarie, was seeking the post of governor of New France, clearly aware of M. de Denonville's lack of energy; he wrote to the minister, detailing his plan of campaign and offering himself to command the expedition. The King replied May 1, 1689, not to M. de Callières but to Governor de Denonville, that it was not time to think of such an expedition, for the King's armies were too busy elsewhere. M. de Seignelay, the minister, wrote on the same day to tell the Marquis de Denonville to get everything ready in case the King decided to order the attack. Louis XIV was not too well satisfied with de Denonville's administration in Canada; he missed the strength and *savoir-faire* of M. de Frontenac. May 31, 1689, the King recalled M. de Denonville and on June 7, restored to New France her great leader, Count de Frontenac.

Although sixty-nine years of age, he was still the energetic, firm "Onontio" so much admired by the Indian allies and feared by the Indian enemies of New France. Louis XIV, at the moment of his departure, gave him instructions to follow exactly the plan proposed by M. de Callières for attack on the Iroquois and the English by way of Lake Champlain.

Thirteen hundred Mohawks were traveling over the Saratoga Trail[9] August 1, 1689, in 250 war canoes to attack the French. They fell upon La Chine, a small village on the island of Montreal, where they massacred the inhabitants, destroyed the houses and harvests and made 130 prisoners on August 5.[10] On August 18, M. de Callières wrote to the minister that the Iroquois returned August 13, with only 150 warriors. They attacked La Chesnaye and the Isle de Jésus, where they killed the inhabitants and took some prisoners. At the same moment the news arrived that New York had decided to support the Prince of Orange. Louis XIV was supporting James II, affording the wished-for occasion for making war against the English and the Iroquois, who had already broken the peace established by M. de Tracy in 1666.[11]

9. See *Appendix A*.

10. Brandow: *Old Saratoga and Schuylerville*, p. 13. Hill: *Old Fort Edward*, p. 12. *Doc. Col. Hist. N. Y.*, IX, p. 431.

11. For the discussion of this period, I have drawn largely from the *Correspondance Officielle*. *The Documentary History of the State of New York* contains a quantity of material covering this period. As for the events in Europe, any detailed history of France or England will suffice.

LOUIS XIV had addressed to Count de Frontenac, June 7, 1689, the "Mémoire pour servir d'instruction au Comte de Frontenac sur l'Entreprise de la Nouvelle-York," accepting with modifications the plan of M. de Callières. De Frontenac and de Callières embarked at La Rochelle, July 22, their departure having been postponed by unforeseen delay in preparing the two warships which were to appear before "Manatte" at the moment of the arrival of the land forces from Canada; they counted on the capture of the port of New York. Obstacles of every nature caused increased delay and, without much confidence in a favorable outcome of the enterprise, de Frontenac at least reached Quebec in October, only to hear of Iroquois attacks in the vicinity of Villemarie. He had boats prepared and went up the St. Lawrence to confer with M. de Denonville at Villemarie. Everything was in confusion and M. de Denonville had even given orders to blow up Fort Frontenac. The new governor, who had had this fort constructed, sent a counter-order immediately, but he was too late. Fort Frontenac, whose destruction an insolent Iroquois ambassador had demanded from M. de Denonville, had been burned and the garrison sent back to Villemarie. French prestige had suffered much from the lack of decision shown by MM. de la Barre and de Denonville.

M. de Frontenac saw his problem clearly: it was to revive the courage of the Canadians and of his troops as much as to impose his authority upon the Indians, allies or enemies. Instead of preparing a punitive expedition against the Iroquois, M. de Frontenac interpreted in his own way the royal instructions. He organized three simultaneous attacks upon the English colonies who had rejected James II as their king, long the ally of the King of France. The Indian allies asked nothing better. The first expedition was assembled at Villemarie to attack Fort Orange; the second at Three Rivers, to fall upon the English on the Merrimack; the third, at Quebec, to advance against the settlements in Maine. The party formed at Villemarie was ready first; the governor only needed active and experienced leaders; he found them in two Canadians, Nicolas d'Ailleboust, Sieur de Mantet, and Jacques Le Moyne, Sieur de Sainte-Hélène. Among the subordinate officers we find Le Moyne de Bienville and Le Moyne d'Iberville, both brothers of the

Sieur de Sainte-Hélène, and Repentigny de Montesson, Le Ber du Chesne, etc. January 15, 1690, a party of 210 men set out for the south; this party was composed of 114 French, 80 Iroquois of the Sault and Montagne missions under their chief, "le Grand Agnier," and 16 Algonquins; apart from the officers there were volunteers among whom are mentioned as most "apt for such a service" the Sieurs de Bonrepos and de la Brosse, reserve lieutenants, and La Marque de Montigny. The party left Villemarie for Chambly on snowshoes, then stopped at Fort Sainte-Anne. At the head of Lake Champlain a council was held (at Crown Point?). The French leaders, well acquainted with the Indian temperament, had kept the goal of the expedition secret until now; at the council they favored an attack upon Fort Orange, capital of the English colony. The Indians believed such a plan somewhat foolhardy, pointing out to the French the difficulties of the enterprise and the weakness of their forces. An Iroquois of the Sault, recalling only too well the disasters of the preceding August, demanded, "Since when have the French become so bold?" The French replied that the purpose of the expedition was to restore French prestige, shattered by the recent Mohawk raids, and that the only means of attaining this goal was to take Fort Orange or die gloriously in the attempt. The council remained undecided; the Indians, more experienced than the French and well acquainted with the country, refused to consent to the attack on Fort Orange; therefore, the party started off toward the English settlements without deciding on a destination, still hoping to reach an agreement before coming to the fork in the trail, leading on the one hand to Fort Orange, on the other to Corlaer (Schenectady).

I do not follow the French on this expedition in detail, because from the moment they cross the Hudson River they are in territory with which this study is not concerned. It is sufficient to say that, in a blinding snowstorm, they fell upon Corlaer on the morning of February 9; in two hours they had killed 60 men, women, and children and taken 80 prisoners; only two homes were spared from destruction by fire. The French lost two men killed and M. de Montigny was twice seriously wounded. The return began at noon; only 27 prisoners marched with the French, the rest being handed over to the Mohawks who had taken no active part in the affray. Fifty horses were a part of the booty seized at Corlaer; in the beginning of the march they facilitated the transportation of the equipment and of the wounded; soon they served a more pressing need, that of food which was very scarce; only sixteen reached Villemarie.[1]

A group of English was organized the very day of the attack. Two days after, joined by 150 Mohawks, they began the pursuit of the French, not giving up hope of overtaking them until they reached Crown Point; a party of Mohawks pursued them still farther.

The French, believing pursuit abandoned and finding that the provisions hidden at the lake had spoiled, began to eat the horses, and to boil their shoe leather with potatoes; exhausted, they marched slowly toward Villemarie. Sixty leagues from Corlaer their Indian allies went hunting, but the starving French were unwilling to wait and struggled on, sending MM. d'Iberville and du Chesne with two Indians to Villemarie with news of their successful attack. Not far from the town several Frenchmen, at the end of their endurance, wandered from the path; their fate was never known; six others died of starvation, having stopped to rest along the trail. The expedition reached Villemarie at three o'clock in the afternoon.

De Frontenac's second expedition, organized at Three Rivers, was composed of 20 Abenakis, 5 Algonquins, and 25 French with François Hertel, Sieur de Rouville, as leader; among the French were his three sons, his two nephews, and the Sieurs Crevier de Saint-François and de Gâtineau. Leaving on January 28, they followed the St. Francis River and its tributary the Magog, crossed Lake Memphremagog, thence went by the Barton River and the Passumpsic to the Connecticut. After three months of exceedingly difficult marching, they attacked the little village of Salmon Falls (now Dover, N. H.), massacred about 30 inhabitants and took 54 prisoners. On the return journey M. de Rouville stopped at the Abenaki village of Kennebec, where he awaited news of the third expedition, undertaken against the settlements in Maine, and led by Sieurs de Portneuf and de Courtemanche. De Rouville joined them with 36 of his men and took part in the capture of Fort Loyal, while the rest of his men returned home by way of Lake Champlain.

The striking success of these three expeditions, although New York still remained English, produced the desired effect upon the

1. For the story of the Schenectady massacre see de Monseignat: *Relation des événements les plus remarquables en Canada, 1689, 1690; Doc. Col. Hist. N. Y.,* I and IX; Parkman: *Frontenac and New France under Louis XIV;* Crockett: *History of Lake Champlain;* Crockett: *History of Vermont,* I; Hill: *Old Fort Edward;* Trumbull: *History of the United States,* I.

Canadians and Indians; French prestige was re-established, fear was vanquished and confidence restored. There was one great misfortune, tragic enough but overshadowed by the joy of the moment; this was the regrettable death of the chief of the Iroquois of the Sault, the Grand Agnier. The Indians of the Sault accompanied by six Frenchmen, among them the Sieur de Beauvais, "son of the Sieur de Tilly," and the Sieur de la Brosse, reserve captain, left Villemarie in canoes May 18, 1690. The journey was without incident until May 26; that day, scouts, sent out in the early morning, heard a gunshot and shortly after, the Indians attacked two cabins and took 14 prisoners, who said that the rest of their party, 30 men with their wives and children, were left on the way to the English fort, the goal of this expedition.[2] The Grand Agnier continued his march and captured this fort by surprise, killing four men and two women. There were eight English women among his 42 prisoners. Informed of the presence of 700 Wolves ahead, the Grand Agnier deemed it wise to order a retreat. Arriving about noon on June 4, "at the Salmon River which empties into Lake Champlain,"[3] they set about building canoes for the return to Villemarie. At vespers this party of French and Christian Iroquois was discovered by another party, composed of Algonquins and Abenakis from Three Rivers. At dawn a skirmish began and the Grand Agnier was killed; two French and two English prisoners were wounded. The party of Algonquins and Abenakis had been detached from de Rouville's forces, and in the darkness the allies had not recognized each other. On the Abenaki side the loss was also tragic as their chief Wohawa or Hopehood, "that memorable tygre," says Cotton Mather, died with several of his warriors.[4] This deplorable affair almost alienated the two Indian tribes most friendly to the French; but, thanks to the influence of the venerable "Onontio," their injured feelings were soothed and the two tribes exchanged gifts designed to assuage the grief of the families of the two renowned chieftains.

The Schenectady massacre and the success of the two other ex-

2. It appears that the Grand Agnier was going toward Salmon Falls by way of the Winooski and Merrimack Rivers.

3. De Monseignat: *Relation des événements les plus remarquables en Canada, 1689, 1690.* This river empties into the lake on the west shore, opposite Valcour Island.

4. Parkman: *Frontenac and New France under Louis XIV*, p. 234.

peditions against the English had made the French aware of the danger of attack by way of Lake Champlain. Until then the valley wilderness as well as the difficulty of travel by the lake had discouraged military maneuvers. Now the route was better known and the dangers of transport lessened. Beginning in March, 1690, the English sent frequent expeditions, sometimes military, more often for exploration. The valley now became the scene of great military activity, followed by persistent effort by each of the two rival nations toward colonization. By clear right of discovery the valley of the lake belonged to New France, but the strategic value of control over this route of direct and comparatively easy communication between the two powers in time of war became quite evident to the English governors, especially after the recent campaigns. The struggle to decide whether Lake Champlain should become English or remain French began in 1690—a struggle which would not cease until the English armies had forced the French withdrawal to the St. Lawrence valley in 1760.

On March 26, 1690, the governor of New York ordered Captain Jacobus de Warm, a Dutchman of Fort Orange, to advance to Crown Point, with a party of 20 Mohawks and 12 English, to watch the French. He was to select a spot other than Crown Point for his base; so on Chimney Point across the lake, he built "a little stone fort" where his party remained for a month. March 30, the governor issued orders to Captain Abram Schuyler to proceed with nine English and a few Mohawks under Chief Lawrence as far as the mouth of Otter Creek, where he was to watch day and night, always keeping in close touch with de Warm at Chimney Point. Schuyler evidently delayed his departure, for supplementary orders were issued to him April 1. After de Warm had completed his stone fort, Schuyler left Otter Creek and went as far as Fort Chambly, where he killed two French and took one prisoner.[5]

The French continued to send Indian bands to take prisoners who might give information of the English plans against New France.[6] The boldness of the Indians was extreme; an Englishman was seized at the very gates of Fort Orange. In the month of August the rumor spread that the English, not only of New York but of all the

5. Hemenway: *Vermont Gazetteer*, I, p. 2. Murray: *Lake Champlain and Its Shores*, p. 213. Brandow: *Old Saratoga and Schuylerville*, p. 17. Crockett: *History of Lake Champlain*, p. 52.

6. *Doc. Col. Hist. N. Y.*, IX, p. 478.

English colonies bordering upon Canada, were preparing an expedition against New France. It appears that this plan was first outlined by the Mohawks—a plan so well conceived that the officials of the several English colonies hastened to put it to the test, but it was difficult to carry out because of the selfish attitudes of the individual governors.[7]

In the month of May, Governor Leisler of New York received representatives from the Plymouth, Massachusetts, and Connecticut colonies, invited to confer with New York officials concerning the strategy of the proposed campaign. The following plan was drawn up: an army of 755 men with the Mohawk allies would assemble at Fort Orange to advance against Canada by way of Lake Champlain; a naval expedition would attack Quebec at the same time. Petty jealousies arose over the appointment of the commander of the colonial army. After almost endless discussion, the choice fell upon Fitzjohn Winthrop of Connecticut, an honest man but lacking in military skill and administrative ability. Discussions continued, and it was agreed that the attacks on Quebec and Villemarie should be simultaneous.

The seizure of Port Royal in Acadia in May warned the French of the danger of attack by way of the St. Lawrence and alarmed the whole colony. The fortitude of de Frontenac when Phipps advanced on Quebec in October contributed to the defeat of the English naval expedition.

On August 7, General Winthrop led his troops to the Petit Sault (Whitehall). There he began the construction of boats for the voyage down Lake Champlain. Captain Sanders Glen, a survivor of the Schenectady massacre, was sent to "Ticonderoga" on the fourth of the month, with 28 men to serve as protection for the construction camp. By October 9, it became evident in Winslow's camp that the season was too far advanced to permit construction of the boats as the bark could no longer be removed from the tree trunks. In addition, provisions were scarce, and the commissaries at Fort

7. New France formed one province governed by direct administrators of the royal authority, while the English colonies each had its own special system of government, in some cases under the direct control of the King, in others administered by governors elected by legislative assemblies or appointed by the directors of the colonizing company. New France presented a united front; the English colonies were often disrupted by inner conflicts, which nullified all efforts toward co-operation.

Orange did not adequately supply the army's needs. Smallpox had made great inroads on the effective strength of Winthrop's force. To add to the general uneasiness Winthrop worried much over not receiving news from the fleet.

Captain John Schuyler, brother of Mayor Peter Schuyler of Fort Orange, soon became convinced that Winthrop would abandon the attack; therefore, Schuyler asked and received permission to attempt a raid on Canada with a band of volunteers. He left the Petit Sault with 29 English and 120 Mohawks on August 13 and was joined at Ticonderoga by Captain Glen and his band of 13 whites and 5 Indians; by way of Lake Champlain and the Richelieu River they reached Chambly, thence going overland to strike La Prairie de la Madeleine on the eve of August 22. Let us leave them near the village to see what the French are doing.

About August 15, La Plaque, nephew of the Grand Agnier and renowned warrior of the Christian Iroquois of the Sault, returned to Villemarie from a scouting trip toward Fort Orange. At Lake Saint-Sacrement he reported seeing many English preparing boats as if for an attack on Villemarie. The Chevalier de Clermont, in command of the guard between Villemarie and Sorel, had received July 31, an order from M. de Frontenac to scout as far as Lake Champlain, "which is the route the enemy has chosen to advance against this country."[8] At the very moment La Plaque was making his report at Villemarie, M. de Clermont discovered fires of the enemy and heard gunshots; he approached the spot and saw during the night 8 boats of the enemy landing 18 to 20 men each on Isle La Motte. De Clermont had no more than 30 men and feared the outcome of an attack; so during the night he sailed around the enemy and stationed his men at the foot of the lake, a league below the English. There he kept watch for two days and then sent two of his boats to Chambly, remaining behind with a third to keep close watch of English movements. From the Falls of Chambly the Sieur de la Bruère was sent to Villemarie with the news of the English advance; he arrived at eleven o'clock in the evening of August 29, unfortunately too late.

M. de Frontenac, at the news brought by La Plaque, crossed the St. Lawrence with 1,200 men to await the enemy at La Prairie. For three days all was calm; scouts found no trace of the enemy lurking

8. De Monseignat: *Relation des événements les plus remarquables en Canada, 1689, 1690.*

in the vicinity, and on August 22, leaving a small garrison in the village, the governor recrossed the river and distributed his troops in the near-by settlements. He had scarcely reached Villemarie when the cannon of La Prairie announced Schuyler's attack on August 23.

Schuyler fell so suddenly on La Prairie that soldiers, villagers, women and children were all harvesting in the fields. The English, with a loss of but one Mohawk ally, killed 6 of the French and took 19 prisoners. They burned all the buildings outside the stockade of the fort and slaughtered 150 head of cattle. On August 30, Schuyler's party safely reached Fort Orange where General Winthrop learned of the successful expedition, which he had not had the energy to initiate or carry out.[9]

1691

After Schuyler's retreat, military operations in the Champlain valley ceased abruptly; winter was approaching and, even more significant, the two rival powers were too poor and too weak to risk further danger. In New France, half the fields remained untilled; although four vessels laden with supplies had arrived at Quebec, double the number had been captured by the English or forced to turn back without landing. As for the troops, they had to be quartered on the villagers who had barely enough for their own maintenance through the winter season. In the English colonies conditions were better in but one respect, *viz.*, no troops were quartered on the colonists since they themselves served as soldiers.

Springtime saw the return of the migratory birds and the raiding Iroquois. The Indians came but rarely in the winter when their bodies could be plainly seen in the bare forests and their path could easily be traced in the snow; their attacks were almost sure to take place at two seasons of the year, those of planting-time and harvest, when results were disastrous.

Since the futile expedition of the preceding year, New York and New England had been at odds; mutual jealousies and political uncertainties had destroyed the possibility of united action against their common enemy. The governor of New York continued activity against the French by inciting Mohawk raids, until the latter became

9. Johannes Schuyler: Journals, *Doc. Col. Hist. N. Y.*, II, pp. 285-288. La Potherie: III, p. 101. De Monseignat: *Relation des événements les plus remarquables en Canada, 1689, 1690.* Fitzjohn Winthrop: Journal, *Doc. Col. Hist. N. Y.*, IV, p. 193.

irritated, being aware that the English were taking no active part in the struggle. Upon realizing their attitude, the English assembled forces at Fort Orange, placing them in command of Mayor Peter Schuyler.

Schuyler left Fort Orange June 21, with 120 English, some 60 Wolves joining him at Stillwater and 15 Mohawks at Saratoga. He arrived at Isle La Motte, June 26, and his "Journal" mentions the old French fort called Sainte-Anne, abandoned several years since. Leaving his boats three leagues from Fort Saint-Louis de Chambly, Schuyler led his men overland toward La Prairie de la Madeleine. After a night of rain, an hour before dawn, Schuyler attacked the 800 men under M. de Callières who had been sent to welcome him. So sudden and well organized were the English movements that the affair turned into a disaster for the French who were forced to withdraw into the fort. The English began a leisurely retreat toward their boats without pursuit. The illness of Governor de Callières and the death of his lieutenant, the Sieur de Saint-Cirque, are not enough to explain the lack of pursuit. After a skirmish en route during which he vanquished a party of 280 Canadians and Indians, Schuyler embarked for Fort Orange, having suffered a loss of 43 dead and 25 wounded, while the French had lost 200 men in the two engagements.[10]

M. de La Chapelle in August led a party of seven or eight men to take prisoners in the vicinity of Fort Orange. Two leagues from the settlement he found two men in a Mohawk cabin which he had seized. Soon after, three other Englishmen arrived with reports of Schuyler's success at La Prairie. M. de La Chapelle decided to kill his prisoners during the night, but, warned by a Christian Indian, three of them escaped. M. de La Chapelle returned to Villemarie with the two others near the end of the month, bringing word of Schuyler's safe return to Fort Orange.[11]

1692

Military operations during this year were confined to frequent skirmishes between the Christian Indians of the Missions and their

10. *Relation de Bénac, 1691. Relation de 1682-1712*, written by an officer of Valrenne. Parkman: *Frontenac and New France under Louis XIV. Doc. Col. Hist. N. Y.*, III, p. 800. Palmer, Butler, and Crockett speak of this expedition in their histories.

11. *Relation de ce qui s'est passé du plus remarquable en Canada, 1690, 1691; Doc. Col. Hist. N. Y.*, IX, p. 525.

cousins, the Iroquois; sometimes the name of an English leader is mentioned with the latter. The Intendant de Champigny speaks of various parties sent out against the English from Villemarie in the month of April, small groups of three, four, eight, ten or twelve, composed of Iroquois of the Sault. One of these groups, in ambush within sight of Fort Orange, surprised three English, killed two and brought the third back to Villemarie where he was forced to divulge the plans of the English.[12]

In October, two French soldiers deserted at Quebec; they had once escaped from prison at "Manatte." They freed three English prisoners and set out with them toward Fort Orange. M. de Frontenac immediately sent some French and Abenakis in pursuit, and ordered M. de Callières to catch the traitors at Lake Champlain. The French pursued them to the head of the lake, only three days' march from Fort Orange, without being able to overtake them. However, they discovered something far more important and menacing than the desertion of two discontented soldiers; near the Petit Sault they had seen a large band of Indian warriors advancing toward the French settlements. A Mohawk, deserted from this band at Villemarie, told the French that 800 Iroquois were moving to attack New France, 400 by the St. Lawrence, the rest by Lake Champlain; at the moment of his desertion these Iroquois were at the lake only five or six days' march from Villemarie. Later, French scouts discovered this war-party on a deserted island in the lake. The cold of winter was imminent, but nevertheless a garrison of 50 Indians and six companies of soldiers was stationed at Chambly. A detachment of these Indians killed one Mohawk in a skirmish near the lake, but two others escaped.[13] M. de Frontenac records nothing else concerning the Lake Champlain country in his official report for this year.[14]

1693

As we have said, the Mohawks habitually attacked when the trees were covered with foliage, affording them natural protection while on the march or fighting; they withdrew in winter into their villages. M. de Frontenac, intent on striking a decisive blow during this period of withdrawal, in January, sent out from Villemarie an army of 625 men consisting of 100 soldiers, 200 Christian Iroquois, and 325

12. *Doc. Col. Hist. N. Y.*, IX, pp. 534-535.
13. *Relation de ce qui s'est passé . . .*, *1692, 1693*.
14. M. de Frontenac à M. de Pontchartrain, 11 novembre 1692.

of "the most active young men in the country."[15]   The Sieurs de
Mantet, de Courtemanche, and de Lanoue, well known for their successful efforts against the English, were the leaders; Sieur de l'Invilliers and a score of other officers joined the expedition to destroy the
Mohawk villages and raid the English in the vicinity of Fort Orange.

Supplied with the necessities for the difficult journey, snowshoes
for the soldiers and sledges for the supplies, the expedition left Chambly, January 30, and advanced by way of Lake Champlain and the
Kayadrosseras Trail,[16] together with the Indian guides.   The movement of the troops was so well concealed that they were undiscovered
until only fifteen leagues from the Mohawk villages.   M. de Lanoue
surprised the first village, February 16, and MM. de Mantet and de
Courtemanche the second on the same day; MM. de Mantet and de
Lanoue seized the third, February 18.   During the first assault a
prisoner escaped, whom the Indian allies of the French had impru-
dently brought with them from Villemarie, John Baptist van Eps,
captured at Schenectady in 1690.   Influenced by this contretemps,
M. de Mantet, with the approval of the other officers, abandoned the
projected attack on Fort Orange and ordered a retreat after spend-
ing one night at the principal village of the Mohawks.   The French
had killed about 20 warriors in the three Mohawk villages and had
taken 280 prisoners, mostly women and children.

The French started back to New France February 22.   Van Eps
talked with Peter Schuyler at Fort Orange with the result that a
party of 300 English, joined by 300 Oneidas, set out immediately to
overtake the French and free the prisoners.   On the third day of the
retreat, the English advance-guard came up with the Christian Iroquois forming the French rear-guard; the Christian Iroquois hastily
set up a barricade of logs.   On February 27, "our Indians" lost eight
warriors during a badly organized sortie; three Canadians were
killed and among the wounded was Sieur de Lanoue.   This engagement is now called "the battle of Wilton" from the name of the village later constructed on the site.   March 1, the French crossed the
Hudson River, still solidly frozen over, and in the evening learned
that the enemy had not given up the pursuit.   The transportation of
the wounded presented the greatest difficulties; often twenty men
were needed to carry one stretcher.   A sudden thaw setting in, the
ice on Lake Saint-Sacrement would not bear a man's weight, and

15. *Relation de ce qui s'est passé . . ., 1692, 1693.*
16. See *Appendix A.*

they were forced to make their way painfully along the wooded shore overgrown with brush and deep in snow. Most of the Indians had left the troops to reach Lake Champlain by way of the Grand Marais. The Mohawk prisoners, encumbered by their "equipages" and their children, remained at Lake Saint-Sacrement, "promising" to come to Canada in the spring. When the French arrived at Chimney Point, March 4, their misery was overwhelming; starvation stared them in the face, the heavy rains having completely spoiled the food hidden there for their return journey. Picture this expedition, deprived of necessary food, forced to carry the wounded in the month of March, and with the nearest French settlement fifty leagues away!

Half-starved and suffering from unexampled hardships, the French reached the Chazy River, March 11, and M. de Mantet sent two of his men to Villemarie for food; the soldiers at the river-mouth thought themselves lucky to find a few potatoes and old shoes to enrich their stew. They spent three days waiting for the return of their envoys; one soldier died of hunger and exhaustion, and many others seemed to be at the point of death. Finally, on March 15, the food sent by M. de Callières arrived at the moment when all those who could had begun the march toward the settlements. The wounded, whom it was impossible to carry farther, had been placed in a hastily constructed redoubt, guarded by Sieurs de Courtemanche and de Villedonné with a few volunteers. On March 15-16 the expedition reentered Villemarie; "only those who saw the soldiers could imagine their condition."[17]

In early spring M. de Callières ordered La Plaque to go with nine Iroquois of the Sault to seize a few English prisoners and find out the enemy plans. Two leagues from Fort Orange the Indians fell upon fourteen men at work in the woods. One was captured and proved to be a Frenchman, taken four years before in Acadia; he divulged that the English were organizing an expedition for a new attack upon Quebec, and at the same time the Mayor of Orange with 600 English was to strike Villemarie by way of Lake Champlain. M. de Callières, thus forewarned, sent scouts along all the trails and stationed two detachments of soldiers, one at Lake Champlain, the other at Lake Saint-François; the threatened attack did not take place.

17. *Relation de ce qui s'est passé . . .*, *1692, 1693.* M. de Callières au Ministre, 7 septembre 1693. Report of Major Peter Schuyler, *Doc. Col. Hist. N. Y.*, IV, p. 16.

The year 1694 was marked by negotiations both frequent and futile. The Iroquois, exhausted by French attacks, did not wish to continue war against New France; first, because they had had no brilliant success; second, because the English, ostensibly their allies, had given them no tangible support, nothing but charming words without the substantial aid of their troops. Consequently, although remaining faithful to the English, they sent ambassadors to Count de Frontenac, inviting him to come to Orange to join a great council of the Five Nations and the English for the consideration of terms of peace. M. de Frontenac curtly refused; with pleasure, at Quebec he would receive two chiefs of each Indian Nation authorized to act for the same purpose. The firmness of M. de Frontenac forced the Iroquois to accept his proposal; the negotiations, once begun, dragged on for months without decisive results.[18] Although peace conversations had not been broken off, Count de Frontenac did not think himself prevented from sending out several scouting parties during the winter of 1694-1695; he aimed at two goals, to give employment to the Canadians and to learn enemy plans.

The first "success" is dated April 15, 1695. That day saw the return of a few Christian Iroquois who had started out with Lieutenant des Chaillons. With Ensign de Boisbriant and fifteen Indians he had set off toward Orange; at Saratoga half the Indians had turned off toward the Mohawk villages, believing that it would be easier to capture Mohawks than English; the officers and the rest of the party had continued toward the English settlement. April 15, the Christian Iroquois returned with three Mohawk prisoners; later, M. des Chaillons and his party reached Villemarie with a Dutchman, captured within a league of Orange; a month later another party of French and Indians brought back another Dutch prisoner. These two Dutchmen were brothers and showed but vague knowledge of English plans, their "residence being quite far from Orange and without direct communication."

A skirmish took place at Isle La Motte, June 13, 1695. M. de Montour, with two French scouts, saw two Indians landing on the island. "Who goes there?" demanded the French. "Mohawks," answered the Indians. M. de Montour and his companions having

18. Louis XIV au comte de Frontenac et à M. de Champigny, Versailles, le 14 juin 1695: *Doc. Col. Hist. N. Y.*, IX, p. 590.

declared "We are French," the Mohawks seized their guns, saying, "Fine, we are looking for you!" They fired on the French, wounding M. de Montour in the abdomen. He had his revenge, for in falling he fired and wounded a Mohawk. His companions fired at the same moment and apparently killed the other Indian who fell on the sand. While aiding M. de Montour, they paid no attention to the Indians, believing both to be dead. Soon shouts were heard from the forest calling for help. The French, fearing Mohawk reinforcements, killed the wounded Indians and began their retreat with prudent haste, without "amusing themselves by scalping their victims." When M. de Callières heard of this skirmish, he lost no time in sending scouts to the lake to discover what the enemy were doing.[19]

September 11, a party of Iroquois from the Sault Mission, returning from Orange, saw 50 Mohawks paddling down Lake Champlain; when the news was reported to M. de Frontenac, he ordered a party under Sieur de la Durantaye to meet the Indians; with 200 Canadians, this officer triumphed over the Mohawks, September 16, "at the end of the wilderness" of Boucherville.

1696

Governor de Frontenac, harassed by his country's enemies, the English and Mohawks, no less than by his personal enemies among the French at Quebec, complained to the King, saying that the efforts of Intendant Champigny together with the enmity of the heads of the Church, nullified his influence and authority over both French and Indians, and that the confidence of the King and the Minister were indispensable if his administration were to be effective. The situation in New France was precarious: on the east, the English of Boston had their eyes turned covetously toward Acadia and the French villages in Maine; on the west, the Indian tribes were secretly aided by English colonists and constantly menaced the weak French outposts; on the south, the Five Nations and the English of New York labored incessantly to destroy New France and gain control over the important Champlain waterway.

On the east, in spite of the brilliant exploits of MM. d'Iberville and de Saint-Castin, ably seconded by the Algonquins in Maine, there was no security. The incapacity of the English leaders and the

19. *Relation de ce qui s'est passé* . . ., *1694, 1695. Doc. Col. Hist. N. Y.,* IX, p. 601.

lack of co-operation between the English colonies rendered their attacks ineffective, not the superior numbers of the French. An unofficial armed truce gave M. de Frontenac the opportunity to turn his attention elsewhere. On the west, the calculating friendship of several Indian chiefs and the presence of a few lieutenants experienced in controlling savages momentarily removed the threat of trouble in that quarter. M. de Frontenac was able to devote his energy to the problem of the Five Nations. Following the plan formerly adopted by the Marquis de Tracy (1666) and by Governor de Denonville (1686), (de Frontenac himself had twice attempted to carry out the same plan in 1690 and 1693), the governor resolved to strike a decisive blow at Onondaga in the heart of the country of the Five Nations, advancing by way of Lake Ontario.

Count de Frontenac, vigorous in spite of his seventy-six years, left Villemarie July 4, with an army of 2,200 men in boats and canoes, transporting a great quantity of war munitions including cannon. He arrived near Onondaga August 1, constructed temporary defenses, and the next day reached the Indian center which the Onondagas had burned the evening before, abandoning all their possessions to take refuge in the forests to the south. M. de Vaudreuil led a detachment to the principal village of the Oneidas which he burned without delay. This expedition like all those which had preceded it, was merely a semi-victory; de Frontenac, overestimating its importance, reported it to the King as a brilliant triumph and received from His Majesty the cross of the Order of Saint-Louis.

The governor had feared that the Mohawks and the English might attack Villemarie during his absence, but fortunately raids were infrequent this year and consisted of a few sudden attempts to secure prisoners. At Sorel the Mohawks captured Madame de Salvaye and her daughter whom they took to Orange.

In October, twenty-one French set out for Orange, but, being discovered, they divided into two groups, which were to join at a certain rendezvous on the return journey. One group of eight or nine, when their comrades failed to appear at the rendezvous, left for Villemarie. At Lake Champlain a party of Iroquois of the Sault, en route also to Orange to "strike a blow there," met the French who were returning. The Indians attacked, believing that they had encountered an enemy party. The French defended themselves vigorously. At the end of the skirmish, the apparent loss was slight, only two Frenchmen being wounded. The real tragedy lay in the fact that the French, unaware that they faced their allies, had killed Chief Tatatiron of the Montagne Mission, "a grave loss because of his courage and the affection which he showed for our service."[20]

The second group was even more unfortunate. After a victory over a band of Wolves and Mohawks, Sieur Dubeau, wounded so gravely that he could no longer keep pace with his companions, surrendered to the English at Orange with two of his comrades. A few English and Mohawks hastened to pursue the rest of the French, so exhausted by hunger and fatigue that the enemy killed or captured all "save two or three, dead probably in the forest." Nothing was ever heard of them. The Sieur Dubeau died of his wounds.[21]

1697

The campaign against the Onondagas, although only a partial success, had its effect. As the Five Nations had sent peace envoys to Quebec after de Tracy's expedition of 1666, so now several Iroquois chiefs came to the French capital asking peace and promising to return the French prisoners in the spring. The ensuing peace was ineffective because of English influence over the Mohawks; the English interests would not be served by lasting peace between the French and the Mohawks.

"Two Mohawks arrived at Villemarie in mid-February with Madame de Salvaye and her daughter, captured during the preceding summer at Sorel, to whom the governor of Manatte had given a safe conduct and these two Indian guides."[22] Cases of such courtesy were rare in those troubled days.

A few soldiers, with the inevitable group of Indians, captured at the gates of Corlaer a noted Onondaga chief. They could not take other prisoners as had been planned because the enemy, more numerous than the French soldiers, immediately set out in pursuit.[23] About fifty Indians from the Missions left Villemarie for the Mohawk villages near Orange, Corlaer, and Esopus, in search of prisoners. Sieur de Batilly, ensign of infantry, "who scarcely ever missed this sort of expedition and had a special aptitude for it," and Sieur de Belestre joined the Indians. These parties returned to Villemarie September 24, with scalps and two prisoners, so beaten by the Indians

20. *Relation de ce qui s'est passé . . ., 1696, 1697.*
21. *Doc. Col. Hist. N. Y.*, p. 233. *Champlain Tercentenary Report*, p. 391.
22. *Relation de ce qui s'est passé . . ., 1696, 1697.*
23. *Relation de ce qui s'est passé . . ., 1696, 1697.*

of the Sault (in revenge it is said for the torture inflicted at London on their relatives captured at Hudson Bay) that the older of the two could no longer stand. The younger spoke of the news of peace in Europe, saying also that the English expected a French attack on Orange and the simultaneous appearance of a French fleet before "Manatte," an echo of the plan so long favored by M. de Callières and his friends.[24]

1698

Toward the end of January, Abram Schuyler reached Villemarie accompanied by a Frenchman resident for twenty-six years at Orange, a Dutchman from Corlaer, a Wolf and a Mohawk. He bore a letter addressed to M. de Callières by Peter Schuyler, commandant at Orange, and by Godfrey Dellius, pastor of that town. This letter announced the treaty of peace between France and England and gave the English version of its provisions.[25] May 8, Colonel Peter Schuyler and Pastor Dellius left Orange with the French prisoners held in New York during the war. Toward the end of the month they reached Villemarie, bringing copies in Latin and French of the Treaty of Ryswick.[26] M. de Frontenac did not receive official news of peace until July when he received from Louis XIV the "Letter of the King ordering a Te Deum to be sung," dated March 12, 1698.

The question of the exchange of prisoners gave rise to heated correspondence between M. de Frontenac and the governor of New York. Peter Schuyler had brought back to Canada all the French captured by the English; on behalf of Governor Bellomont he had demanded in exchange the English and Mohawks captured by the French. To surrender the Mohawks or to receive Frenchmen captured by the Mohawks would admit English sovereignty over the Five Nations; de Frontenac bluntly refused. The Earl of Bellomont in fury threatened to rouse the Five Nations against the French, to arm them, and to send all the English colonists to help the Indians. Bellomont's letters reached Quebec with Captain John Schuyler in September. M. de Frontenac refused to comply with the demand of the Earl of Bellomont, was not intimidated by his threats and, having caused the Te Deum to be sung as ordered by Louis XIV, proclaimed peace. At the ceremonial dinner, to which John Schuyler

24. *Ibid.*
25. *Relation de ce qui s'est passé . . ., 1697, 1698.*
26. Hill: *Old Fort Edward*, p. 14.

was invited, M. de Frontenac drank to the health of King William and John Schuyler to that of King Louis. The next evening de Frontenac handed Schuyler his reply to Governor Bellomont's threats; although his hand trembled, the strong will and pride of the old soldier remained as firm as in his prime. "I insist on holding to my course without flinching; and I beg you not to try to turn me from it by useless efforts. All the protection and all the aid which you have given and which you will continue to give to the Iroquois contrary to the Articles of the Treaty will not alarm me to any great extent nor make me change my plans, but on the contrary will spur me to greater effort in carrying them out." November 28, 1698, Count de Frontenac died at the age of seventy-eight.

After the death of Count de Frontenac, the new governor, Louis-Hector de Callières, former governor of Villemarie, concluded peace with the Five Nations in 1700, carrying out the will of his great predecessor. Through his efforts, in the following year all the Indian tribes from Maine to the Great Lakes entered into a general agreement. The Treaty of Ryswick established such friendly relations that in the spring of 1699, William III of England sent a letter to the Earl of Bellomont by the French ships which bore the orders of Louis XIV of France to Governor de Callières. Under date of April 29, Louis XIV ordered M. de Callières to have the English King's letter delivered to its address, which the governor did, choosing for this mission Sieur de la Vallière and the Jesuit Father Bruyas; the King gave his approval of the choice of ambassadors in his letter of May 5, 1700.

In 1676, in his instructions to the governors of New France, Louis XIV provided for the settlement of French colonists throughout the territory, especially by the grant of seigniories along the St. Lawrence and Richelieu Rivers. Soon the banks of these water highways were peopled by Frenchmen struggling to snatch from the forest a few acres of land fit for cultivation. About the same time England cast covetous looks on the fertile valleys of the Hudson River and Lake Champlain; in 1684, Governor Dongan had granted the Saratoga Patent to Peter Schuyler. September, 1696, Pastor Godfrey Dellius, the envoy of 1698 mentioned above, had received an enormous grant extending from the Saratoga Patent on the south to Split Rock on the north, 70 miles front by 12 miles in depth, situated on the west shore of Lake Champlain.

I find no record of grants made by the governors of New France in the Champlain valley during this period; it is certain, however, that there were French settlers in the region. After the death of King Philip in 1676, the French had given shelter to the Abenakis and their relatives, the Sokokis, "realizing the value of such accessions."[27] The village of Saint-François de la Chaudière, founded in 1683, became the refuge and rendezvous of all the Indian tribes driven out of New England. Of almost equal importance was the village of Missisquoi, situated on the bay of the same name at the north end of Lake Champlain. Saint-François and Missisquoi were centers of an active hostility against the English, carefully kept alive by the French; as we have seen, the Indian braves were almost invariably led by French officers. Peter Schuyler says in his letter to Governor Dongan of September 7, 1687: "They put our Indians upon the way hither giving them provisions as much as carried them to a castle of Penacook Indians, where they wanted for nothing."[28] The *Jesuit Relations*, October 10, 1682, speaks of a village of Abenakis on Lake Champlain. *The History of the Catholic Church in the United States*, by J. G. Shea, states: "Fort St. Thérèse was abandoned in 1690. It is about this time that the Abenaki Indians appeared on the Missisquoi river, on the Winooski, and on Otter Creek, having been driven from Maine in 1680." It is said that M. de Vaudreuil persuaded the Abenakis to settle in New France.[29] From the village of Saint-François the route by Lake Memphremagog and the Connecticut River led to the English settlements of New England; from Missisquoi the route by way of Lake Champlain led directly to Orange. The Abenakis were constantly passing over these trails from 1700 to 1760.

In 1700, the whole valley of Lake Champlain drew the attention of the governors of the two neighboring colonies, French on the north, English on the south. The French had penetrated into the valley farther than the English; Fort Sainte-Anne, although abandoned, became a regular stopping-place for travelers and military expeditions; settlers there had been attacked in 1695. Missisquoi was gaining colonists and the fertile lands at the mouths of the Winooski and Otter Creek were becoming known; Crown Point together with

27. Crockett: *History of Vermont*, I, pp. 73-80.
28. These Indians had visited Villemarie and were returning to Orange, apparently stopping at Missisquoi.
29. Drake: *Border Wars of New England*, p. 150.

Chimney Point was to be the site of a permanent trading-post; an outpost was even considered at the Petit Sault of the "rivière du Chicot."[30] The English had shown their interest in the valley by grants to Peter Schuyler and Godfrey Dellius; they had sent captains to assure, momentarily at least, possession of Crown Point and the mouth of Otter Creek. Separating the two opposing claimants, there was a more or less undeveloped region some sixty leagues in length which the rival colonies from then on attempted to control by means of outposts and settlers established in the valley.

CHAPTER VII. *Queen Anne's War*

IN England, Queen Anne succeeded her brother-in-law, William III, and war was declared anew between England and France, at Westminster on May 4, 1702. In North America, at the beginning of the struggle, the frontier between New England and Acadia was so often the scene of conflict that it was spoken of as "Villebon's War," from the name of the governor of Acadia. It was not until 1704 that attacks were made on the Massachusetts frontier, at Deerfield, Northfield, Hadley, and elsewhere.

In 1703, it was proposed in Canada to destroy the English settlements along the entire New England frontier, from Northfield on the Connecticut River to the coast of Maine; the destruction was already complete in the east from Casco Bay to Wells. The western villages were undisturbed; Deerfield believed herself protected against surprise by miles of wilderness. Sieur Jacques Hertel de Rouville, able leader of expeditions of this type, accompanied by his four brothers and Pierre Gaultier de Varennes, Sieur de la Vérendrye, left Villemarie at the head of a party of 200 French and 142 Christian Iroquois. In February, they marched toward Deerfield on snow-shoes, over the deep snow, through the forest, over the ice of frozen lakes and rivers. They hollowed out little caves in the snow around their fires to shelter them from the wind and keep them warm during sleep. They followed the route so familiar to the French and their Indian allies, called "the French Road" by the English, because of the numerous French expeditions which passed over it.[1] De Rouville's party was two miles from Deerfield the evening of February

30. At the village of Whitehall, N. Y., on Wood Creek.
1. See *Appendix A*.

28, 1704. The attack was sudden, the village defenseless, the surprise complete. The French killed 47 settlers, took 112 prisoners, and burned the village, sparing only two houses. They set out to return to Canada by the same route. At the mouth of the White River, the party divided, half going by the Connecticut and Lake Memphremagog to Three Rivers, the rest continuing toward Lake Champlain. They required twenty-five days to reach Chambly, killing 19 prisoners on the way. Judging from the number of bodies found in the neighborhood of Deerfield, the French losses were placed at 40, and M. de Rouville was among the wounded.[2]

May 13, a band of French and Indians surprised the garrison of Passacomuc (Easthampton, Massachusetts); they killed 20 English and took a few prisoners. About July 1, M. de Beaucour left Quebec at the head of 800 French and Indians to lay waste the valley of the Connecticut. Following the Lake Memphremagog route, they finally reached the river where a discontented Frenchman deserted to the English. Surprise being no longer possible, half the party turned back to Canada, the rest continuing toward the south. On July 31, M. de Beaucour fell upon Lancaster. The burning of the houses alarmed the countryside and forced the French to beat a retreat. M. de Vaudreuil threw M. de Beaucour into prison, then summarily dismissed him, taking his sword from him; all this because of the desertion of one disgruntled soldier.[3]

The valley of Lake Champlain remained peaceful during the next four years; Governor de Vaudreuil had received definite orders to undertake no enterprise against the Mohawks. He had complete freedom to organize attacks on New England.

July 26, 1708, a party of 100 Canadians with an equal number of Indians left Villemarie; they were to meet a band of Abenakis at Lake Winnepesaukee. M. de Vaudreuil had chosen his leaders well —Hertel de Rouville, Saint-Ours, des Chaillons, and Boucher de la Perrière, all experienced leaders in border warfare and thoroughly acquainted with the wilderness to be crossed. Traveling by the French Road, they reached Lake Winnepesaukee where the Abenakis failed to put in an appearance. With their original number of 200, the party attacked Haverhill, August 29. Nine Frenchmen were

2. Crockett: *History of Vermont*, I, pp. 95-97. S. R. Hall: *Geography and History of Vermont*, p. 102. Wrong: *The Conquest of New France*, p. 110, et seq. Drake: *Border Wars of New England*, pp. 173-186.
3. *Ibid.*, pp. 206-207.

killed, among them Sieurs de Verchères and de Chambly; 18 were wounded. The English lost between 30 and 40 men; 16 villagers were killed, the rest taken prisoners. Pursuit was immediately organized and was so active that the French were forced to abandon the booty taken at the village.[4]

M. de Vaudreuil, informed that the English were planning an attack in 1709, often sent Indians toward Orange to get news of English plans. He also maintained scouting parties on Lake Champlain to warn him of surprise attacks.[5]

Lieutenant Governor Ingoldsby of New York, May 31, 1709, appointed Francis Nicholson commander-in-chief of the expedition planned against New France.[6] An undated manuscript in the New York State Library contains the orders given Nicholson by the Council of New York: "You will march from Albany to Wood Creek with as many workmen as you shall think convenient to build storehouses, canoes and boats at Wood Creek. And you, if in conjunction with Colonel Schuyler shall find it practical, (will) cut a road from Albany to the Wood Creek for the marching of the men and carrying of the provisions." The plan of this advance against Canada revived that of 1690; only the names of the chief actors and the number of combatants were changed. An English fleet was to attack Quebec; Nicholson's army was to proceed by Lake Champlain in the attempt to capture Villemarie.

In June 1709, the Iroquois of the Sault asked M. de Vaudreuil's permission to strike a blow against the English of the Connecticut, who were spying on French movements, they said. The Indians requested fifty "of the most active" French and Sieurs Hertel de Rouville and Boucher de la Perrière as leaders. M. de Vaudreuil took pleasure in granting all their requests in order to show them "that he held close to his heart their interests just as much as those of the French" and an attack against his allies was enough to persuade him to organize a counter-attack. One hundred and eighty men, including the 50 French and two leaders requested, set out for the forks of the "Pynictigouk" (Connecticut). Not encountering any English scouts, they reached "Guerrefille" (Deerfield) where they succeeded in taking two prisoners in ambush. On the return journey,

4. *Ibid.*, pp. 239-249. Palfrey: *History of New England*, p. 254. Crockett: *History of Lake Champlain*, p. 54.
5. M. de Vaudreuil à M. de Pontchartrain, le 27 avril 1709.
6. Hill: *Old Fort Edward*, p. 19.

M. de Rouville and his party joined the troops of M. de Ramezay at Lake Champlain.[7]

Colonel Schuyler left Orange (Albany) June 1, 1709, with the advance guard of Nicholson's expedition. On June 29, he wrote from Fort Nicholson, which he had just built at the south end of the Great Carrying Place (Fort Edward, N. Y.), telling the Council of New York that the promised provisions had not arrived, and that he had sent his brother, John Schuyler, with 228 soldiers and Indians to Otter Creek to meet an enemy party en route to the Connecticut; without doubt this was M. de Rouville's party. General Nicholson soon followed his troops and waited at Fort Nicholson for news from the fleet sent against Quebec.

Upon receiving reports of Nicholson's advance, M. de Vaudreuil busied himself with preparations for the defense of the Champlain waterway. An Indian, sent to Albany for news, reported that the English were building boats at Wood Creek. Ignorant of the position of the English fleet sent against Quebec, M. de Vaudreuil believed he should oppose Nicholson's approach at any cost. Early in July, a message from Sieurs de Rouville and de la Perrière justified this decision by announcing that the English fleet had not yet left England. Thus relieved of any anxiety about Quebec, M. de Vaudreuil organized a force of 1,500 men under the command of Sieur Claude de Ramezay, which was to proceed to Lake Champlain and attempt the seizure of Nicholson's supplies.

M. de Ramezay planned to establish his headquarters at Crown Point. Proceeding up the lake, he learned that John Schuyler's detachment was in the neighborhood and sent his nephew, M. de la Peyrade, on reconnaissance. Unfortunately this impetuous young man advanced too far, and a party of 100 English discovered him. M. de Ramezay, his plans upset, effected his landing three-quarters of a league to the north of the Point. Soon reports came that the English were advancing to attack the Point. M. de Ramezay was disposing his troops in order to give the enemy a warm welcome, when a scout came to tell him that there were a great number of English in the forest. Prevented from attacking the enemy by boat as he had planned, M. de Ramezay fired upon the English at the moment they became aware of his presence, about 30 being killed.

7. M. de Vaudreuil à M. de Pontchartrain, le 14 novembre 1709. Drake: *Border Wars of New England*, p. 259. Hutchinson: *Massachusetts*, II, p. 163. The English accounts say that the enemy killed one and wounded four.

In speaking of this affair, M. de Vaudreuil regretted that the English had discovered the French advance through M. de la Peyrade's lack of caution; otherwise, M. de Ramezay would have surrounded the enemy; and, moreover, this misfortune prevented M. de Ramezay from going further toward Wood Creek. That very evening, hearing gunshots and believing them to be a call for help by a wounded Englishman, M. de Ramezay sent M. de Rouville with two or three boats full of soldiers to the spot whence came the shot. Two Dutchmen, thinking these soldiers were of their own party, came to the shore of the lake. Realizing that the soldiers were French, the two tried to escape, but M. de Rouville had them seized and took them to camp August 1, 1709, where M. de Ramezay questioned the prisoners, and one Carel Rolantse gave exact information about what was going on among the English.[8]

M. de Ramezay sent a letter to Governor de Vaudreuil by M. de Joncaire, September 10, and with him went an Indian recently escaped from the English. The English army of 1,600 men was still in camp awaiting news of the fleet and preparing to attack Chambly before taking Villemarie. Therefore, M. de Vaudreuil, with a large force, went to Chambly on September 15, remaining a month, when he was forced to send back 600 militiamen on account of scarcity of food. He left 350 marines at Chambly to wait there for the arrival of two parties of 50 men each still on the watch at Lake Champlain.[9]

M. de Ramezay returned to Villemarie where he wrote to Governor de Vaudreuil, October 19, giving a digest of the English plans and preparations against New France. This information had come to M. de Ramezay through Lieutenant Barent Staats, captured by Chief Catnaret near Fort Orange on October 12.[10] This prisoner told M. de Ramezay that the English had learned of the French arrival at Crown Point within twenty-four hours, that they had organized a detachment of 1,000 men within an hour of the alarm; that they had hastily constructed earthworks fearing an attack by "our troops" during the night; and, finally, that three days later 350 Mohawks had come to join the expedition against the French.[11]

8. Procès-verbal de l'examen de Querel Roulonse par M. de Ramezay à la Pointe à la Chevelure, le 1er août 1709.

9. M. de Vaudreuil à M. de Pontchartrain, le 14 novembre 1709.

10. Hill: *Old Fort Edward*, pp. 19-21. *Doc. Col. Hist. N. Y.*, IX, p. 834. Barent Staats was a relative of the Schuylers.

11. M. de Ramezay à M. de Vaudreuil, le 19 octobre 1709.

We mentioned above two detachments of fifty men each, left by M. de Vaudreuil at Lake Champlain, the commanders being Sieurs de Montigny and des Chaillons. M. de Montigny had visited Fort Schuyler, October 8, to count and measure the boats during the night and had seen the enemy leave by detachments; as he had only seven men with him he was unable to take prisoners. M. de Vaudreuil wrote to the minister that the enemy, knowing that the French were at Chambly, had hastened their retreat in fear of an attack by "all the troops of New France"; as more striking evidence of their definite withdrawal, the English had burned all the forts built during the campaign, all their boats, canoes, and provisions.[12]

In order to be sure that the enemy had left, in the winter, M. de Vaudreuil, under pretext of an exchange of prisoners, sent Sieurs de la Perrière and Dupuis to Orange accompanied by six Frenchmen and one Christian Indian. They were to visit Fort Schuyler to find out if the English had really burned the forts and the boats, then to send two Frenchmen to report to the governor as soon as possible. MM. de la Perrière and Dupuis did their best, sending by letter a report that they had seen, in the ruins of the storehouses, bits of pork which the fire had not entirely consumed. At Orange these officers were told that the presence of M. de Vaudreuil at Chambly had so terrified the Mohawks and English that the Mohawks had refused to spend the winter in their own villages and had taken refuge in Corlaer (Schenectady).[13] The French officers returned to Villemarie in May, 1710.[14]

The English had two other reasons for ordering a retreat: an epidemic of smallpox was costing the lives of many men each day; England had sent the fleet destined for Quebec to Portugal. Discouraged, Schuyler and Nicholson saw no other way out but that of retreat. Nicholson went immediately to London to persuade the Queen to continue the struggle against New France.[15]

In Canada, Governor de Vaudreuil, finally convinced that French success in the last resort would depend upon the possession of the

12. M. de Vaudreuil à M. de Pontchartrain, le 1er mai 1710.
13. M. de Vaudreuil à M. de Pontchartrain, le 1er mai 1710.
14. *Ibid.*, le 31 octobre 1710.
15. For the English activities in 1709, see Drake: *Border Wars of New England*, pp. 251-254; Carpenter: *Summer Paradise in History*, p. 98; Hoyt: *Indian Wars*, p. 200; Palfrey: *History of New England*, pp. 256-257; Crockett: *History of Lake Champlain*, p. 54; Hill: *Old Fort Edward*, pp. 19-21, and any good history of the English colonies.

Champlain valley, began the task of perfecting the defense of the colony by building a stone fort at Chambly. Simultaneously he sent a party to Lake Champlain to protect the workmen at the fort and to oppose the advance of fifty men sent to the lake by the English governor at Boston.[16] M. de Vaudreuil insisted on sending parties toward Boston and Orange every week during the summer of 1710, for he felt it to be of prime importance that he should know what was going on in those centers. These parties carried out their task so well that the governor received reports "every one or two weeks ordinarily by means of prisoners captured in the vicinity of the English settlements."[17]

M. de Subercase surrendered Port Royal to the English October 13. Shortly after, Nicholson sent Baron de Saint-Castin and Major "Levingston" through the forests of Maine with a letter to M. de Vaudreuil. As bearers of his reply the French governor chose two renowned colonial leaders, Sieurs Dupuis and de Rouville, "being delighted to use these two officers on this occasion in order to have intelligence of the movements of our enemies, and at the same time to teach them to know the country and the most favorable routes for sending war parties." Sieurs de Rouville and Dupuis returned to Chambly from Boston about April 15, 1711, traveling over the French Road.[18] They reported that without doubt Queen Anne would grant Nicholson's request for a fleet sufficient to besiege Quebec.[19]

This news influenced M. de Vaudreuil to seek information at Orange; for this purpose he used a pretext, that of sending back under escort, Mr. Livingston's servant, who had fallen ill in the autumn and had been cared for ever since at Three Rivers. To even more effectively conceal his real purpose, he sent along an English prisoner to be exchanged for Sieur de Beaunny, confined at Boston for three or four years. October 25, M. de Vaudreuil writes that "they have kept in Orange up to the present time, the three Frenchmen whom I sent to bring back these men, and I have since had no news of the English prisoner whom I sent on parole" to be exchanged. Information also came from another source: M. Coste-belle wrote from Acadia August 6, that a prisoner taken at Plaisance

16. M. de Vaudreuil à M. de Pontchartrain, juin 1710.
17. *Ibid.*, le 31 octobre 1710.
18. See *Appendix A*.
19. M. de Vaudreuil à M. de Pontchartrain, le 25 avril 1711.

had reported that "2000 men were going to attack Ville Marie this year."[20]

During the summer of 1710 and the following winter and spring, while secretly engaged in negotiating peace in London, the English government was openly preparing to conquer New France. The plan was again a well-developed renewal of that of 1709 originally conceived as early as 1690. The fleet was at Gaspé August 18, 1711, and two nights later, in a thick fog was wrecked in the St. Lawrence with a loss of eight transports and 1000 men. Admiral Hovenden Walker gave up the attempt and sailed away for England.[21]

General Nicholson, again commander-in-chief of the land forces, marched with about 2,000 men directly to ruined Fort Schuyler which he rebuilt, naming it Fort Anne; the French called it Fort la Reine. The news of the naval disaster reached Fort Anne in September. There was nothing left for Nicholson to do but once more to give up his cherished plan of taking Villemarie. After destroying Fort Anne, he withdrew to Orange, leaving Fort Saratoga the most advanced outpost of the English.[22]

As far as the Lake Champlain valley is concerned, the war ended with the retreat of General Nicholson. The treaty of Utrecht, signed April 11, 1713, marked the end of the conflict between France and England; by this treaty France gave up her rights of sovereignty over the Five Nations, and Split Rock was recognized as the northern limit of English claims, but New France never accepted this limit.

The result of eleven years of fighting and of enormous expense is insignificant when territorial expansion alone is considered. The real effect of these disturbed years becomes evident during the developments which follow. The English and the French saw more and more clearly that the valley of Lake Champlain was to play a most important rôle in the history of their colonies in North America; they would never be able to share sovereignty over this important waterway. Thus, during thirty years of official peace, we shall see careful preparation on both sides for the inevitable struggle; it was to be war to the death, the death of one sovereignty in the valley and the triumph of the other.

20. *Ibid.*, le 25 octobre 1711.
21. Drake: *Border Wars of New England*, pp. 267-281.
22. Hill: *Old Fort Edward*, pp. 21-22.

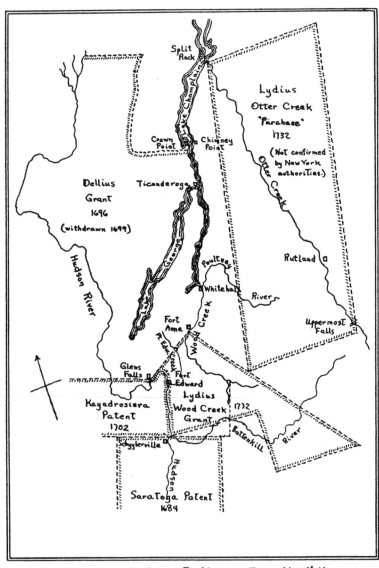

Map of the English grants in the Valley

WE have noted the grant of the Saratoga Patent in 1684 to Peter Schuyler and the grant of an enormous property to the west of Lake Champlain in 1696 to Godfrey Dellius. Schuyler had established settlers within the limits of his grant, but the few inhabitants of Saratoga had seen their homes and farms ruined in 1698;[1] in 1713 nothing remained of the villages but a small fort, dangerously exposed even in times of peace. The Dellius grant, not having been developed by the settlement of colonists within its limits and considered as "an extravagant favor to one man,"[2] reverted to the province of New York in 1699.[3] In 1702, David Schuyler purchased from the Mohawks, the Kayadrossera tract on the right bank of the Hudson River at the south end of the Great Carrying Place; in 1708, Queen Anne confirmed to Samson Shelton Broughton, purchaser of David Schuyler's rights, the "Kayadrossera Patent," renewing about the same time the Saratoga Patent in favor of the Schuyler family. Philip Livingston undertook to build a fort at Saratoga in September 1721, Captain William Helling becoming its first commandant.

It appears that the Mohawks had for some years been carrying on trade with the French fur-buyers who came to the head of Lake Champlain for that purpose. Whether the merchandise offered by the French was more to the Mohawk taste than that offered by the English or whether the Indians received better value for their furs at Lake Champlain is not stated. Governor Burnet of New York believed it his duty to prevent this trade and to encourage that between the English and the Indians who hunted in the forests of the Champlain country. He wished to build up the trade of Albany, rivaling that of Montreal, and by so doing increase English influence and control over the Indian tribes. To this end he established a small fortified post at the Great Carrying Place on the site of Fort Nicholson.[4] The location was chosen with clear knowledge of the strategic value of the site which was the junction of the two main routes followed for centuries by the red men going to and fro between the hunting grounds and their homes along the Mohawk River, and in the last century constantly traveled by the French on

1. Brandow: *Old Saratoga and Schuylerville*, p. 23.
2. Crockett: *History of Vermont*, I, p. 132.
3. Governor Burnet to the Board of Trade in London, October 16, 1721.
4. It is a question whether this site ever rightfully belonged to New York.

their numerous attacks on Mohawk or English settlements. From the Champlain country two routes led south; the first, leaving Lake Champlain at Ticonderoga, over the Little Carrying Place to Lake George and from the head of that lake to the Hudson River at Glens Falls; the second, continuing by Lake Champlain to Whitehall, then by Wood Creek to Fort Anne and over the Great Carrying Place to the Hudson River at Fort Edward, from which point Albany or the Mohawk country were within a few days' march over comparatively easy trails. But Governor Burnet's post was short-lived.

John Henry Lydius may be called the father of Fort Edward. Of Dutch origin, a native of Orange and nephew of Pastor Godfrey Dellius, Lydius had settled in Montreal as a merchant. After some years of apparently successful trade, he incurred the displeasure of the French authorities; possibly he was suspected of espionage, which so often explained the presence of traders in both Montreal and Albany; he was exiled from New France in 1730. With intimate knowledge of Indian and French customs, he decided to establish a new trading-post at the Great Carrying Place, halfway between the French and English centers, where he would be in a position to tap the lines of trade flowing in either direction. There he built his home in 1731, a palisaded blockhouse, flanked by storehouses for his wares and four or five cabins for his employees.[5] In 1732, the English authorities granted him his so-called "Wood Creek Tract," including the site of his house.

War broke forth anew in 1723, not between France and England this time or even between their American colonies; peace continued officially. The Indians, banished from New England, had come to settle in New France, preferably along the frontier of the wilderness which separated them from their former homes; thus we have seen the founding of Saint-François and Missisquoi. The struggle begun in 1723 was only a series of attacks by these exiled Indians upon their English enemies. Probably these attacks were inspired if not directed by the French who viewed English expansion toward the north with hostility.

From 1723 to 1725, the celebrated Indian chief Gray Lock, so named from the color of his hair, was the scourge of the English settlements along the Connecticut. Driven from New England after the death of King Philip, famous Indian chieftain, he had built a fort

5. Hill: *Old Fort Edward*, pp. 27-49. The life of Lydius reads like a romance.

at Missisquoi Bay not far from the Abenaki village and from this base he spread terror among the English of Deerfield, Westfield, and Northampton.[6] As long as Gray Lock lived, the Champlain valley was the principal scene of war activity against the English, peace being restored after his death.

Governor de Vaudreuil, "who was supposed to countenance, if not to aid the savages in the war,"[7] died October 25, 1725, and his death "broke the mainspring"[8] of Indian activity.

CHAPTER IX. *The Seigniories*

HAVING prepared the way by military expeditions for the occupation of the valley of Lake Champlain by the French, Louis XIV with his governor and intendant of New France set about the task of colonizing the fertile shores of the lake. A far-reaching policy inspired their labors: first, that of establishing French settlers in a climate more suited to Europeans than that of the St. Lawrence River; second and much more important, that of insuring French control over this route between the French and English centers, important from the military as well as the commercial point of view.

Beginning with the establishment of a royal colony, the King and his representatives had granted seigniories to the noted leaders of New France. May 20, 1676, the King promulgated an ordinance pertaining to the grant of lands along the St. Lawrence, the Richelieu (often called the Chambly) and Lake Champlain. Little by little these seigniories spread along the banks of the St. Lawrence as far as Villemarie; there were a few further west reaching to the shores of Lake Ontario. January 18, 1694, Count de Frontenac granted to "Jean-Baptiste Hertel, écuyer, sieur de Rouville," the seigniory of Rouville on the banks of the Richelieu River. Between 1694 and 1732 grants were made along this river to many whose names were to become famous in the history of Lake Champlain—François Lefebvre Duplessis-Fabert, Louis de Gannes de Falaise, Antoine de Pécaudy de Contrecoeur, Jean-Louis de Chapt de Lacorne, Pierre-Joseph Celoron de Blainville, François Daine, Joseph Boucher de Montarville, François Hertel de la Fresnière, Jacques Hertel de Cournoyer,

6. Crockett: *History of Vermont*, pp. 82-89.
7. Hoyt: *Indian Wars*, p. 219.
8. *Ibid.*, p. 89.

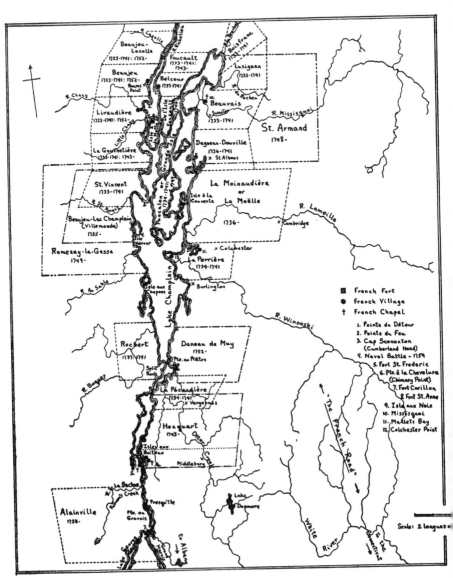

Map of the French grants in the
Champlain Valley

G. Coolidge –

Pierre-Noel Le Gardeur de Tilly, Claude de Ramezay, Pierre Boucher de Boucherville, and many others.

July 6, 1711, the King ordered "that in one year from the publication of this present as final delay, those to whom have been granted lands in seigniory in New France, will be held to place them under cultivation and to locate settlers on them, in default of which the said time passed, that the said lands shall be reunited to his majesty's domain."[1] It seems that these "concessions in fief and seigniory" well fulfilled the desired function of protecting and encouraging trade between French and English colonies. Louis XV writes to Governor de Vaudreuil June 8, 1722, that he "desires that the Sieur de Vaudreuil continue his orders to the commandant at Chambly and to the officer with the detachment of foot at Lake Champlain to examine attentively the pelts loaded into each boat and to draw up an inventory, noting well the quantity, the names of the savages and of the mission whence they come; to make a like visit at their return from Orange, and to have a list made of the merchandise which they will bring back . . ."[2]

As we have seen in the last chapter, the English had taken steps to acquire the valley of the lake; in addition, they coveted the fertile shores of Lake Ontario. M. de Vaudreuil writes, May 22, 1725, that the English had proposed a settlement at the mouth of the River Choueguen (site of the present city of Oswego), on the banks of Lake Ontario, land which had always belonged to New France. The new Governor, the Marquis de Beauharnois, sent M. de la Chassaigne, Governor of Three Rivers, with one officer and four gentlemen to Governor Burnet of New York on July 20, 1727, "to place in your hands this letter" protesting formally against the English settlement at Oswego, "and to inform you of my intentions."[3]

In 1730, Governor de Beauharnois, irritated by the news that the English were coming to Lake Champlain to trade with the Indians, sent an officer and thirty soldiers with orders to drive them from the lake.[4] M. de Beauharnois sent a letter to the King, October 15, 1730, proposing the construction of a fortified post at Crown Point; with his letter he sent a memorandum by Jean-Louis de Chapt de Lacorne, King's lieutenant at Montreal, a memorandum on the im-

1. *Archives de Québec:* Inventaire des Concessions, etc., IV, p. 208.
2. Louis XV à MM. de Vaudreuil et Bégon, le 8 juin 1722.
3. *Doc. Col. Hist. N. Y.*, IX, p. 969.
4. *Ibid.*, IX, p. 1021.

portance of this Point on Lake Champlain.[5] From Marly, May 8, 1731, Louis XV wrote Governor Beauharnois and Intendant Hocquart giving his approval of the plan "to construct at Crown Point a palisaded fort" until they were able to build one of stone.[6] The construction of this post would favor the development of seigniories along Lake Champlain,[7] and MM. de Beauharnois and Hocquart set to work at once.

April 3, 1733, saw the beginning of an "offensive directed by the governor and intendant of New France against the wilderness." On that day Clement de Sabrevois, Sieur de Bleury, received a grant of a seigniory along the "river of Chambly, . . . going up toward Lake Champlain," bordered on the north by the lands of the Hertels.[8] On the 2nd, 3rd, and 4th of April, seigniories "going up toward Lake Champlain" were granted to Sieurs Pierre-Jacques Chavoy de Noyan, François Foucault, and Charles de Sabrevois.[9] Two seigniories were granted April 5, 1733. The first received the name of "Boisfranc," according to the act of concession to François Daine, "chief clerk of the Superior Council of this country, of the extent of one and a half leagues front in the Bay of Missiskouy which is in Lake Champlain, by three leagues depth."[10] The seigniory of Boisfranc bordered on the west that of Sieur de Noyan. The second grant was made to Sieur Jacques de Lafontaine, "five quarters of a league front on the Chambly river . . . by the depth which will be found reaching to the Bay of Missiskouy . . ., bordered on the north by the seigniory newly granted to Sieur Foucault."[11] It received the name of "Belcour." This is the first grant wholly within the present limits of the State of Vermont.

On April 6, two more seigniories were granted. The first to Paul-Louis Dazemard, Sieur de Lusignan, bordered on the south by that of François Daine, "two leagues front by three leagues depth in the Bay of Missiskouy at Lake Champlain."[12] (These are the usual dimensions of a seigniory.) The second, to Gaspard-Joseph Chaus-

5. This memorandum appears in translation in *Doc. Col. Hist. N. Y.*, IX.

6. Louis XV à MM. de Beauharnois and Hocquart, le 8 mai 1731.

7. See Chapter XI for the history of this post.

8. *Archives de Québec:* Inventaire des Concessions, etc., IV, p. 244.

9. *Ibid.*, pp. 247-251.

10. *Ibid.*, IV, p. 255.

11. *Ibid.*, IV, p. 257.

12. *Ibid.*, IV, p. 258.

segros de Léry, "King's chief engineer in the places of New France," lay on the Richelieu River bordering the lands of the Seigneur de Longueuil.[13]

On April 9, Sieur Louis Denys de la Ronde received the grant of a seigniory south of that of M. de Léry.[14] The same day, lands of equal extent were granted to Sieur Louis Liénard de Beaujeu south of the seigniory of Sieur de la Ronde.[15] The next day, it was the turn of Hugues-Jacques Péan, "écuyer, Sieur de Livaudière," who received the seigniory south of Sieur de Beaujeu, "and in addition the isle called La Motte which is opposite the said lands in Lake Champlain."[16] South of the lands of Sieur Péan, Sieur Daniel Migeon de la Gauchetière became proprietor of a seigniory of the usual extent, April 11.[17] The next day, the seigniory immediately south became the property of Sieur Henri-Albert de St. Vincent, the younger, ensign of marines.[18]

In twelve days, the Marquis de Beauharnois and M. de Hocquart had made thirteen grants "in fief and seigniory, with high, middle, and low justice." The purpose of the governor and the intendant was to establish, along the route which led directly to the English settlements, a series of homes, probably fortified, and inhabited by officers of experience in the command of troops—homes which would serve as defense outposts in case of hostilities.

The following year, 1734, four other grants were added to the list. July 1, Sieur de Contrecoeur, the elder, received the isle "popularly called Grande Isle or Pancalon."[19] (This grant covered the islands now known as Grand Isle and North and South Hero.) July 6, grant was made to Sieur René Boucher de la Perrière of lands at the mouth of the Winooski River, one league above and one below, making two leagues front by three leagues depth, under the name of "La Perrière."[20] July 7, the seigniory of La Pécaudière was granted to Pierre-Claude de Pécaudy de Contrecoeur, eldest son of the Seigneur of Pancalon mentioned above; it included the mouth of Otter

13. *Ibid.*, IV, p. 260.
14. *Ibid.*, IV, p. 263.
15. *Ibid.*, IV, p. 266.
16. *Ibid.*, IV, p. 268.
17. *Ibid.*, IV, p. 270.
18. *Ibid.*, IV, p. 272.
19. *Ibid.*, IV, p. 276.
20. *Ibid.*, IV, p. 279.

Creek.[21]   Finally, July 20, the seigniory of Beauvais was granted to Philippe-René le Gardeur de Beauvais, the younger; this grant was of the usual extent just south of the seigniory of Lusignan.[22]

October 8, 1736, Sieur Pierre Raimbault, "lieutenant-general of the jurisdiction of Montreal," received "the extent of four leagues front by five leagues depth in Lake Champlain," bordering on the south the seigniory of La Perrière and including the mouth of the river "called La Moëlle."[23]   On the same day, Michel Dagneau, "écuyer, Sieur Douville," was granted a seigniory of the usual extent north of the grant to Sieur Raimbault.[24]

June 13, 1737, the Marquis de Beauharnois and Honoré-Michel de la Rouvillière, "governor and administrator in New France" (in the absence of M. Sieur Hocquart, intendant), granted to Louis-Joseph Rocbert, King's store-keeper at Montreal, a seigniory at the Boquet River, "terminating near the Split Rock."[25]

Louis XV signed the act of confirmation of these grants.   The grantees, with notable exceptions, could not or would not place their lands under cultivation or settle colonists within their limits.   Consequently, MM. de Beauharnois and Hocquart were forced to promulgate on May 10, 1741, an ordinance which restored the majority of these grants to the King's domain, "by failure on the part of the grantees to have developed their grants"; this was in accord with the King's ordinance of July 6, 1711.[26]

The seigneurs did not accept the reversion of their grants to the Crown domains without protest.   One wrote "that he could not find any farmers, up to this time, to place in his seigniory, that if he should find any, he is ready to furnish them with axes and picks for clearing, with one year's provisions; that he will do his best to find some and that he intends to form a demesne there."[27]   The Sieurs de Contrecoeur, father and son, and de la Perrière informed the King "that they have done everything to settle their grants; that it was impossible to find individuals to accept lands though they offered them some on very advantageous terms and were willing to give even 300 livres to engage such individuals . . ., that they intend, moreover,

21. *Ibid.*, IV, p. 280.
22. *Ibid.*, IV, p. 282.
23. *Ibid.*, V, p. 34.
24. *Ibid.*, V, p. 36.
25. *Ibid.*, V, p. 47.
26. See pages 216 and 217 of this work.
27. Crockett: *History of Vermont*, I, p. 127.

to do all in their power to find farmers to settle said seigniories and they hope to succeed therein." M. de la Fontaine offered "to go this summer on the grant with three men to build there and begin clearances and to give to those whom he will find willing to settle there, grain and even money, asking from them no rent, in order to obtain from them by the allurement of this gift what he cannot obtain from them by force." Sieur Rocbert de la Morandière stated "that he had neglected nothing to induce some young farmers to go and settle there by procuring for them great advantages and many facilities."[28]

Among all the grants in the Lake Champlain valley there are thirteen whose history is of especial interest, seven granted before the ordinance of 1741 and six granted between 1743 and 1758.

CHAPTER X.   *Vermont Under the Feudal System*

LA MOINAUDIÈRE, OR LA MOELLE

October 8, 1736.

Act of concession by Marquis de Beauharnois and Gilles Hocquart, Governor and Intendant of New France, to the Sieur Pierre Raimbault, Lieutenant-General of the Jurisdiction of Montreal, of "the extent of four leagues front by five leagues depth in Lake Champlain, on the east shore, the said four leagues to start at the limit of the seigniory granted to the Sieur de la Perrière July 6, 1734, going down the lake, in which is comprised the river called La Moelle with the islands, islets and adjacent waters, right of fief and seigniory, high, middle and low justice."[1]

April 30, 1737.

Act of ratification by His Majesty of the concession granted by MM. de Beauharnois and Hocquart, Governor and Intendant of New France, to the Sieur Raimbault, Lieutenant-General of the Jurisdiction of Montreal, October 8, 1736.[2]

28. New York State Historical Association, *Proceedings*, X, p. 90.

1. *Archives de Québec:* Registre d'intendance no. 8, folio 16; published in *Pièces et documents relatifs à la tenure seigneuriale*, p. 160. *Archives de Québec:* Inventaire des Concessions, etc., V, p. 34.

2. *Archives de Québec:* Insinuations du Conseil Souverain ou Supérieur, cahier 10, folio 5; published in *Appendice HHHH de l'Assemblèe Législative*, 1853, p. 22.

September 23, 1757.

Deed of gift by Paul-François Raimbault, seigneur de Saint-Blin, de la Moelle and other places, to his son Paul-François Raimbault, commandant of the fort of Rivière-au-Boeuf, near the fort of Presqu'isle, of the fief and seigniory of La Moinaudière, or La Moelle, on Lake Champlain.

Seal of Gervais Hodiesne, notary of Chambly.[3]

September 27, 1766.

Deed of sale by the heirs of the late Sieur Pierre Raimbault, during his life Lieutenant-General of the Jurisdiction of Montreal, to Benjamin Price, Daniel Robertson and John Livingston, of the seigniory La Moelle, for the sum of 90,000 livres.[4]

FROM 1736 to 1766, three generations of the Raimbault family are named as proprietors of this seigniory: Pierre Raimbault (1671-1740), Paul-François Raimbault de Saint-Blin (1696-17—) and Paul-François Raimbault (1725-17—), all three of whom were active participants in the administrative or military departments of the colony. From the bare record of the documents it is evident that the owners had made some successful efforts "to place their seigniory under cultivation" and settle colonists within its limits, for La Moelle did not revert to the Crown in 1741. The first English settler to arrive after the Treaty of Peace discovered clearings of considerable extent between the Isle of Pines and the Lamoille River.[5] Possibly Captain Mallet held his lands under grant from the Raimbault family.[6]

The extent of this grant was enormous: "we have given him (a grant) of this extent because of his numerous family which consists of fourteen children, for ordinary grants are of only two leagues."[7] In our day it comprises the shore of the lake from the head of Mallet's Bay to a point about three miles south of the City of St. Albans; on the east the boundary extended from a point three miles south of Cambridge to the village of East Fairfield.[8] Until further discov-

---

3. *Archives de Québec:* Inventaire des Concessions, etc., V, p. 35.

4. *Doc. Col. Hist. N. Y.,* I, pp. 363-364.

5. Hemenway: *Vermont Gazetteer,* I, p. 756.

6. See Chapter XIII.

7. MM. de Beauharnois et Hocquart au Ministre, le 15 octobre, 1736.

8. I have cited all documents in detail, concerning this seigniory; for the others I shall only give titles with the necessary references.

eries are made, the number of settlers and their names must remain unknown, but their presence is undoubted.

When the Raimbault heirs finally disposed of the seigniory of La Moelle, Benjamin Price and his associates paid 90,000 French "livres" (the "livre" was approximately twenty cents, and purchase price $18,000). That sum represents to-day a purchasing power of from five to eight times that of the eighteenth century value, or between $90,000 and $144,000. Benjamin Price was a well-known land speculator, named as the purchaser of the seigniory of Saint-Armand and others, usually lands comprising mineral or power resources.

FOUCAULT

April 3, 1733. Act of concession.[9]

April 6, 1734. Act of ratification.[10]

June 14, 1737. Record of Janvrin Dufresne, accredited surveyor.[11]

May 10, 1741. Ordinance regulating reversion to the Crown.[12]

May 1, 1743. Act of reconcession of the same seigniory with the addition of one league front on the south, i.e., almost the entire seigniory of Belcour.[13]

November 1, 1744. Act of concession of a peninsula of two leagues front (formerly granted to Sieur de l'Isle and "abandoned immediately"), adjoining on the south the grant of May 1, 1743.[14]

March 25, 1745. Act of ratification.[15]

Sieur Foucault had worked hard to develop his seigniory and to settle families there, for the Act of May 1, 1743 mentions seven inhabitants already established: François Laporte alias Labonté, Chris-

9. *Archives de Québec:* Registre d'intendance no. 7, folio 9.

10. *Ibid.,* Insinuations du Conseil Souverain . . ., cahier 7, folio 45.

11. *Archives de Québec:* Inventaire des Concessions, etc., IV, p. 248.

12. *Ibid.,* Ordonnances des Intendants, cahier 29, folio 28: published in *Edits et Ordonnances relatifs à la tenure seigneuriale,* II, p. 555.

13. *Ibid.,* Registre d'intendance no. 9, folio 12.

14. *Ibid.,* Registre d'intendance no. 9, folio 30.

15. *Ibid.,* Registre français des enregistrements, cahier D, folio 145.

tophe de St. Christophe alias Lajoie, Thomas Caret, David Corbin, Joseph Xaintonge, Pierre Marmet, Michel St. Julien.

There is some confusion as to the date of the founding of this settlement. Some historians mention 1731, two claim 1730.[16] The Foucault grant as finally constituted in 1744 comprised three separate concessions: the original seigniory of Foucault, dated April 3, 1733; the seigniory of Belcour, dated April 5, 1733, and acquired by Sieur Foucault May 1, 1743; and the seigniory of De l'Isle, mentioned only in the Act of November 1, 1744, when it was added to the lands already held by Sieur Foucault. The settlement at the Pointe du Détour was located within the limits of the grant to Jacques de la Fontaine de Belcour. It must have been clear in 1740 to the authorities in New France that M. de Belcour had not fulfilled the conditions of his grant; if he had succeeded in establishing settlers there, the property would not have reverted to the Crown domain by the Act of May 10, 1741. He claimed some effort at settlement, however, when he protested vainly against the reversion, stating that he would "go this summer on the Grant with three men to build there and make clearances,"[17] offering special "allurements" to persuade colonists to settle on his lands, and hoping to obtain by "gift what he could not obtain from them by force." It seems scarcely logical to me that Sieur François Foucault, the admitted founder of this settlement, would have established colonists and have built a mill for their use, etc., on land which was not yet his property. Therefore, I am convinced that the activity of Sieur Foucault at the Pointe du Détour began no earlier than 1740.

In 1740, there were eight settlers to form the nucleus of the little village planned by M. de Foucault; the following year, a stone mill costing 4,000 livres was built near the lake shore, three new settlers joining the settlement; a church 20 by 40 feet was begun by M. de Foucault to be completed in the spring ready for the arrival of the missionary. In addition, the proprietor had made free grant to the Bishop of Quebec of a plot two "arpents" front by forty arpents depth, comprising the site of the church and the priest's house with sufficient land for farming and for setting off a cemetery.[18] At the time of the visit to Lake Champlain of the Swedish professor, Peter

16. Coolidge and Mansfield, Hemenway, Crockett; also Hiram A. Huse: *State Papers of Vermont*, II, p. 251.

17. Crockett: *History of Vermont*, I, p. 128.

18. These developments are all noted in the Act of 1744.

Kalm, in July, 1749, the Pointe du Détour presented the following appearance: "a windmill, built of stone, stands on the east side of the lake on a projecting piece of ground. Some Frenchmen have lived near it; they left it when the war broke out (1744), and are not yet come back to it. The English, with their Indians, have burned the houses here several times, but the mill remained unhurt."[19] He saw it from the boat taking him to St. Johns. Captain Phineas Stevens who was traveling by way of the lake in 1749 observes that "at the emptying of the lake into the Shamblee River there is a windmill built of stone; it stands on the east side of the water, and several houses on both sides built before the war, but one inhabited at present."[20]

After the peace in 1763, Sieur Foucault sold the seigniory to General Frederick Haldimand, who granted it to Mr. Henry Caldwell of Belmont, near Quebec.[21] The first English settlers found the mill in ruins, a pile of masonry; quite near was a hole evidently the cellar of a building, and growing in this hole were found trees forty years old. In 1868, the cellar and mill walls, about four feet high, were still fairly well preserved.[22]

HOCQUART

April 20, 1743. Act of concession by His Majesty.[23]

April 1, 1745. Act of concession by His Majesty to Sieur Hocquart, Intendant of New France, "in order to give him a new mark of the satisfaction he has in his service," of a territory "of three leagues front situated on Lake Champlain, starting from the boundary of the land already granted him by brevet of April 20, 1743, drawing toward the north by the same depth of five leagues . . ."[24]

Sieur Gilles Hocquart deserves special mention. The family originated in Champagne; Jean Hocquart, Seigneur d'Essenlis et de Mus-

19. Kalm: *Travels into North America*, II, p. 213.
20. Quoted in Crockett's *History of Vermont*, I, p. 129.
21. Hemenway: *Vermont Gazetteer*, II, pp. 488-489.
22. *Ibid.*
23. *Archives de Québec:* Inventaire des Concessions, etc., V, pp. 57-58. Insinuations du Conseil Souverain, cahier 9, folios 7 and 34; Appendice HHHH . . ., 117 and 121; *State Papers of Vermont*, II, pp. 254-255.
24. Original Manuscript in Bennington Historical Museum.

court, great-grandfather of our intendant, married a cousin of the great Minister Colbert; their eldest son became his chief clerk; their grandson, Jean-Hyacinthe Hocquart, born in 1649, member of the King's Council and Intendant of Marine since 1716, had married, December 10, 1681, Marie-Françoise, daughter of François Michelet-du-Cosnier by Marie Talon, cousin of the famous intendant of that name; Hocquart died in Paris October 17, 1723, leaving eight children, his third son becoming intendant of New France.

Gilles Hocquart was born toward the end of the seventeenth century, probably at Nantes; having served in France as commissary of the Marine, he was named commissary-general of the Marine and "administrator of New France March 8, 1729." M. Hocquart reached Quebec in August, and his predecessor, Claude-Thomas Dupuy, recalled by the King, left the colony October 1. M. Hocquart acted as intendant until January 21, 1731 when Louis XV appointed him to that position. "Under his administration and in spite of the financial embarrassment of the mother-country the colony seemed to prosper." The King maintained him in his functions until January 1, 1748, when François Bigot was named his successor. M. Bigot arrived in Quebec August 26, and M. Hocquart left New France at the annual departure of the boats about November 1. On April 1, 1749, he became intendant of Brest and Councillor of State, December 29, 1753. He married August 23, 1750, Anne-Catherine, daughter of Claude de la Lande, Comte de Câlan, Chevalier of St. Louis. A flattering biographical note is recorded by the Marquis de Montcalm who was cordially received by M. Hocquart at Brest in 1756: "As for M. and Madame Hocquart, they are a well-matched couple; respectable people, virtuous, well-intentioned, keeping a good home. Also M. de Hocquart was twenty years intendant in Canada, without having increased his fortune, contrary to the custom of intendants of the colonies who make too great profits at the expense of the colony."[25] The last time the name of Gilles Hocquart appears in Canada is on April 7, 1763, when he sold his seigniory of Hocquart to Sieur Michel Chartier de Lotbinière for 9,000 livres.[26] He probably died soon after.[27]

25. *Journal de Montcalm*, p. 30.

26. *State Papers of Vermont*, II, pp. 294-295. *Doc. Col. Hist. N. Y.*, I, pp. 351-352, 375.

27. Roy: Les Intendants de la Nouvelle-France, in: *Mémoires et Comptes-Rendus de la Société Royale du Canada*, 2e serie, IX, p. 65.

The seigniory of Hocquart included within its limits the present towns of Ferrisburg (southern part), Panton, Addison, Bridport (northern part), the City of Vergennes, Waltham, Weybridge, Middlebury (northern part including the village), New Haven, and the western parts of Monkton and Bristol, an area of some 115,000 acres. On the Lake Champlain shore was included Chimney Point opposite Fort St. Frederic; in the center flows Otter Creek whose falls at Middlebury and Vergennes might have furnished unlimited water-power for commercial development. The property was probably never thoroughly explored since the value of its natural resources received no mention in documents dealing with this seigniory.

Tradition persists that the French first came to Chimney Point soon after the construction of Fort Sainte-Anne in 1666 and built a small fort and village there. It is certain that the Point was a frequent campsite for those traveling through the Champlain valley. The English made an attempt to control the waterway in 1690 by the temporary occupation under Captain Jacobus De Warm. From vague references to the Point in the *Official Correspondence* it appears that the French and Indians habitually met here for trading and that proposals for the establishment of a permanent post were frequently under consideration. Sixteen hundred and thirty-one, 1724, and 1726 are given as the possible date of the founding of a Chimney Point settlement, but no supporting evidence has come to light. The first efforts at colonization recorded in official documents were undertaken between the years 1726 and 1731.

About 1730, a few French families settled near Chimney Point, where they built a stockaded fort, probably using the materials from the ruined "little stone fort" built by Jacobus De Warm in 1690.[28] This was the first permanent settlement made by the French in the valley of the Lake "in pursuance of their plan to extend their settlements and fortifications and set limits to those of the English."[29] These first settlers immediately began the construction of a windmill near the site later occupied by the old tavern now owned by the Hon. M. F. Barnes.[30] When the troops arrived in 1731, sent to build a military post on the point opposite, the settlers at Chimney Point heartily approved since this fort would assure them a much more peaceful existence. Soon others, associated with the garrison in some

28. *Americana:* XXVIII, 23. *State Papers of Vermont:* II, pp. 249-250.
29. Swift: *History of Middlebury and Addison County*, pp. 44-50.
30. Reid: *Lake George and Lake Champlain*, p. 360.

capacity, came to this region and settled on the two points and on "the Isles aux Boiteux" (since disappeared), which were located between Chimney Point and Hospital Creek.[31]   The land had been cleared along the lake shore toward the north, the wood being used in the construction of the fort and houses.   As was usual in New France, small land-owners held only narrow frontage on the lake, their lands extending far back from the shore; their houses were built close to the shore and consequently close to each other as a means of defense as well as a source of social enjoyment.   The proprietor reserved between 200 and 300 arpents square on Chimney Point as inalienable domain, separated from lands granted to divers tenants "by a marsh formed by a stream which empties there" (Hospital Creek?).[32]

May 5, 1756, Robert Rogers reports a scouting trip to a little village on the east shore of the lake about two miles from Crown Point. He found no inhabitants there, remained for a day and a half and went away; however, before leaving, the record says that his rangers killed twenty-three head of cattle.[33]   In August, Rogers landed his rangers on the east shore of the lake eight miles north of the fort; he marched south to a "village lying east of the fort," where he seized a man, his wife and their daughter.[34]   Speaking of the population along the shores, Rogers mentions "300 men, chiefly inhabitants of the adjacent villages."[35]

During the years from 1749 to 1759 the settlers built their houses and cabins along a road extending four miles north from the point; they sowed grain in the fields near their homes and planted fruit trees and flowering plants foreign to the country.[36]   In 1867, the cellar holes and deserted gardens indicated a much more populous "street" during the French régime than in that year.[37]   Samuel Swift, author of the *History of Middlebury and Addison County*, visited the site of these villages in 1859; at that time the earthen ramparts which had protected the fortified mill still existed; old plum

31. Hemenway: *Vermont Historical Gazetteer*, I, p. 2.

32. O'Callaghan: *Doc. Hist. of N. Y.*, I, p. 538.

33. Crockett: *History of Vermont*, I, p. 130.   *Journals of Robert Rogers.*

34. *Ibid.*, I, p. 131.   *Journals of Robert Rogers.*

35. *Journals of Robert Rogers.*   Murray: *Lake Champlain and Its Shores*, p. 91.   The estimates of population vary.

36. Robinson: *History of Vermont*, p. 20.   Hemenway: *Vermont Historical Gazetteer*, I, p. 1.

37. Hemenway: *Vermont Historical Gazetteer*, I, p. 1.

and apple trees could be seen as well as the cellar holes of houses; four were on the farm of John Strong, three or four on the Vallance farm,[38] ten or twelve on the Barnes property. The French inhabitants followed the troops in the retreat of 1759, leaving their farms forever; before leaving they burned the barns, the cabins, the houses, everything.[39] When the English arrived nothing remained of the French villages but the blackened chimneys, "standing as grim sentinels amid the surrounding ruin."[40] From these ruined chimneys came the name Chimney Point, given by the English; the first English settlers used the ruins of the French buildings in the construction of their own homes.[41]

M. Hocquart's efforts in developing the settlements in the environs of the fort were recognized and rewarded by the grant of the seigniory of Hocquart, April 20, 1743, one league frontage opposite Fort St. Frederic. Two years later he received an additional grant of three leagues frontage adjoining the first grant on the north, "in order to give him a new mark of the satisfaction he (His Majesty Louis XV) has in his service." M. de Lotbinière, purchaser of these lands April 7, 1763, made great efforts to establish his claims, giving as evidence of the validity of his title the "frequent clearances" and "various settlements" on these lands. In 1776, the British government admitted his claims, awarding him the grant of equivalent lands within the province of Quebec.

La Gauchetière[42]

April 11, 1733. Act of concession to Daniel Migeon, de la Gauchetière.[43]

February 8, 1735. Act of ratification.[44]

May 10, 1741. Ordinance regulating reversion to the Crown.[45]

38. Swift: *History of Middlebury and Addison County*, pp. 44-50.
39. *Ibid.*
40. Palmer: *History of Lake Champlain*, p. 5.
41. Hemenway: *Vermont Historical Gazetteer*, I, p. 4. Swift: *History of Middlebury and Addison County*, pp. 40-50.
42. *Archives de Québec:* Inventaire des Concessions, etc., IV, pp. 270-272.
43. *Ibid.*, Registre d'intendance, cahier 7, folio 19.
44. *Ibid.*, Insinuations du Conseil Souverain . . ., cahier 7, folio 77.
45. *Ibid.*, Ordonnances des Intendants, cahier 29, folio 28.

January 15, 1744. Act of concession to Sieur Guillaume Estèbe, member of the superior council of Quebec.[46]

March 25, 1745. Act of ratification.[47]

On the west shore of the lake opposite the south end of Isle La Motte lay the seigniory of La Gauchetière; included within its boundaries were Pointe au Roche and Monty Bay. The original grantee, Daniel Migeon de Bransac, chevalier de Saint-Louis, was a member of a distinguished family of Montreal, a lieutenant and aide-major, later commandant at Fort Saint-Frederic. Evidently whatever efforts he may have made to develop his grant were unavailing and the title reverted to the Crown in 1741.

In 1744, the property was granted to Sieur Guillaume Estèbe, a member of the Superior Council of Quebec, merchant and King's storekeeper at Quebec in 1755. No evidence of reversion to the Crown appears, and it must be supposed that the proprietor was successful in his efforts to exploit his grant; however, there are no documents to show the final disposition of La Gauchetière.

SAINT-ARMAND[48]

September 23, 1748. Act of concession to Sieur Nicolas-René Levasseur of an extent of six leagues front along the River Missiskoui, by three leagues depth "on each side of the latter."[49]

April 30, 1749. Act of ratification.[50]

November 17, 1763. Deed of sale by Alexandre Saint-Hilaire de la Rochette, in the name of and as attorney for René-Nicolas Levasseur and Dame Marie-Angélique Just, his wife, to Henry Guynand, merchant at London, accepting for him Jean Passelier and John Henry Eberts, bankers at Paris, of the fief and seigniory of Saint-Armand.[51]

May 23, 1766. Deed of sale to William McKenzie, Benjamin Price, James Moore and George Fulton.[52]

46. *Ibid.*, Registre d'intendance, cahier 9, folio 21.
47. *Ibid.*, Insinuations du Conseil Souverain, cahier 10, folio 80.
48. *Archives de Québec:* Inventaire des Concessions, etc., V, pp. 61-64.
49. *Ibid.*, Registre d'intendance, cahier 9, folio 35.
50. *Ibid.*, Insinuations du Conseil Souverain . . ., cahier 9, folio 74.
51. *Ibid.*, Inventaire des Concessions, etc., V, p. 63.
52. *Ibid.*, V, pp. 63-64.

James Moore purchased the rights of McKenzie and Price, April 4, 1786, and sold an undivided three-quarters of the seigniory of St. Armand to the Hon. Thomas Dunn, July 4, 1786. Thomas Dunn, a member of the Legislative Council of Quebec and later acting lieutenant governor, purchased the remaining quarter from the legatees of George Fulton, February 11, 1787. On May 12, 1789, Dunn was recorded as proprietor of the fief and seigniory of St. Armand; he and his heirs retained title as late as December 1, 1860.[53] Although a great part of this grant lay within the limits of the State of Vermont, where French rights were not recognized, Dunn was able to collect fees from some of the early English settlers along the Missisquoi River.

St. Armand comprised the whole of the grants previously made to Sieurs de Lusignan and de Beauvais, as well as parts of those made to François Daine and to Michel Dagneau-Douville, all of which had reverted to the Crown Domain under the terms of the Act of 1741.

Tradition among the St. Regis Indians during the early nineteenth century told "of the first visit of a priest, in the summer of 1613, to Swanton, and thence to all the scattered encampments along the eastern shores of the placid lake discovered four years earlier by Samuel Champlain."[54]

A village of Abenakis had grown up near the falls of the Missisquoi during the latter part of the seventeenth century.[55] In all probability this settlement was an outgrowth of the mission settlement on the St. Francis River. Jesuits are supposed to have been here as early as 1700 and brought about the establishment of a second village, located on the right bank some two miles below the falls. During a quarter of a century the Indian village grew and prospered. In 1730, a "mortal sickness" attacked the Abenaki and French villages. The superstitious Indians left "their beautiful fields which extended for four miles along the river," and fled to their relatives at St. Francis. For a few years they returned only for the hunting season.

By 1736 the Abenakis had returned to Missisquoi in full numbers to remain there permanently; in that year Chauvignerie reports 180 warriors in the village. About 1741 or 1742, the French settlers

53. *Ibid.*, V, p. 64.

54. Hemenway: *Vermont Gazetteer*, IV, p. 1090: *The Catholic Church in Swanton*, by Mrs. Julia C. Smalley.

55. *Jesuit Relations*, Oct. 10, 1682.

returned and built a stone chapel at the lower village, which was served by the Jesuits.[56]   Building material was found in a marble quarry near the river.   Reference is made to the establishment of the Missisquoi Mission in the King's Instructions, May 24, 1744.   MM. de Beauharnois and Hocquart are enjoined to aid Father Lauverjat in whatever efforts he may make to detach the Loups and Abenakis of that region from the English; full co-operation of the officer in command at Fort St. Frederic is assured.   Again, April 28, 1745, the King expresses pleasure in the progress made by the village of Missiskouy and the attitude displayed by the Indians in reference to the war with the English then going on.   He also encourages the governor to urge the Indians to raid the English settlements, in this way fulfilling the principal purpose in the establishment of the mission, that is, to destroy any friendly relations between the Abenakis and the English.   M. de la Jonquière reports in 1749 that the village is entirely restored, that the cabins of the savages and the house of the missionary are in good condition, and that there is reason to believe that the settlement will gain in strength.[57]

The Abenakis of Missisquoi were active during King George's War and the Seven Years' War, constantly furnishing men for the raids on the English settlements along the Connecticut River and the Massachusetts frontier.   One band of warriors encamped near the St. Frederic settlement and supplied men for many of the raiding parties led by the officers of that post.

René-Nicolas Levasseur was a naval constructor who had been sent to New France in May, 1739, to direct shipbuilding in the colony.   His work was so satisfactory that the King granted him an annuity of 500 livres.   He was commissioned Chief of Construction in Canada in 1749 and Inspector of Timber and Forests in 1752. In the spring of 1744 and during the following winter, Levasseur visited the shores of Lake Champlain in search of timber for shipbuilding, particularly of pine suitable for masts.   He was successful in his quest, locating extensive stands of pine along the Saranac and Au Sable Rivers.   On both journeys, Levasseur stayed for some days at Missisquoi, where the possibilities of water-power at the falls probably attracted his interest.   He petitioned the King for the grant of this region and received title in 1748.

M. Levasseur constructed his mill at the foot of the falls soon after

56. Hemenway: *Vermont Gazetteer*, IV, pp. 953-955.
57. M. de la Jonquière au ministre, le 9 octobre 1749.

1749. This was the first sawmill built by the French in the Champlain valley. The site was unusually favorable as no dam was necessary since the natural fall was such that a simple channel cut along the bank furnished ample power; the course of this channel could still be traced in 1868 on the right bank above the falls.[58] Natural protection was afforded by the approach from the lake, a six-mile journey; sailing between wooded banks, fifty-ton vessels could come up to the mill. Timber and power were abundant, and transportation by water to Montreal and Quebec was comparatively easy by way of Lake Champlain, the Richelieu and St. Lawrence Rivers. On the crest of a hill on the right bank near the mill a wooden stockade was set up for the protection of the mill and the villages. This fort, with a palisade of white cedar (still visible in the nineteenth century), was hastily built in the hope of concealing the operations from the English. Not far from the mill and fort a thriving French and Indian village soon came into being; about fifty houses clustered around a stone church. In 1754 the King granted Intendant Bigot permission to purchase lumber from the mill owned by the Sieur Levasseur.

When the Seven Years' War was at its height, shipbuilding lagged. M. Levasseur asked for recall to France in October, 1757, but the pressure of war-time activities caused his request to remain unanswered for the time being. Intendant Bigot wrote to the Minister the same month telling of the difficulty of getting out masts in the Lake Champlain district owing to the constant activity of the enemy. The English learned of the existence of the Missisquoi mill and resolved upon its destruction. Five men were sent out from northern Massachusetts to carry out this plan. While the French mill-workers were at dinner in their homes on the east hill near the fort, the English forded the rapids and succeeded in setting fire to the mill. Three of the attacking force were killed during the subsequent pursuit; the two survivors found their way back to Massachusetts to tell of their success.[59]

November 1, 1757, M. Levasseur completed his last shipbuilding contract in New France. The authorities in France believed that Levasseur's ability could be put to profitable use in constructing the Great Lakes fleet which M. de Montcalm considered desirable. De-

58. Hemenway: *Vermont Gazetteer*, IV, pp. 959-960.
59. Hemenway: *Vermont Gazetteer*, IV, pp. 956-958: account of one of the survivors.

lays intervened, and before this plan could be put into effect the defeat of the French at Quebec destroyed French dominion over the country. M. Levasseur returned to France with Governor de Vaudreuil.

Robert Rogers, at the time of his Ranger raid against St. Francis, October, 1759, left boats and provisions at the mouth of the Missisquoi, which were found and destroyed by the French from the settlement at the Falls. Rogers was then pursued by a party from the Missisquoi village—French settlers reinforced by a detachment of soldiers.[60] Probably every able-bodied resident joined in the pursuit. At the height of its career, the French village counted 50 families at the most; the Abenaki village numbered some 200 persons.[61]

Joseph Powers, who later lived and died in Ferrisburg, was a soldier at the capture of Quebec, September 18, 1759; he chose the Missisquoi route for his return home. He found the Jesuit church flourishing; among its parishioners were a large number of Christian Indians. Further research may reveal the names of the priests who served this church; only the name of Father Léon-Basile Roubault, missionary among the Abenakis from 1742 to 1764, is now known. In the neighborhood of the villages there were tilled fields, and as late as 1795 apple-trees fifty to sixty years old were found on this site. Between 1765 and 1775, James Robertson and Simon Metcalf employed fifty men of French descent in the lumber industry at Missisquoi; his mill was built on the site of the old French mill. John Hilliker settled near the Missisquoi River in 1779. He found the Abenaki village still in existence, the Jesuit Father still busy with his flock. According to the statement of John Hilliker, Jr., in 1862, his father held his lands under a lease granted by the Christian Abenakis of Missisquoi.[62]

PANCALON, OR GRANDE ISLE[63]

July 1, 1734. Act of concession to François-Antoine Pécaudy de Contrecoeur "of an island situated in Lake Champlain, popularly called Grande Isle, with the islands, islets and waters dependent upon it."[64]

60. *Ibid.*, IV, p. 960: *Journal of Robert Rogers*.
61. Crockett: *History of Lake Champlain*, pp. 110-111.
62. Hemenway: *Vermont Gazetteer*, IV, p. 972.
63. *Archives de Québec*: Inventaire des Concessions, etc., IV, pp. 276-279.
64. *Ibid.*, Registre d'intendance, cahier 7, folio 30.

February 8, 1735. Act of ratification.[65]

March 4, 1736. Act of Faith and Homage.[66]

March 5, 1736. Avowal and census.[67]

May 10, 1741. Ordinance regulating reversion to the Crown.[68]

The family of M. de Contrecoeur was one of the most celebrated in the military annals of New France. The founder of the family in this country was a noted soldier in the French armies for twenty-five years before his arrival in the colony. Antoine Pécaudy de Contrecoeur was born in 1596. A distinguished officer at the age of sixty-four under the famous Marshal de Turenne in Europe, he continued his service in New France as captain in the regiment of Carignan with M. de Tracy's expedition against the Mohawks in September, 1666. A widower of seventy-one, he married Barbe Denys de la Trinité, a girl of fifteen, daughter of an influential family of Quebec. In 1672, his services to the colony were recognized by the grant of the seigniory of Contrecoeur on the Richelieu River. At his death shortly after 1681, he left one daughter Marie, wife of Jean-Louis de la Corne, and one son François-Antoine, born in 1680. François-Antoine Pécaudy de Contrecoeur married Jeanne de St. Ours, whose father was proprietor of a nearby seigniory and whose family became equally famous. Chevalier and captain, he became commandant of Fort St. Frederic in 1734, and died on duty at that post June 24, 1743. His five surviving children married into the families of Daine de Boisfranc, Péan de Livaudière, Boucher de la Perrière and Boucher de la Bruyère, all proprietors of Champlain Valley seigniories. The son and heir, Claude-Pierre Pécaudy de Contrecoeur, captain in the Marine, received the grant of the seigniory of La Pécaudière (Otter Creek), July 7, 1734. His two wives were chosen from Champlain valley families: Marie-Madeleine Boucher de la Pérrière and Marguerite-Barbe Rocbert de la Morandière. In 1754 and 1755 he served as commandant at Fort Duquesne, where illness prevented his active participation in the glory of Braddock's defeat. King Louis XV raised him to the dignity of chevalier de St.

65. *Ibid.*, Insinuations du Conseil Souverain . . ., cahier 7, folio 76.
66. *Ibid.*, Pois et hommages, régime français, cahier 2, folio 168.
67. *Ibid.*, Aveux et denombrements, régime français, cahier 2, folio 430.
68. *Ibid.*, Ordonnances des Intendants, cahier 29, folio 28.

Louis in 1756. After a distinguished career, he died in 1775, leaving six children.

In the Ordinance of 1741, mention is made of a remonstrance by the Sieurs de Contrecoeur, father and son, in which they declare that they have done their best to fulfill the conditions of their grants; it had seemed impossible to find settlers willing to accept lands even on very advantageous terms, etc.; they intended to continue their efforts without much hope of success; they asked a delay in consideration of their offers to conform to His Majesty's intentions. This remonstrance had no effect and their seigniories reverted to the Crown. In 1772, the Sieur de Contrecoeur presented a request that the British government recognize his rights to the seigniories formerly granted to his father and to himself by the French government. Basing its decision on the Ordinance of 1741, the English authorities refused this request.[69]

November 1, 1749. Act of concession to François Daine, formerly seigneur de Boisfranc, of the seigniory granted to M. de Contrecoeur, senior, July 1, 1734.[70]

It is interesting to note on May 25, 1745 the Act of Faith and Homage of François Daine, *by power of attorney from Pierre-Claude Pécaudy de Contrecoeur,* for the fief of St. Denis. Was there a secret understanding between M. Daine and the Contrecoeurs in 1749? François Daine, Royal Councillor and Chief Clerk of the Sovereign Council, married at Boucherville, March 8, 1742, Louise, daughter of François-Antoine Pécaudy de Contrecoeur; in 1749, M. Daine received grant of the seigniory formerly owned by M. de Contrecoeur; and in 1772, M. de Contrecoeur, as shown in his petition to the English King, believed that he still had rights over these lands.

May 31, 1750. Act of ratification.[71]

September 22, 1763. Deed of sale to Jean Marteilhe, merchant of Québec.[72]

69. *Archives de Québec:* Registre d'intendance, cahier 9, folio 45.
70. *Archives de Québec:* Registre d'intendance, cahier 9, folio 45.
71. *Archives de Québec:* Insinuations du Conseil Souverain . . ., cahier 9, folio 80.
72. *Ibid.,* Deed included in Inventaire des Concessions.

*September 22, 1763. Act of Faith and Homage of Jean Mar-
teilhe.*[73]

*January 8, 1767. Act of concession to Jean Thomas of four
"arpents" front by thirty depth in the seigniory of Grande Isle,
to start "from the Point called Colins going toward the Bay of
Michiscouk."*[74]

Sieur Daine, whether acting for himself or his wife's family, evidently fulfilled the conditions of his grant, otherwise it would have
reverted to the Crown Domain. François Daine was named Director of the Crown Domain in 1752, and perhaps enjoyed freedom
from regulations which would have been strictly enforced in the case
of less influential persons. The title to the seigniory remained in his
name until the deed of sale to Jean Marteilhe in 1763. After the
retreat of the French, M. Marteilhe granted lands on Grande Isle,
which shows that the presence of settlers within the limits of the
seigniory guaranteed title to the proprietors until 1767.

RAMEZAY-LA-GESSE[75]

*October 25, 1749. Act of concession to "demoiselle Louise la
Gesse" of six leagues front by six leagues depth on Lake Champlain, "starting one league above the river au Sable and five
leagues below the said river."*[76]

On the margin of this grant is a note stating that "this limit has
been changed at the request of the said Demoiselle and the brevet
which came this year (1750) has been sent back to be placed in conformity." The contemplated limits included the grant made in
1733 to M. de St. Vincent, located opposite Grande Isle, and a considerably larger area to the south. Louise de Ramezay was a daughter of Sieur Claude de Ramezay, governor of Three Rivers and administrator of New France. The seigniory was granted to his
daughter in recognition of his eminent services to the colony.

The *Archives of Quebec* contain no record of the arrival of the
new brevet nor is there any record of the final disposition of the
grant. Apparently the lands were still considered a part of the

73. *Ibid.*, Inventaire des Concessions, etc., IV, pp. 278-279.
74. *Ibid.*, Inventaire des Concessions, etc., IV, p. 279.
75. *Ibid.*, Inventaire des Concessions, etc., V, pp. 68-69.
76. *Ibid.*, Registre d'intendance, cahier 9, folio 44.

Crown Domain, since the northern part of Ramezay-la-Gesse was granted to the Sieur de Villemonde in 1755.

BEAUJEU[77]

April 9, 1733. Act of concession to Sieur Louis Liénard de Beaujeu of lands bordering those of Sieur de la Ronde on the south.[78]

February 8, 1735. Act of ratification.[79]

May 10, 1741. Ordinance regulating reversion to the Crown.[80]

March 6, 1752. Act of reconcession to Sieur Daniel-Hyacinthe-Marie Lienard de Beaujeu of the seigniory of his father.[81]

June 1, 1753. Act of ratification.[82]

August 14, 1765. Deed of sale by Dame Eléonore de Beaujeu, widow of Daniel Liénard de Beaujeu the younger, . . . to Gabriel Christie.[83]

Louis Liénard de Beaujeu, chevalier de St. Louis and major of the troops, was the son of an official of the household of King Louis XIV. After his arrival in New France he married a sister of Daniel Migeon de Bransac, seigneur de la Gauchetière.[84] At the time his seigniory of Beaujeu reverted to the Crown Domain he was fifty-nine years old and probably died shortly afterward.

Denise Migeon de Bransac, his wife, is mentioned in a letter from Comte de Maurepas to the Marquis de Beauharnois, May 24, 1728: "There has been granted to Dame de Beaujeu a passage on the transport 'Eléphant,' to return to France to perform the duties of 'Remueuse' [cradle-rocker] to the Royal children (of Louis XV), to which she has succeeded."

His son, Daniel-Hyacinthe-Marie Liénard de Beaujeu (1711-1755), became a distinguished officer in the military service of New

77. *Archives de Québec:* Inventaire des Concessions, etc., IV, pp. 266-267.
78. *Ibid.*, Registre d'intendance, cahier 7, folio 17.
79. *Ibid.*, Insinuation du Conseil Souverain . . ., cahier 7, folio 53.
80. *Ibid.*, Ordonnances des Intendants, cahier 29, folio 28.
81. *Ibid.*, Registre d'intendance, cahier 10, folio 4.
82. *Ibid.*, Insinuations du Conseil Souverain . . ., cahier 10, folio 6.
83. *Ibid.*, Inventaire des Concessions, etc., IV, p. 265.
84. See page 235.

France. He succeeded M. de Contrecoeur in the command of Fort Duquesne and commanded the French during the ambush of Braddock's forces; both leaders lost their lives in the engagement. He married a daughter of François Foucault, seigneur de Foucault and Royal Councillor. March 22, 1743, he received grant of the seigniory of Lacolle (formerly the property of the Sieur Denys de la Ronde), bordering his father's lands on the north. His younger brother Louis Liénard de Beaujeu, Sieur de Villemonde, became Seigneur de Beaujeu-Lac Champlain, January 20, 1755.[85]

Daniel Liénard de Beaujeu recovered his father's seigniory in 1752 by a new grant. Between 1752 and 1765 he and his heirs developed his property to a sufficient extent to retain title. One settler on these lands is recalled by the name of a village of our day, Rouses Point, N. Y. Jacques Rouse established his home on the site of the present village in 1753.[86] Undoubtedly he was soon joined by other colonists, as title to the seigniory remained in the Beaujeu family until 1765, when Eléonore, widow of Daniel Liénard de Beaujeu, Jr., sold the property to Gabriel Christie.

June 6, 1760, Robert Rogers with 200 Rangers from Crown Point was surprised at Rouses Point by 350 French from Isle aux Noix under Sieur Pépin-La Force. In the ensuing engagement, the English lost 17 killed and 11 wounded, inflicting upon the French a loss of 40 killed and a few wounded, including the French leader himself. Rogers withdrew to Isle La Motte, remaining there until June 9, when he stealthily passed Isle aux Noix unperceived and took 25 prisoners during a surprise attack on Fort St. Thérèse. The English safely withdrew to Crown Point.

Walter H. Crockett in his *History of Lake Champlain,* page 59, speaks of a "deed of transfer" May 2, 1754, from Sieur Péan to Sieur de Beaujeu of the seigniory of "Péan."[87] Mr. Crockett does not give the source of this information. The seigniory of Livaudière (the *Archives of Quebec* list no seigniory called "Péan") was granted to M. Péan April 10, 1733, and reverted to the Crown by the Ordinance of May 10, 1741;[88] the same seigniory was granted to Sieur Bedout November 1, 1752, "which concession was formerly granted to the late Sieur Péan."[89]

85. See page 248.
86. Reid: *Lake Champlain and Lake George,* p. 7.
87. Quoted also in N. Y. State Historical Association, *Proceedings,* X, p. 89.
88. *Archives de Québec:* Inventaire des Concessions, etc., IV, pp. 268-270.
89. *Ibid.*

April 10, 1733. Act of concession to Sieur Hugues-Jacques Péan, Sieur de Livaudière. This grant included Isle La Motte.[91]

February 8, 1735. Act of ratification.[92]

May 10, 1741. Ordinance regulating reversion to the Crown.[93]

November 1, 1752. Act of concession to Sieur Bedout of the grant "formerly made to the late M. Péan."[94]

June 1, 1753. Act of ratification.[95]

Sieur Hugues-Jacques Péan, Seigneur de Livaudière, married Marie-Françoise Pécaudy de Contrecoeur, sister and daughter of the Sieurs de Contrecoeur, who received grants on the shores of Lake Champlain. At first captain in the troops of the Marine, chevalier de St. Louis, then "major" of the city and Château of Quebec and member of the Superior Council, he received grant of the seigniory of Saint-Michel, August 14, 1736, and that of the seigniory of Livaudière-en-Québec, September 20, 1744. At his death, about 1752, he left one son, Michel-Jean-Hugues Péan, Seigneur de Saint-Michel, captain in the troops of the Marine and "aide-major" of Quebec. The Péans failed to develop their grant sufficiently to guarantee the title, and the seigniory reverted to the Crown Domain, 1741.

Sieur Jean-Antoine Bedout, Seigneur de Livaudière and member of the Superior Council of Quebec, must have developed his property. At the mouth of the Chazy River, ten leagues south of St. Johns, Professor Kalm, in 1749, saw a few houses evidently constructed without authorization of the Seigneur who did not become proprietor until 1752.[96] "When we were yet ten French miles from Fort St. John, we saw some houses on the western side of the lake, in which the French had lived before the last war, and which they abandoned, as it was by no means safe; they now returned to them again."

90. *Archives de Québec:* Inventaire des Concessions, etc., IV, pp. 268-270.

91. *Ibid.,* Registre d'intendance, cahier 7, folio 18.

92. *Ibid.,* Insinuations du Conseil Souverain . . ., cahier 7, folio 69.

93. *Ibid.,* Ordonnance des Intendants, cahier 29, folio 28.

94. *Ibid.,* Registre d'intendance, cahier 10, folio 12.

95. *Ibid.,* Insinuations du Conseil Souverain . . ., cahier 10, folio 1.

96. Kalm: *Travels into North America,* II, p. 212.

These houses, then, were built before 1744, perhaps under the Péan régime before 1741. In any case the settlers did not desert their homes permanently, if one may judge from the fact that M. Bedout remained proprietor.

Before 1768, Livaudière was sold to Francis McKay;[97] Mr. McKay confirmed to Jean La Framboise (often written "La Frombois" by the English) two homestead lots at the mouth of the Chazy River, where the said La Framboise had lived under the French régime before 1763 and where he still lived. This pioneer had built a house there, from which the English drove him in 1776. He returned in 1786, rebuilt his home, and died there in 1810. Joseph La Monte, in 1774, settled close to Jean La Framboise; driven from his home in 1776, he returned to Chazy in 1784.[98]

DANEAU DE MUY[99]

September 28, 1752. Act of concession to Jacques Pierre, Sieur de Muy, captain of infantry, of a seigniory of three leagues front by four depth, starting from the great "Otter River, said river included."[100]

Jacques-Pierre Daneau, Sieur de Muy (1695-1758), was the son of Nicolas Daneau de Muy and Marguerite Boucher de Boucherville of the Richelieu River family, so prolific and so influential in seventeenth century New France. Chevalier, captain and commandant at Detroit, he served his country for many years. From 1741 to 1754 his signature appears on the parish register of St. Frederic. Frequently he led war-parties to and from Fort St. Frederic during King George's War; after 1754 he became active in the western province and died in Detroit. His wife Louise-Geneviève Ruet d'Auteuil, was closely related to the important Juchereau family of Quebec. In his death record we read, "Having received the sacraments with all the piety which we could wish at the end of a life which had always been of the most edifying."

The seigniory of De Muy included the mouth of Otter Creek,

97. Crockett: *History of Lake Champlain*, p. 111. Limits of land grants were none too accurately indicated, but it seems clear that the mouth of the Chazy River lay within the boundaries of Livaudière, not of La Gauchetière.
98. *Ibid.*, p. 111.
99. *Archives de Québec:* Inventaire des Concessions, etc. . . . The English sources give an incorrect spelling, "Deumy."
100. *Ibid.*, Registre d'intendance, cahier 10, folio 11.

which had been for a century a favorite stop for travelers through the Champlain valley. It was the lake terminus of a well-blazed trail from New France to the settlements on the Connecticut River. An Indian village had been established here about 1690. In the present town of Ferrisburg there was a stone chapel, equipped with a bell, according to Shea's *History of the Catholic Church in the United States*. Near the center of the shore-line was the Pointe au Plâtre, frequently mentioned in contemporary documents. In the Act of Concession appears an interesting phrase, "to be enjoyed by him, his heirs and assigns, in perpetuity," which does not appear in any grant before 1752. Perhaps it is because of this supplementary phrase that we find no record of the sale or reversion of this seigniory.

BEAUJEU-LAC CHAMPLAIN[101]

July 20, 1755. Act of concession to Louis Liénard de Beaujeu, Sieur de Villemonde, of lands four leagues by the same depth, starting from the boundary of the seigniory of Sieur Estèbe, "going to the east as far as the river Sainte-Anne."[102]

The Act of Concession carries the same supplementary phrase as was noted in the grant of Daneau de Muy. The identity of the grantee has been discussed under the heading of "Beaujeu." The extent of the grant was double that of the usual seigniory, comprising the entire St. Vincent concession of 1733 and an equal area to the south, opposite Valcour Island, which had been included in the seigniory of Ramezay-la-Gesse in 1749.

ALAINVILLE[103]

November 15, 1758. Act of concession by Pierre Rigaud, Marquis de Vaudreuil, and François Bigot, governor and intendant of New France to Michel Chartier de Lotbinière, of an extent of land four leagues front by five leagues depth, part on Lake Saint-Sacrement and part on "la rivière à la Barbue."

This act is quoted in the letter from the Lords of Trade in London to Cadwallader Colden, lieutenant governor of New York, July 13, 1764; there is no trace of it in the official French archives of France or Canada.

101. *Archives de Québec:* Inventaire des Concessions, etc.; cf. page 244.
102. *Ibid.*, Registre d'intendance, cahier 10, folio 20.
103. *Archives de Québec:* Inventaire des Concessions, etc., V, pp. 88-97.

The grantee, Michel Chartier de Lotbinière was of distinguished lineage. His grandfather, René-Louis Chartier de Lotbinière, Royal Councillor and lieutenant-general, had served in his youth with M. de Courcelles' expedition in 1666; he was the author of a rhymed account of the disastrous exploit. Through his grandparents Michel Chartier was related to the well-known families of Lambert-Dumont and Damours de Louvières. His mother was Marie-Françoise Renaud-Davennes; his wife was daughter of Gaspard Chaussegros de Léry and Marie-Renée Le Gardeur de Beauvais. Lieutenant and chevalier de St. Louis, he was sent to survey the terrain at Carillon in 1752, and recommended, to M. de Vaudreuil, fortification of the site. He served with Montcalm in 1755 and was entrusted with the direction of the works at Carillon in 1756. In 1763 he purchased the seigniory of Hocquart.

M. de Lotbinière claimed Alainville in affidavit submitted to the English authorities in London. "I, undersigned, affirm and declare on oath that the Seigniory of Alainville, four leagues and more in front by five leagues in depth to the West, commences at La Pointe des Habitans (one league and a half or thereabouts above the Fort at Pointe à la Chevelure, and on the same side of the River) and that it terminates at Pointe du Bivac (Bivouac Point) of M. de Contrecoeur's camp, the lower point above l'Isle au Mouton near the entrance of Lake St. Sacrement; that the said Seigniory belongs to me in virtue of the Grant which the Marquis de Vaudreuil made to me dated 15th November of the year One thousand seven hundred & fifty Eight; that this deed of Concession was left, in the Original, by me in July 1764 with Mr. Pownall, Secretary of the Board of Trade & the Colonies, to be registered in said Office; that Sr. Henry Guinaud, my agent in London, informed me by letter that the Title deeds deposited by the Honble Mr. Cholmondeley on my behalf and by me at the said office had been returned to him all registered."[104] In a letter of May 6, 1764, M. de Lotbinière claimed "he had made divers establishments that have been successively ruined by the English armies."[105]

The seigniory of Alainville is the subject of a long correspondence between M. de Lotbinière and the English authorities.[106] M. de Lotbinière, Seigneur d'Hocquart and d'Alainville, finally received

104. O'Callaghan: *Documentary History of New York*, I, p. 546.
105. *Ibid.*, I, p. 541.
106. *Doc. Col. Hist. N. Y.*, VII, p. 642; VIII, pp. 577-669.

from the British government lands in Canada of the same area as the seigniory of Hocquart; as for the grant of Alainville, since the archives contained neither the act of concession nor the act of ratification by His French Majesty, the government recognized no obligation to compensate M. de Lotbinière. Alainville included within its limits Fort Carillon, the Pointe aux Gravois, the north end of Lake George and the little River à la Barbue; the area of this seigniory was only surpassed by that of St. Armand.

BOISFRANC[107]

Apr. 5, 1733. Grant to François Daine, chief clerk of the Superior Council of Quebec, of one and one-half leagues front by three leagues depth on Missisquoi Bay in Lake Champlain, bordered on one side by the mouth of the River "du Brochet," on the other by a line one and one-half leagues east of the mouth of the said river, running N. E. and S. W.

Apr. 6, 1734. Act of Ratification.

Dec. 20, 1733. Grant by François Daine to Nicolas Boisseau, notary at Quebec, of 3 arpents front by "the depth of the said seigniory," at the mouth of the River "du Brochet," to be held in perpetuity as "arrière-fief."

Dec. 20, 1733. Grant by François Daine to François Perreault, merchant and citizen of Quebec, of 3 arpents front by "the depth of the said seigniory," bordering the 3 arpents granted the same day to the Sieur Boisseau at the mouth of the River "du Brochet."

May 10, 1741. Ordinance regulating reversion to the Crown.

Although the Sieur Daine made efforts to develop his seigniory by the grant of lands to prospective settlers, the tenants evidently neglected to carry out the conditions of their grants. Nearly the entire area of Boisfranc lay north of the present boundary between Vermont and Canada. The two sub-grants noted above were at the northern extremity of Missisquoi Bay.

The seigneur de Boisfranc continued his interest in the Champlain valley long after his grant had reverted to the Crown. By Act of

107. *Archives de Québec:* Inventaire des Concessions, etc., IV, pp. 255-257.

Nov. 1, 1749, he received the grant of the seigniory of Pancalon (or Grand Isle), formerly the property of his father-in-law, M. de Contrecoeur.[108]

The history of the seigniories in the Lake Champlain valley is closely bound to the story of the development of Fort St. Frederic; as long as the troops controlled the lake, the settlements prospered; from the moment military protection was withdrawn, the settlers followed the soldiers in retreat.

Chapter XI. *Fort St. Frederic*

THE "Pointe à la Chevelure," the name which designated the two points facing each other on opposite sides of the lake (now known as Crown Point on the west, and Chimney Point on the east), was the subject of frequent proposals on the part of both French and English. Governor Dongan of New York, in a report to the English King in 1687, advocated the fortification of "the pass in the Lake 150 miles from Albany."[1] Two years later Governor Leisler sent sixty men "to the pass in the Lake Champlain to maintain this as an outpost."[2]

"A large and important province was planned by the French political geographers whose eastern boundary should be the Connecticut and whose western boundary should be Lake Ontario. North was the St. Lawrence River, and the southern confine was rather misty, except that it should be all that could be kept from the English. The metropolis was to be a place situated at that peculiar bend of Lake Champlain where there was a projecting tongue of land, making a fine site for settlement, fortification and development. In other words, it was to be Crown Point. . . ."[3]

As early as the summer of 1700, the French established a trading post at the Pointe à la Chevelure for the important commerce between the French and the English—the latter bringing articles of English manufacture, the former furs.[4] Doubtless they built a simple fortification on the point, a blockhouse or fortified storehouse; it is evidently to this construction for the protection of trade to which

108. See "Pancalon," p. 241.
1. Stevens: *French Occupation of the Champlain Valley*, pp. 44-45.
2. Hemenway: *Vermont Gazetteer*, I, p. 2.
3. Hammond: *Quaint and Historic Old Forts of North America*, p. 67.
4. Watson: *Essex County, N. Y.*, p. 117.

reference is made by General George Clark in writing to Governor Clinton, September 16, 1738: "The French have built a strong fort at Crown Point about fifteen years ago."[5] Rev. Hosea Beckley writes: "A fort at Crown Point had been previously (to 1724) built by the French from Montreal."[6] In spite of numerous plans for fortification suggested before 1725, it was only in 1730 that English policy forced the French authorities into action to protect their interests by the establishment of a military post. M. de Beauharnois wrote to the Minister at Versailles, October 15, 1730, that he had been informed that the English were coming from Albany to trade with the Indians at Lake Champlain. He had sent to the lake M. de la Corne and thirty soldiers to drive the English from the region.[7] M. de Beauharnois feared that the English might seize the Pointe à la Chevelure as they did Oswego, if attention was not given to this possibility; in that case, it would take an army to drive them out. To prevent English aggression M. de Beauharnois proposed the construction of a military post at the point; once finished, lands might be granted to settlers willing to go there and reinforce the garrison. The King gave his approval for the building of a "stockade fort" until a stronger fortification could be erected; M. de Beauharnois should station there a garrison sufficient in his opinion to maintain the post, and should grant lands to the farmers requesting them.[8]

The governor sent the Sieur Hertel de la Fresnière and another officer (perhaps M. de la Corne, who was there in 1730) with a detachment of twenty soldiers and workmen to build the authorized stockade fort. M. de la Fresnière reported that he left Montreal August 16, 1731, returning the second of November.[9] Construction was completed September 22, 1731.[10] In reporting to the King the establishment of the post, MM. de Beauharnois and Hocquart mentioned the stockade and the necessary buildings to house the garrison, sending His Majesty the plans.[11] In October, the governor chose M.

5. New York State Historical Society, *Proceedings*, X, pp. 108-113.

6. Beckley: *History of Vermont*, p. 66.

7. *Doc. Col. Hist. N. Y.*, I, p. 444.

8. Mémoire du Roy aux Srs. de Beauharnois et Hocquart, le 22 avril et le 8 mai 1731.

9. *Archives du Dominion:* Correspondances Officielles—Série F, Vol. 54, p. 207.

10. *Ibid.*, p. 245: M. de Beauharnois au ministre, le 10 octobre 1731.

11. *Ibid.*, pp. 211-212: MM. de Beauharnois et Hocquart au ministre, le 14 novembre 1731.

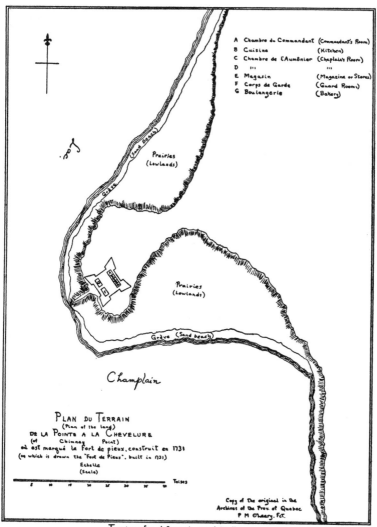

A Chambre du Commandant (Commandant's Room)
B Cuisine (Kitchen)
C Chambre de l'Aumônier (Chaplain's Room)
D " "
E Magasin (Magazine or Stores)
F Corps de Garde (Guard Rooms)
G Boulangerie (Bakery)

Prairies
(Lowlands)

Prairies
(Lowlands)

Grève (Sand beach)

Champlain

PLAN DU TERRAIN
(Plan of the land)
DE LA POINTE A LA CHEVELURE
(of Chimney Point)
où est marqué le Fort de pieux, construit en 1731
(on which is drawn the "Fort de Pieux", built in 1731)
Echelle
(Scale)

Toises

Copy of the original in the
Archives of the Prov. of Quebec
P M O'Leary. Fct.

Tracing of a photograph owned by the
Hon. M. F. Barnes

G. Coolidge
1938

Hertel de Moncours (younger brother of M. de la Fresnière) to command the garrison of twenty men during the winter with the aid of the Sieur Hertel de Rouville, his nephew; ten men would strengthen the garrison in the spring. M. de Beauharnois made strong representations to the Minister concerning the permanent garrison of the new post; it should be of thirty soldiers at least since this fort was the nearest to the English.[12] His Majesty, Louis XV, signified his approval of these efforts by a memorandum dated April 22, 1732.[13]

The English immediately protested, especially through diplomatic channels. Mr. Rip Van Dam wrote to the Lords of Trade, November 2, 1731: "The French have already encroached and built a fort at a place called Crown Point."[14] The government of New York let it rest there, being busily engaged in a controversy with the colony of New Jersey at the moment. However, the English ambassador to the Court of Versailles wrote in this fashion: "The Earl of Waldegrave, Ambassador Extraordinary and Plenipotentiary of his Britannic Majesty, has the honor to represent that the Board of Trade established in London having laid diverse complaints before the King, his Master, that the French in America continued to encroach on the Territory of their neighbors, has just complained again that the said French have recently commenced seizing on certain territory within the Province of New York, and that they have caused a fort to be built there at a place called 'Pointe de la Couronne,' in English 'Crown Point,' situated within the Country of the Iroquois, which Fort is only three days' journey from the town and city of Albany . . ., there is no doubt but his Most Christian Majesty will issue the necessary orders that said Fort be razed, and that the subjects of the French Colonies do not henceforward undertake anything contrary to Treaties. At Compiègne, this 13th. June, 1732."[15] Of course, "his Most Christian Majesty," Louis XV, did not give "the necessary orders" that the new fort be destroyed, especially since the question of the frontier had always been unsettled, no exact limit being recognized by either power.

Louis XV answered these representations of the Earl of Walde-

12. M. de Beauharnois au comte de Maurepas, le 1er octobre 1731: Lettre commune de MM. de Beauharnois et Hocquart au ministre, le 12 octobre 1731.

13. Mémoire du Roy aux Srs. Marquis de Beauharnois . . . et Hocquart . . ., le 22 avril 1732.

14. New York State Historical Society, *Proceedings*, X, pp. 108-113.

15. *Doc. Col. Hist. N. Y.*, IX, p. 1034.

grave by a letter approving the efforts of M. de Beauharnois, February 18, 1733.[16] The King notes that the fort is in good condition. Although he has not yet learned that the English consider building a fort on the opposite point, as had been rumored, he orders that the commander at the fort keep close watch on the enemy—if necessary he will strengthen the garrison. MM. de Beauharnois and Hocquart recalled to His Majesty's attention, November 14, 1731 (when the fort has scarcely been completed) his suggestion that it was to be only a temporary establishment, and proposed to him the construction of a redoubt "à mâchicoulis"[17] of which the design was enclosed. This redoubt was contemplated "as much for the safety of the post as to avoid the considerable expense necessary to construct a regularly designed fort."[18] M. Chaussegros de Léry, the King's Engineer in New France, approved the plan, and the King's approval was granted in 1734. That fall, M. de Beauharnois sent workmen to the fort to prepare the materials for the construction of the redoubt, which would be started in the spring. All precautions were taken to prevent any accident, during the spring thaws, which might delay the completion of the project.[19] "I have also ordered the Sieur de la Gauchetière, who is in command at Pointe à la Chevelure, to be on his guard with the 30 men of his garrison. We cannot put more men there, because of the small size of the fort; until the redoubt is completed, larger forces cannot be maintained there during the winter."[20] If the English attack in that season, a few French and Indians will reinforce the garrison; the Indians will keep the governor informed. When the redoubt is finished, the governor suggests a permanent garrison of 120 men.[21] The Comte de Maurepas, Secretary of State for the Marine, replied, May 10, 1735, approving the activity of M. de Beauharnois at Pointe à la Chevelure, and hoping that the redoubt would be finished by the next year.[22] This redoubt became the citadel, the central stronghold of the post of St. Frederic.

16. *Ibid.*, p. 1037.

17. This was a redoubt furnished with an overhanging rampart or battlement, of which the floor was pierced with holes for dropping heated liquids or stones on the heads of attackers. At the same time the rampart served as a sentry-walk for the citadel, which was supplied with fairly strong armament.

18. MM. de Beauharnois et Hocquart au ministre, le 14 novembre 1731.

19. M. de Beauharnois au roi, le 10 octobre 1734.

20. *Ibid.*

21. M. de Beauharnois au comte de Maurepas, le 10 octobre 1734.

22. Le ministre à M. de Beauharnois, Versailles, le 10 mai 1735.

The Recollect priest, Father Emmanuel Crespel, was sent from Canada to serve as chaplain at Pointe à la Chevelure; he has left an interesting description of the post as it appeared at his arrival, November 17, 1735. "The fort's situation is advantageous, for it is built on an elevated point about 15 leagues northerly from the extremity of the Lake. It is the key to the colony on that side: that is to say, on the side of the English, who are only 20 or 30 leagues off. . . . The building where they put us was not yet finished and we were only partially sheltered from the rain, and the walls, which were 12 feet thick, having been finished only a few days, added still more to our troubles which the snow and rain gave us. . . . We finished our building as soon as the season would permit. . . ."[23] Father Crespel was recalled to France, leaving the Pointe à la Chevelure, September 21, 1736.

The redoubt was completed during the summer of 1736, according to Father Crespel's report. The governor and intendant report in their reply to the King's memorandum of 1737 that "the fort and the redoubt at the Pointe à la Chevelure have reached perfection. We enclose the plan, profiles, elevations, and an account of the expense incurred for the construction of these works." In explanation of the large expense reported, we learn that "the first plan of a simple redoubt with a covered way could not be carried out, the terrain not permitting," and that the builders "have been obliged to enclose the redoubt in a fort."[24]

Up to this time travel by the lake had been by bateaux (large, flat-bottomed boats propelled by oars) and canoes. Now Fort Beauharnois—a name had finally been selected for the post at the Pointe à la Chevelure—became of increasing importance, and since communication with Canada should be as rapid as possible, the inauguration of regular service by sailing vessels between St. John and St. Frederic was contemplated. M. de Beauharnois had a study made of the possibilities of navigation on the lake, and wrote on October 12, 1736: "If Lake Champlain be navigable for sloops, it will be very useful to have one built for the conveyance of the supplies for the Pointe à la Chevelure. We do not yet possess knowledge respecting its rocks and sand bars, which may render the building of such vessels hazardous. Up to the present, only one has been discovered; it lies north

23. *Champlain Tercentenary Commission Report*, pp. 394-395.
24. *Archives du Dominion:* Correspondances Officielles, Série F, Vol. 67, p. 101.

of Isle la Motte, and is three quarters of a league wide, opposite the Pointe au Fer [Champlain, Clinton County, N. Y., eighteen miles north of Plattsburg]. In other respects sloops will, apparently, be able to sail through this Lake."[25]

Soon after the completion of the redoubt, troubles began to arise. M. de St. Ours asked to be relieved of his post as commandant, because life at the fort was too difficult and the reward was insufficient. M. de Beauharnois persuaded him to remain,[26] but urged that His Majesty grant an annual reward or bonus to the commandant at this post, "and that would persuade officers to ask to be sent there." Evidently the governor felt the need of an "Intelligence Service" for the safety of the post, as he recommended that "a certain number of cadets" of good family be sent there to warn of incipient sedition.[27] By the same courier, the governor and intendant strongly represented to the minister the advisability of encouraging settlements near the fort, the chief advantage being that the settlers would supplement the King's rations by furnishing the garrison with much-needed wheat, beef and pork. In this despatch the authorities requested permission to name the fort (hitherto called Fort Beauharnois) after Frederic, Comte de Maurepas, Secretary of State for the Marine and active administrator of colonial affairs.[28] Since most of the forts in Canada were named after saints, the word was also used here—Fort St. Frederic.

The importance of Fort St. Frederic increased rapidly. The garrison was generally composed of 120 men; on both sides of the lake land grants grew in number; the two villages of the Pointe à la Chevelure opposite the fort spread toward the north and south; the vicinity of the fort became dotted with cultivated plots of land, kitchen-gardens and small homes; there was a priest in residence to minister to the spiritual needs of the growing settlements. M. Chaussegros de Léry, military engineer, spoke of the armament of the newly finished post in his letter of Oct. 20, 1738. "Monseigneur, the fort of St. Frederic and the redoubt were finished last year, and as the artillery which had been requested in France for this post has not been sent, and as war with the English was expected, I requested a few small pieces from the General: he granted me 6 four-pounders

25. MM. de Beauharnois et Hocquart au ministre, le 12 octobre 1736.
26. M. de Beauharnois au ministre, Québec, le 5 octobre 1737.
27. M. de Beauharnois au ministre, Québec, le 16 octobre 1737.
28. MM. de Beauharnois et Hocquart au ministre, Québec, le 11 octobre 1737.

with balls and 6 swivels, which I had brought with me. At my arrival, I had a few carriages made which were lacking, and placed everything in the Redoubt; only the fort is not armed. Those who command in this post must devote themselves to keeping good watch, surprise only is to be feared."[29] The swivel found near the gate of the fort (now preserved in the Crown Point Museum) was probably one of those mentioned by M. de Léry. In October, 1739, M. Hocquart reported the expenditure for the maintenance of Fort St. Frederic of 20,414 livres (a French livre was the equivalent of approximately 20 cents), 18 sous, 1 denier; an additional sum of 19,344 livres, 18 sous, 1 denier, to be itemized later.[30] During the same year the windmill was built near the fort on the site now occupied by the Champlain Memorial. MM. de Beauharnois and Hocquart recommended, November 5, 1740, that the additions suggested by M. de Léry "to perfect Fort St. Frederic, the construction of a barque on Lake Champlain, of a hangar (store-shed) above the Rapids of St. John, and of a road from Chambly to the hangar" be put into effect by the King.[31]

The Chevalier de Beauharnois, nephew of the governor, made a visit to Fort St. Frederic in September, 1740. His letter to his uncle, detailing his experiences, merits quotation in entirety:

My very dear uncle; I arrive just now from Fort St. Frederic after 24 days since leaving Montreal and having experienced much contrary wind and much rain. Nothing deserving your attention took place between my departure and my arrival at the fort. Upon reaching the fort, according to the orders of M. de Beaucour, I inspected the soldiers' armament, which I found in very bad condition, there being but four guns in shape to be used. The second fine day I spent part at table and part in inspecting the redoubt and the environs and the settlement of the Intendant, which is very fine and well-advanced.

If you will permit me, my dear uncle, that in giving a faithful account of my journey I have the honor of telling you what I think of Fort St. Frederic, I shall have the honor of saying that I find it much to my taste, but, however, that I should find something to criticize:

29. *Archives du Dominion:* Correspondances Officielles, Série F, Vol. 70, p. 114.

30. *Ibid.*, Vol. 72, p. 32.

31. MM. de Beauharnois et Hocquart au ministre, Québec, le 5 novembre 1740.

I mean an inner court in which one's foot sinks 6 inches when it rains, and which would be worth the trouble to have paved; in the second place, a well which gives no water and which might be deepened with advantage; fortifications without ditches and without ramparts—simply curtained on the inner side with clay, upon which one cannot walk when it has rained; no barracks, guard-rooms on the third floor, no cells, no prison, the environs of the fort not sufficiently cleared; that, my dear uncle, is about all that I should criticize. The third day of my stay, M. Duplessis, the Officers of the post and I, two cannoneers, the blacksmith and the carpenter inspected together the cannon, swivels, gun-carriages and swivel-mounts, which, after having plumbed, inspected, and put into condition for use, I found mounted the former on carriages too low and without iron-work, the latter on mounts too high and without base; having also made inspection of the ramparts with these gentlemen, I found the embrasures without platform for the recoil of the cannon. I did not wish, my dear uncle, to have anything done without your orders; however, there is great need for some work to be done; I simply carried out the orders of M. de Beaucour, which were to have the cannon and swivels mounted if necessary.

I left Fort St. Frederic the 23rd of September, after having been received by M. Duplessis with all imaginable politeness; allow me to urge you, my dear uncle, to be so kind as to mention it to him when you do him the honor of writing him. I reached Fort Chambly the 23rd of the said month, where I was received,—to put it in two words,—as the nephew of the general. The next day, I inspected the artillery, which I found in rather good condition, with the exception of the gun-carriages and swivel-mounts: I have the honor of sending you herewith two reports, one on the artillery of Fort St. Frederic and the other of Fort Chambly. If you judge it proper, my dear uncle, to have some work done in these two posts and if you believe me capable of carrying on this work, I beg of you to be good enough to entrust it to me: I shall be delighted if I can thereby prove to you how close the service lies to my heart and how desirous I am of finding ways to please you.

I am, my very dear uncle, with the most profound respect,
Your very humble and very obedient servant,

Montreal, le 30 7bre 1740   *Le Cher de Beauharnois.*[32]

32. *Archives du Dominion:* Correspondances Officielles, Série F, Vol. 79, p. 224.

The improvements recommended by M. de Léry and some of those suggested by the Chevalier de Beauharnois were proposed to the minister by M. de Beauharnois, October 5, 1740—"a covered way, interior walls in the fort, and two buildings beside the entrance gate: a covered way is necessary as well as the increase in buildings in order to be able to lodge the 50 men in garrison with their 4 officers independently of the 100 others the fort can accommodate. In reference to the interior wall, it appears necessary to support the terre-plein of the fort's enclosure, upon which is the sentry-walk which the officers assure us is impracticable in winter: we join herewith the plan and estimate of these works. . . ."[33]

In 1741, the difficulty of finding satisfactory commandants again arose. M. Hocquart, in a letter of October 20, 1741, says that "up to the present, most of the officers have considered these commands as a burden, or at least unprofitable, however honorable they may be." The intendant believes that the minister could, by explaining his attitude concerning the importance of the service in the outposts, stir up a little eagerness among the officers for such service; the example of the minister's devotion to the colonial service might arouse a spirit of emulation. The difficulty at that moment seems to have been that military commands were sought for the sole reason that they might be lucrative; "on the other hand," says M. Hocquart, "the poverty of the country prevents one from thinking more nobly of them." M. Hocquart's own devotion to the service of his King should have spurred on the others; he seems to have been the only intendant who did not attempt to enrich himself at the expense of the colony. His intelligent insight into the nature of the colonial officers, however petty their motives, is clearly shown as he continues: "Since it has been built, scarcely have the officers detached to command there remained one year, often they have not waited until the year had expired to ask to be relieved; it is not possible that in such a short space of time an officer may seriously concern himself with what may interest the service; he can deserve neither praise nor censure. . . . I should think it fitting, that those who are placed in charge should remain at least three years; they would not hesitate to remain even longer if they thought that this service would secure for them the King's favor."[34]

Just as the construction of Fort Carillon (Ticonderoga) in 1755

33. M. de Beauharnois au ministre, Québec, le 5 octobre 1740.
34. M. Hocquart au ministre, Québec, le 20 octobre 1741.

reduced Fort St. Frederic to a position of secondary importance, so in 1741 the latter was "the advanced post by means of which Fort Chambly becomes almost useless." M. Hocquart advocated the abandonment of Fort Chambly as a military post, and suggested sending there a reserve officer and five or six men to act as guardians of the King's property placed there in storage.[35] It would mean a considerable saving for the King, since the military function of Chambly had ceased; its only service was that of storehouse for Fort St. Frederic.

By 1742, the construction of the additions had been completed, and Fort St. Frederic, enlarged and strengthened, had become a stronghold of strategic value second only to Quebec. A quarry of limestone had been discovered nearby; little by little the high, thick walls had risen, the redoubt had become the citadel—so solid that it was used for the storage of bombs and other war munitions; on the upper floors were the apartments of the commandant. Within the enclosure of the fort a church and stone barracks for officers and men had been constructed.[36] Now M. de Beauharnois found no difficulty in the choice of commandants for this post other than that of selecting the best out of several capable volunteers for the service.[37]

A report was sent to France, July 30, 1742, on the armament of the military posts in New France; "At Fort St. Frederic,

12 iron	4 pounders with	15 marine carriages and 690 balls
1 iron	2 pounder	1 carriage
2 small	grenade mortars	2 carriages and 200 grenades
13 swivels	mounted on parapets	31 case-shot and 160 iron balls."

Fort Chambly still served as a depot for war munitions.[38] Shortly after, the cannon of that post were added to the armament of Fort St. Frederic.

The clouds of war were already gathering. M. de Beauharnois informed M. de Maurepas of the weakness of Quebec's defenses in case of a naval attack; at the same time he discussed the situation of Fort St. Frederic. "I have, moreover, reinforced the garrison of Fort St. Frederic, which is composed of 72 soldiers and cadets, and 9 officers. . . ."[39] Reports from scouts sent toward the English

35. M. Hocquart au ministre, Québec, le 20 octobre 1741.
36. Kalm: *Travels into North America*, II, p. 208.
37. M. de Beauharnois au ministre, Québec, le 24 septembre 1743.
38. *Doc. Col. Hist. N. Y.*, IX, p. 1095.
39. *Doc. Col. Hist. N. Y.*, IX, pp. 1103-1104.

settlements were not encouraging. Tecanancoassin, chief of the Christian Iroquois of Sault St. Louis, informed M. de Beaucour that the English built at "Sarastau" (Saratoga) a garrisoned fort similar to the blockhouses and stockade of La Prairie de la Madeleine.[40] Reports came to St. Frederic that the English intended to settle on Wood Creek the next spring (1745), building a sawmill and gristmill at the Petit Sault.[41]

By 1748, the armament of Fort St. Frederic had been considerably increased—62 guns are listed:

2 iron cannon	6 pounders	1 iron cannon	2 pounder
17 iron cannon	4 pounders	1 mortar	
23 brass cannon	2 pounders	18 iron swivels & 25 iron shells[42]	

After King George's War, 1744-1748, the Swedish academician, Peter Kalm, a distinguished naturalist, came to travel in North America. He arrived at Philadelphia, September 26, 1748, and did not leave America until February 13, 1751, traveling in Pennsylvania, New Jersey, New York, and eastern Canada. The letter of introduction sent by Cadwallader Colden to Colonel William Johnson will also serve to present Peter Kalm to us in his proper quality.

Fort George, New York, May 27, 1749
Colonel Johnson—
The bearer of this, Mr. Kalm, is a Swedish gentleman, a professor in the Academy of Science there, and is now traveling in order to make discoveries in botany and astronomy. For this purpose he is on his way to Canada with a design to return in the fall. The purpose for which he travels, the advancement of useful knowledge, will be a strong motive to you to give him any assistance he wants, and he wants no other but that of advice in what manner to travel to Canada most conveniently and with the least danger, whether by Oswego or Crown Point. He comes strongly recommended to me by the King of Sweden's physician and other friends in Europe and therefore what civility you show him will lay an obligation on me.
Your most humble servant—
Cadwallader Colden.[43]

Fortunately for us, Professor Kalm decided to reach Canada by way

40. M. de Beauharnois au comte de Maurepas, le 29 octobre 1744.
41. Statement signed by Beaubassin, Fort St. Frederic, Mar. 2, 1744.
42. H. P. Smith: *History of Essex County, N. Y.,* p. 64.
43. Hill: *Old Fort Edward,* p. 57 (Citation from the Johnson Papers).

of Lake Champlain. He describes Fort St. Frederic as he saw it in 1749—and we must remember that he was a trained observer, which gives us an accurate picture of the post. "July 19. Fort St. Frederic is a fortification on the southern extremity of Lake Champlain, situated on a neck of land, between that Lake and the river which arises from the union of the river Woodcreek, and Lake St. Sacrement.[44] The breadth of this river is here about a good musket-shot. . . . The fort is built on a rock, consisting of black lime-slates . . .; it is nearly quadrangular, has high and thick walls, made of the same limestone, of which there is a quarry about half a mile from the fort. On the eastern part of the fort is a high tower, which is proof against bomb-shells, provided with very thick and substantial walls, and well stored with cannon from the bottom almost to the very top: the governor lives in the tower. In the terre-plein of the fort is a well built little church, and houses of stone for the officers and soldiers. There are sharp rocks on all sides towards the land, beyond a cannon shot from the fort, but among them are some which are as high as the walls of the fort, and very near to them. . . . Within one or two musket shots to the east of the fort, is a windmill built of stone, with very thick walls, and most of the flour that is wanted to supply the fort is ground here. This Wind-mill is so contrived as to serve the purpose of a redoubt, and at the top of it are five or six small pieces of cannon."[45] Then he goes on to speak of the choice of location for the fort, saying that it should have been built on the mill-site in order to cover the approach from the English settlements.

In 1755, war again threatened New France. Governor de Vaudreuil proceeded to carry out his cherished plan of building a fort at Carillon at the fork in the route south to the English settlements— the eastern path reached the Hudson by the Grand Marais, Wood Creek and the Great Carrying Place; the western, by the Little Carrying Place and Lake St. Sacrement. At this time, Fort St. Frederic enjoyed among the English a reputation for strength far greater than the condition of the fortifications merited. Colonel Ephraim Williams, in writing from Fort Edward to his relative, Colonel Israel Williams, August 23, 1755, stated that "not less than ten or twelve thousand men are needed to reduce Crown Point."[46]

44. Kalm calls "river" that part of the lake above Fort St. Frederic.
45. Kalm: *Travels into North America*, II, pp. 207-209.
46. Hill: *Old Fort Edward*, p. 77.

Both Abercrombie and Amherst evidently put faith in this judgment in making preparations for their attacks of 1758 and 1759. A report to Governor de Vaudreuil stated that Fort St. Frederic was ready to fall in ruin, because the walls were crumbling, being too weak to support gun platforms.[47] On May 1, 1758, the Sieur Hugues, officer with Montcalm, wrote to the Marshal de Belle-Isle that Fort St. Frederic could not hold out after the capture of Fort Carillon, that four cannon shot would make it fall in ruins.[48] At Amherst's approach, the French garrison left the fort, July 31, 1759, blowing up the magazine. In 1813, the fort was only a mass of débris.[49] In our day, ably conducted excavations have revealed the ancient ramparts still quite well preserved; one may discover within the enclosure the foundations of the citadel and the other buildings, but the revetment with its thick walls twelve feet high has served as a "quarry" for the construction of houses in the neighborhood—even on Chimney Point across the lake.

CHAPTER XII.   *The Chronicle of St. Frederic*

POINTE de la Couronne" and "Pointe à la Chevelure" (thus named about 1689 because of the abundant foliage of the trees and shrubs which covered it) have no separate history and will be considered together in this study. Already in discussing the seigniory of Hocquart we have spoken of the settlements on Chimney Point; in what follows the reader should remember that the parish of St. Frederic included both shores of the lake; it is impossible to-day to determine whether an inhabitant lived on one shore or the other; all the inhabitants formed the community of which the fort and its church were the center.[1] Additional information may come to light in official documents which have not yet been made available to the student of history.

47. Reid: *Lake George and Lake Champlain*, pp. 224-227.

48. M. Hugues au maréchal le Belle-Isle, le 1er mai 1758. Cited by Crockett: *History of Lake Champlain*, p. 87.

49. Spofford: *Gazetteer of 1824*: paragraph on "Crown Point."

1. This chapter is based on the *Register of the Chaplains at Fort St. Frederic*, in the archives of the Secretary of State at Ottawa. Father J. U. Baudry has given excerpts from the register in *Mémoires et Comptes-Rendus de la Société Royale du Canada*, 1887, Vol. V, Section I, p. 93.

At St. Frederic, as elsewhere, the soldier did not long await the arrival of a missionary. The first commandant, M. Hertel de Moncours, appointed in October, 1731, was replaced in November, 1732, by Sieur René Boucher de la Perrière, whose name appears so often in these pages. With him came Father Jean-Baptiste La Jus, Recollect priest. In the exercise of his functions, Father La Jus kept his parish register on loose sheets, of which one example has been preserved; it is worth quoting in entirety both in the original French and its English translation.

L'an de grace mil sept cens trente deux, le 23 novembre a ete par moy aumonier du fort de la Pointe a la Chevelure Baptise Antoine, fils du Sr. Charles Monarque Sergent dans Les troupes et Chirurgien Major dans Le dit Poste de La pointe a La Chevelure et de Marie Daze. Le Parain a ete Monsieur de Laperriere, capitaine des Troupes du Detachement de La Marine et Commandant pour Le Roy au Fort de La pointe a La Chevelure. La marain a ete Marie-Anne Cuillerier, Religieuse hospitaliere a Montreal. Le Parain a signe avec moy Le jour et L'an que dessus.

Laperriere   *Monarque*
F. Jean-Bapt. La Jus, Recoll.
Aumonier du Fort de La pointe a La Chevelure.

The year of Grace one thousand seven hundred thirty-two, the 23 November has been by me chaplain of the fort of the Pointe à la Chevelure Baptised Antoine son of the Sr. Charles Monarque Sergeant in The troops and Surgeon Major in the said Post of The pointe à la Chevelure and of Marie Dazé. The Godfather has been Monsieur de Laperrière, captain of the Troops of the Detachment of the Marine, Commandant for the King at the Fort of The pointe à La Chevelure. The godmother has been Marie-Anne Cuillerier nursing sister at Montreal. The godfather has signed with me The day and The year as above.

Evidently the godmother was not present; she did not sign "with me."

It is certain that with the French troops at the fort there was a band of Indians; in 1733, Father La Jus made three entries in his register, all being death records of Indians. During that year he was replaced by Father Pierre-Baptiste Resche, whose first entry is undated, the baptism of Charles Jérôme, Abenaki Indian; before the end of 1733 the good Father had three other baptisms, without god-mothers; at the last, December 27, the godfather was the comman-dant Sieur Hertel de Beaulac. The same chaplain served in 1734 and recorded three baptisms, two Abenakis, the other a son of Surgeon-Major Charles Monarque. The company of M. de Contrecoeur, at least in part, was in garrison at the fort. The reports to the Crown state that the establishment of this post has had the effect of stopping smuggling on Lake Champlain. Before the month of March, 1735, Father Resche had been replaced by Father Bernardin de Gannes, whose first entry is dated March 16; his second and last is the baptism of Abenaki twin girls, July 24. November 25, we find at the fort Father Emmanuel Crespel, who officiates at the burial of "Frappe-d'abord" (nickname meaning "strike-first"), sol-dier of La Perrière's company, "removed by sudden death"; this is the first burial of a Frenchman at Fort St. Frederic.

Father Emmanuel reached the fort November 17, 1735; he has left a memorandum of his trip to and sojourn at St. Frederic: "The day of my departure from Chambly, a post about 40 leagues from Fort Beauharnois, we were obliged to sleep out, and during the night, about a foot of snow fell. The winter continued as it set in and al-though lodged we did not suffer less than if we were in the open field. The building where they put us was not yet finished[2] and we were only partially sheltered from the rain, . . . many of our sol-diers were seized with scurvy, and our eyes became so sore that we were afraid of losing our sight without resource. We were not bet-ter fed than lodged. Scarcely can you find a few partridges near the fort and to eat venison you must go to Lake St. Sacrement to find it, and that is 7 or 8 leagues off. We finished our building as soon as the season would permit, but we preferred to camp out in summer than remain any longer. Yet we were not more at ease, for the fever surprised us all and not one of us could enjoy the pleasures of the country."[3]

During his stay at Fort Beauharnois, Father Emmanuel recorded five baptisms, the last September 8, 1736. Four were little Indians, the other a child of the same Charles Monarque, without doubt per-manently at the fort. The godfather of this child was Gaspard Chaussegros de Léry, chief engineer in New France. M. de Contre-

2. This evidently means the citadel, finished the following year.
3. Champlain Tercentenary Commission: *Report*, pp. 394-395.

coeur, commandant for the past two years, was replaced by the Sieur
Pierre de St. Ours. Father Emmanuel was recalled to France and
left the fort, September 21, 1736. Soon his successor arrived, Father
Pierre Verquaillié, who made his first entry in the register December
4, the burial of Pierre "Prêt-à-Boire" ("Ready-to-drink"), soldier
in the company of M. de Serigny.

In 1737, the register shows seven baptisms and three burials. The
second baptism was that of Pierre-Charles, son of Commandant de
St. Ours, christened March 15; this child was buried April 26, of the
same year. "The Sieur Chevalier de St. Ours, commandant at the
Pointe à la Chevelure wished to be relieved, I persuaded him to remain, and I shall give special attention to the choice of officers to be
sent there."[4]

In August the Reverend Father, tired of the system of detached
sheets for his records, procured a weighty volume and on the first
page we read:

Register

*Of baptisms, marriages and burials Made in The Fort Beauharnois,
at The Pointe à La Chevelure diocese of Quebec Begun the twenty-
third of November of The year one thousand seven hundred thirty-
two, Containing one hundred and ninety nine sheets of paper all
marked.*

"*B*	*Baptêmes*
M signifit	*Mariages*
E	*Enterrements*"

*I undersigned Recollect priest chaplain for the King of this Fort
Beauharnois, at The pointe à La Chevelure certify all these records
true for I have found them so on detached sheets. In testimony
whereof I have signed. This 4th. of August 1737*

F. Pierre Verquaillié, R. Ind.

The last record of this year is the burial November 17, of Antoine
Lubet Duplessis, storekeeper, died suddenly at the age of thirty-six.

Early in 1737, M. Hocquart proposed plans for the settlement of
the lands near Fort St. Frederic and on the eastern shore opposite the
fort. "These lands are well-suited for cultivation, as much by their
quality as by their situation in the most southern part of the colony.

4. M. de Beauharnois au ministre, Québec, le 5 octobre 1737.

. . . Among the sorts of produce to be raised, tobacco will be the one to receive the most favor because of the mildness of the climate."[5]

In urging upon the minister the advantages of establishing these settlements, M. Hocquart presents a plan carefully and logically developed. The lands to be settled extended on the east shore 3 leagues north and 3 leagues south of Chimney Point; on the west shore, from the fort south to the River "à la Barbue" (now "Put's Creek," a name given because the river-mouth was the site of an engagement in which Gen. Israel Putnam was vitally concerned). Each grant would be of 3 arpents front by 40 depth, at a charge of 1 sol for each arpent frontage, 20 sols for each arpent of area, and a half minot (a minot equalled 1.11 bushels) of wheat for each 40 arpents of area, "which will bring in to the King 10 livres for each settler." Two hundred settlers may be established on these lands and still reserve for the King's domain the "whole peninsula of the new fort . . ., where M. de Léry has had cleared an area of 50 arpents . . ., 15 are at present plowed, the rest sown to grass. We have been obliged to build within range of the guns of the fort a barn, a stable and a cow-stable . . ., so that it will cost but little to put under cultivation 120 arpents of the King's domain." The new settlers will be encouraged to take up lands by various methods—subsidies consisting of farm tools and rations up to a value of 150 livres during the first year, remission of taxes for two or three years, reduced prices for munitions and provisions from the King's stores at the fort, etc. A windmill will be built on a site chosen by M. de Léry—"a jutting point protected by the cannon of the fort, the most suitable spot and the most exposed to the wind." The maintenance of the mill will be an expense at first, but as soon as the terrain in question is well settled, the income from milling-fees will maintain a miller, "who besides will pay the King for a farm." The cost of the mill is estimated at 2484 livres, 16 sols and 8 deniers. A priest is in residence at the fort and will extend to the settlers the spiritual aid "which they need"—an extremely efficient move to encourage settlement.

M. Hocquart then suggests a "make-work program" for the settlements. "A soldier of the fort's garrison will . . . grind the first settlers' grain for 50 livres a year wages." The garrison of the fort will be employed in clearing land and in assisting the new settlers to make their grants productive. In return, the settlers will be "a

5. MM. de Beauharnois et Hocquart au ministre, Québec, le 11 8bre 1737.

prompt aid to the fort in case of attack," and will furnish eventually the necessary wheat, beef and pork for the subsistence of the garrison. "It would also be advisable, My Lord, for the safety of this post, to send there a certain number of cadets to warn of information or sedition which might arise, but as they are all young men of family and not used to the work, and as the soldiers are obliged each to get out 15 or 20 cords of wood, by paying with goods from the stores for the getting out of the wood for each cadet (which costs 18 to 20 sols a cord), it would not cost the King much by the year; the soldiers who would do the work for them (the cadets) would find profit in it and the commandant would find peace."[6] An additional suggestion of a typically thrifty nature is offered—the annual taxes will be used for the maintenance of the fort; it is hoped that the post will become self-sustaining.

These settlements will cause others to be established "along the east and west shores of the lake and will one day join together in villages within the government of Montreal a great number of settlers who are today spread along the rivers." The provisions furnished to the garrison by the settlers will save the King the considerable sum now expended for the transportation of food by water from Montreal to Fort St. Frederic—"this single item amounts to more than 3000 livres a year."

M. Boisberthelot de Beaucours reported, October 13, 1738, that the commandant at Fort St. Frederic had "inspected the lands in the environs; he notes that they are very fine and very well suited to cultivation, and to constitute a fine domain and mills for wheat and rye, only the families of good farmers are needed to make them productive."[7] The mill on the west side near Fort St. Frederic was completed in 1740, the mill-wheel being sent from France.[8]

In the summer of 1738, M. Hocquart sent Médard-Gabriel Vallet de Chevigny, for twenty-eight years King's scrivener at Quebec, to work on the lands "for the sole purpose of establishing a domain for the King."[9] M. de Chevigny had forty arpents planted to wheat and other grains in 1739—"finer grain cannot be seen than what it

6. M. de Beauharnois au ministre, Québec, le 16 octobre 1737.

7. Correspondances Officielles, Vol. 70, p. 107.

8. MM. de Beauharnois et Hocquart au ministre, Québec, le 5 novembre 1740.

9. M. Vallet de Chevigny au ministre, Fort St. Frederic, le 12 septembre 1739.

produced." He reports that there is sufficient pasturage near the fort for 200 cattle. Upon the receipt of M. de Chevigny's report, M. Hocquart sent M. de Boiscler with four "former inhabitants" (probably former settlers on Chimney Point) to make an additional examination, which confirmed on all points that of M. de Chevigny.

In 1738, Father Verquaillié is still chaplain. He has three burials, of which one, April 5, is that of the storekeeper, François-Xavier Despointes. Then there are seven baptisms, among them still another son of the same Charles Monarque; it is certainly his tenth child.

The same missionary has five baptisms and one burial in 1739. Among the first let us note that of Marie-Josephte, daughter of Médard-Gabriel Vallet de Chevigny, King's scrivener and keeper of stores. He was a "good colonist" in this country where the King sent gifts to the fathers of large families. M. de Chevigny had already two daughters, Marguerite-Ursule and Marie-Angélique, and one son, Michel-Médard, and the baptisms of four other children appear in the register. The godfather of Marie-Josephte Vallet de Chevigny was Sieur Joseph Le Moyne, Seigneur de Longueuil, de Soulanges "and of other places," the new commandant, who was replaced that same year by François Lefebvre, Sieur Duplessis-Fabert, captain of a company of the Marine.

Inevitably, the interests of commandants who sought only personal profit from their positions of authority would clash with those of officials concerned primarily with the good of the King's service. M. de Chevigny, after many years of devoted service in Quebec, was sent to St. Frederic in 1738 as storekeeper at a salary of 600 livres a year; "faithful and persevering, he wishes to do good work. . . . I have found no one better fitted for the position."[10] During his second year at the fort, he believed it necessary to send to M. Hocquart a confidential report on the activities of the commandant.

Monsieur, I have the honor of speaking to you in private; it is not to me that M. Duplessis, Commandant in this post, addressed himself when he told me that no one was to, nor had the right to, have his company treated as the others, when he asked me to give him a detailed account of the prices of provisions and merchandise, of what the soldiers of his company have received for two years and a half, in order to draw up the information which he believes necessary for the

10. M. de Beauharnois au ministre, Québec, le 3 septembre 1740.

great memorandums he sends to the minister concerning the ideas and advantages he expects to gain from this post if he may remain in command for three years as he expects: 1. to have the post as M. Lansagnac had Chambly; 2. that there should be no Storekeeper; 3. to undertake the clearing and cultivation of 200 arpents of land, to have 50 cattle, 100 sheep, and 80 men in garrison, which would be for him a little government: and to gain his ends and to make his reasons appear sound, he represents to the minister the poor quality of the provisions sent to this post, the consumption which is caused by the poor quality.

To succeed in his purpose, he will find worse quality than is possible; since his arrival he has caused 300 pounds of pork to be thrown out of 150 pounds which was delivered. The flour he considers very bad, and I think, according to what I see, that before long he will have it condemned; there is 21,000 pounds of it; he has it noised about by some of the soldiers that the bread is not good.

He would have liked to have a great deal of work done, but I told him that as for me I had no orders and that I should take nothing upon myself (that I did not wish to take any responsibility); he wishes to have the rooms in the redoubt floored; he would like to control what is in the Storehouse.

You do not give him, Sir, what is due him, for according to the ordonnance if you consider him as naval lieutenant, you must give him 4 rations per day and 1½ rations for his valet, and as commandant he should be on a different footing.

According to the ordinance of the Marine, which he cites in entirety, the whole garrison, officers as well as sergeants and soldiers in the post, as soldiers detached for service on sea should have their rations gratis, have all they have in the way of refreshments, a cask of wine and their ration of beef, the King giving out no pork when his troops are on land: that is the subject of his memorandums to the Minister. All this being as he thinks, he asks to be commandant there, which is not a place to which any one wishes to come. He could not be so secretive that he should not act as Samson whom love caused to admit everything, and he at table after having eaten well let me know and see everything which he was writing, believing me at that time agreeable to acquiesce in everything he said (since I was), saying to him neither yes nor no. I believe, Sir, that I am obliged to call all this to your attention in the interest of the service, and also to point out to you for the good of the post that those whom you name

*Storekeepers should be so by formal commission, which would up-
hold them in their functions and they would not be treated in the way
that I have been treated, that one would make his servant storekeeper
whom one would consider, as I, being placed there by the Intendant.
I am, etc., Signed: Chevigny[11]*

The year 1740 leaves few records on the register. The same
commandant and the same chaplain are maintained on duty. There
are two baptisms of Indians and the burial of Dame Geneviève Le
Tendre, wife of Sieur Etienne Volant de Radisson.[12] Madame de
Radisson by her first husband, Jean-François-Xavier Le Pelletier,
was mother of Catherine-Geneviève Le Pelletier, wife of the commandant: in their marriage contract they are given by the Sieur de
Radisson and his wife three islands situated at the mouth of the
Richelieu River.[13]

Father Verquaillié remained at Fort Beauharnois until May, 1741;
before leaving, he recorded four baptisms and one burial, all Indians.
During his stay at the fort distinguished personages signed the register
as witnesses: Pierre de St. Ours, his son François, his wife Marie-
Claire Douville; Chevalier de Gannes de Falaise; Hertel de Beaubassin; Charles de Sabrevois; Joachim de Sacquespée, his wife Jeanne
de Lorimier; Le Fournier du Vivier; Louis de Beaujeu de Villemonde; Longueuil; Chevigny; Duplessis-Fabert, his son Joseph-
François, his daughter Geneviève; the Sieur de Montigny; François
de Bailleul. All these persons were for some time members of the
parish of St. Frederic.

The new missionary was Brother Daniel Normandin, who was not
lucky in his first entry; it was a baptism and Brother Daniel had
already made three attempts when he finally succeeded with the
following:

*The year one thousand seven hundred forty and one the nineteen
of the month of june has been Baptised by me priest Recollect The
son of Médard Gabriel Vallet de Chevigny keeper of the Stores of
the King at fort St. Frederic and of Marguerite Mailhou his Wife
born the twenty of ———— [January has been inserted] The*

11. Sr. de Chevigny, Garde magasin du Roy au fort St. Frederic, le 8 septembre 1740.

12. From the record in the register one might read "Batisson."

13. *Archives de Québec:* Inventaire des concessions, etc., IV, article "Volant
de Radisson."

present year at four o'clock in the morning his name is Gilles frederic
The godfather has Been Messire Gilles hocquart Chevalier Council-
lor of the King in his Council Intendant of Justice police and Finance
In new france Represented by françois Le febure Sieur duplessis
fabert Commandant of fort St. frederic And the godmother has Been
Geneviève françoise du plessis fabert Who have all signed with me
The days and year as above.

    Chevigny   *maillou Chevigny*
      Duplessis Faber   *Boulaserre*   *Repentigny*
frencoise genevieve Duplessys faber   *Chr faLaise*
                                f Daniel Normandin

With a success to the priest's credit, it seems that this time everyone wanted to sign the register, even those who were not required to
do so. It is unfortunate for the reader that no one saw fit to insert
a few commas. The principal point to note in this entry is the name
"fort Saint-Frederic" which appears for the first time; until now it
has been merely the fort at Pointe à la Chevelure or Fort Beauharnois.

Turning the page of the register we find the record of what must
have been a sensation in the little world of St. Frederic, the first
marriage! The ceremony uniting François Varlet, alias La Vertu,
and Marie-Josette Durbois took place in the presence of Commandant de Contrecoeur, MM. de Chaillon and de Villiers, officers of
the garrison and M. and Madame de Chevigny. (This time Father
Daniel put three commas in his record!) The bridegroom was
granted permission to marry by the vicar-general, the banns being
published once as the Bishop granted dispensation for the omission
of the two other publications under date of September 20. We note
that the commandant has been changed; M. de Contrecoeur has returned to the post he occupied until his death.

In 1741, M. Hocquart reports that M. de Contrecoeur, the new
commandant at the fort, has made an excellent record in encouraging
the new settlements as well as in military matters. The post is in
fine shape, although still a source of considerable expense to the King.

The two following entries in the register are also marriages; "de-
cidedly the colony is awakening," says Father Baudry. The marriages are of Antoine Brailly and Marguerite Bourdet; then on the
same day, November 14, that of François Moquier and Marie
Dumesnil. During the same year François Moquier was granted

land of five arpents front near the fort.[14]   A feature to be noted all through the register is that the officers of the post, doubtless obeying orders from Quebec and perhaps from Versailles, gave the greatest possible éclat to these wedding ceremonies, being present in a body.

This year Father Daniel has two baptisms, three marriages and one death.   In 1742, we have the same commandant and chaplain; the latter performs eleven baptisms, three marriages and two burials. One day he begins a baptismal record which breaks off with "Marguerite Louise, daughter of ————": whether he was called to attend the sick or whatever the interruption the record ends.   When his successor arrived, the blank space struck his attention, and with exemplary devotion, Father du Buron completed the entry from information given by the witnesses (later this certification was crossed out; it is very difficult to read because of the poor quality of the ink).

This year the fort was visited by M. Chaussegros de Léry, chief engineer in New France, who acted as godfather September 16, for Marguerite-Charlotte, slave of the Brochet nation, belonging to François Brébion, alias Sans-Cartier.

Father Daniel has eleven baptisms, one marriage and four deaths in 1743, his last entry being October 1.   One entry merits special mention: June 24, 1743, in the baptismal record of a son of M. de Chevigny we read "all signed with me Excepting my said Sieur de Contrecoeur whom God has Withdrawn from This World. . . ." Father Baudry observes: "Let us accept the excuse of this poor commandant who did not sign because God had withdrawn him from this world."   This is the only record of the death of M. de Contrecoeur.   Father Daniel failed to sign this record, but Father Alexis, always observant, and with his characteristic good will, undertook to remedy the omission by the following certificate inserted between the signature of the last witness and the next entry:

The R. P. Daniel having failed to sign the Baptism of the infant above named after information taken from the godfather and godmother I certify That the Baptism was conferred with the forms Required by the Holy Church in testimony of which I have signed in his place this 25th. of November 1743.

This certificate was later crossed out, but it gives the approximate date of Father du Buron's arrival.

The principal signatures during the time of Father Daniel Nor-

14. Stevens: *French Occupation of the Champlain Valley*, p. 52.

mandin are these: Duplessis-Fabert, his daughter Geneviève; Boulaserre; de Gannes de Falaise; de Repentigny; Chevigny; de Contrecoeur; Lacorne; de Villiers; La Perrière, the younger; Hertel de Beaubassin; Montizamber; Déchaillon; de Muy; Chaussegros de Léry, de Léry, the younger; Montessont Croizille; and let us not forget Marguerite-Ursule de Chevigny, ten times godmother between August 5, 1739 and March 3, 1744.

About this time Sieur Hertel de Beaubassin became proprietor of four arpents frontage on the lake south of the fort; this land was bordered by the grants of François Moquier and Charles Labadie.[15]

I have noted above that M. Chaussegros de Léry had acted as godfather of a slave. The fact that slavery existed at St. Frederic is shown by this record as well as by the following records:

August 9, 1739. Baptism of a Panis belonging to M. La Marq.
September 5, 1747. Baptism of a negro of M. Barsalou.
November 20, 1747. Burial of the same.
April 10, 1753. Burial of a half-breed slave of M. Douville.
November 6, 1753. Baptism of the child of a slave of M. de Blainville.

These records give us also the names of persons resident at St. Frederic.

After the death of M. de Contrecoeur, Sieur Michel Le Gardeur de Montesson et de Croisille was named commandant and served until the end of 1746. His wife, Françoise Boucher de Boucherville, was a relative of M. de Contrecoeur.

The first entry of Father du Buron is of December 24, 1743. The good Father had most imaginative spelling and he often leaves half pages blank. On sheet 19 are three entries begun, then crossed out; on sheet 22, a blank at the top of the page, immediately below it, an entry begun, crossed out and begun again. He sometimes writes "memeeme" for "même," "fillie," for "fille," "Grabrielle" for Gabriel, and so on.

During 1744, there were no deaths; the only entries by Father Alexis are ten baptisms. It was a deceptive calm, however, for March 15 had brought a declaration of war after twenty years of official peace. M. de Beauharnois wrote the Minister that English spies had been seen near Fort St. Frederic; he immediately strengthened the garrison.

15. Stevens: *French Occupation of the Champlain Valley*, p. 52.

On the register, the year 1745 begins with the baptism of a daughter of Michel Naouanarogin "Hiroquois du Sot St Loui" (Sault St. Louis). Father Alexis performed ten baptisms and ten interments. In April the garrison of the fort numbered six officers, five sergeants and 88 soldiers. The officers were Captain de Noyan, lieutenants Dumot, de Boucherville and Herbin, ensigns de Millon and de Montigny.[16]

On October 11 or 12, 1745, a party of about 60 French and 12 Indians attacked the fort at Great Meadows, not far from Putney; after an hour and a half of fighting David Rugg lay dead and Nehemiah How was a prisoner. The English pursued the enemy as far as Fort No. 4 (Charlestown, N. H.), where the French turned off to St. Frederic, taking seven days for the return from Great Meadows to Lake Champlain.[17]

Sieur Marin, having returned from Acadia after the capture of Louisburg, came to St. Frederic, November 13. His party, organized to attack the English settlements on the Connecticut, arrived shortly after.[18] A letter from Abbé François Piquet tells us: "The English are making warlike preparations at Saratoga and are pushing their way up to Lake St. Sacrement." He suggests that the governor send troops there "at least to intimidate the enemy, if we could do no more."[19] Upon this warning the goal of Marin's expedition was changed; Saratoga was made the objective. Marin's party, 280 French and 229 Indians, accompanied by Abbé Piquet, "a mischievous and active priest,"[20] moved from Fort St. Frederic. They left their boats at the head of Lake Champlain and, over the Great Carrying Place, they reached Fort Lydius, November 27. Prisoners seized in the vicinity told of a garrison of 80 men at Saratoga. Sieur Marin, ably aided by Sieurs de Boucherville, de Niverville, and de Courtemanche, attacked Saratoga November 28; all the buildings in the village were destroyed; 12 persons were killed and 109 prisoners taken during the assault.[21] On the return journey they burned

16. Reid: *Lake George and Lake Champlain*, pp. 224-227.
17. Hall: *History of Eastern Vermont*, p. 36. Crockett: *History of Vermont*, I, p. 103.
18. Hill: *Old Fort Edward*, p. 34.
19. *Doc. Col. Hist. N. Y.*, I, p. 429.
20. Drake: *History of the French and Indian War*, p. 87.
21. *Doc. Col. Hist. N. Y.*, VI, p. 228 and X, p. 76. Brandow: *Old Saratoga and Schuylerville*, pp. 31-41. Butler: *Lake George and Lake Champlain*, p. 107.

the houses and fort of Lydius. They reached St. Frederic December 3, and started at once for Montreal.

Lydius wanted vengeance on St. Frederic; he made several trips to Boston to urge the English to capture the fort, and Shirley, governor of Massachusetts, proposed a coalition of the northern colonies for this purpose, but the plan fell through. M. de Beauharnois, aware of these machinations, sent as aid to M. de Croisille at Fort St. Frederic, two parties, one of 50 French and 300 Indians led by M. de Muy, the other of 400 men commanded by M. Rigaud de Vaudreuil. In the month of January 1746, M. de Beauharnois sent M. de La Corne de St. Luc with 150 men to join M. de St. Pierre's party and to protect St. Frederic. The English colonies, not wishing to lose time waiting for royal troops, resolved to attack. The governor of New York asked the aid of the Five Nations. Beginning in the spring the French kept sending out bands of Indians, always accompanied by a few French officers, in order to keep the English as busy as possible and thus prevent formation of the coalition. These groups started out from Missisquoi as well as from St. Frederic, French capital of the Lake Champlain valley.[22] Between March 16, and June 21, Indian parties left these two centers to make sudden raids upon the English villages; Lieutenant de St. Blain is mentioned as leader May 10, and Sieur de Carqueville, June 21. The latter brought from Albany the report that 13,000 English were setting out for St. Frederic. M. de Beauharnois at Montreal sent M. de Léry to the fort with two cannoneers taken from the warship Auguste. He gave orders to prepare 15,000 to 16,000 men to support the garrison at the fort. July 24, M. de Croissille wrote that the Wolves had killed and scalped a French soldier who had gone from the fort unarmed. The register informs us: "the 24th. of July died at fort Saint-Frederic Jean-Gabriel alias Bosoleille soldier of the company of M. de Saint-George, aged sixteen and a half, who had his scalp taken by the enemy." This is the last entry of Father Alexis du Buron as well as the last of the year, during which there were five baptisms and two burials.

Meanwhile, although their numbers were enormously exaggerated, the English were not inactive. August 4, Colonel William Johnson sent out two parties of Iroquois of the Five Nations: the first massacred settlers on Isle La Motte and attacked Chambly where

22. *Doc. Col. Hist. N. Y.*, X, pp. 32-35. Butler: *Lake George and Lake Champlain*, pp. 58-62.

most of the inhabitants were killed or captured;[23] the second, of twelve men, scouted near St. Frederic. Colonel Johnson wrote to Governor Clinton, August 19, that this party, on the return from St. Frederic spent two days within sight of an enemy camp of 600 men on Long Island in Lake St. Sacrement. It was the camp of M. de Rigaud de Vaudreuil who commanded two parties covering St. Frederic, one stationed at the head of Lake Champlain, the other at Lake St. Sacrement.[24] A detachment of his troops in command of M. de St. Luc had been as far as Saratoga. August 10, M. de Repentigny wrote Quebec of the capture of eleven prisoners near Schenectady.

Toward the end of August, 1746, M. Rigaud de Vaudreuil, finding the English too inactive to suit his taste, resolved to attack Fort Massachusetts, built by the English near Williamstown in 1744, about ten days' march from Fort St. Frederic. At the head of 400 Canadians and 300 Indians, he arrived August 29, before Fort Massachusetts, whose garrison consisted of Colonel Zadock Hawks and 33 persons including women and children. M. Rigaud attacked. After a most heroic defense of twenty-six hours the garrison surrendered and was taken to St. Frederic.[25] M. Rigaud was himself wounded in the right arm. On the return trip they ravaged the country for a space of fifteen leagues. After the attack, M. Rigaud sent Sieur de Montigny, August 31, with 14 Abenakis to scout near Saratoga. They attacked a convoy of 20 men and, at the very gates of Fort Clinton, killed four men and took four prisoners.[26]

In October, Sieurs de St. Blin, de l'Epervanche and de Langy set off toward Saratoga. On the 11th M. de Repentigny left Fort St. Frederic for the same destination with 4 French and 33 Indians. On the 23d, he attacked two wagons of a convoy between Albany and Saratoga, killed and scalped the drivers, and disappeared.[27] M. de Repentigny returned to St. Frederic, November 9, reporting that he had seen great numbers assembling at "sarasto" and transporting great quantities of munitions, probably the party of Colonel Johnson returning from Lake St. Sacrement.[28] About the end of the year

23. Champlain Tercentenary Commission: *Report*, pp. 131-132.

24. Butler: *Lake George and Lake Champlain*, p. 61. *Doc. Col. Hist. N. Y.*, X, pp. 114, 132, and 148.

25. Robinson: *History of Vermont*, pp. 20-21. H. Hall: *Early History of Vermont*, p. 2. Crockett: *History of Vermont*, I, p. 104.

26. Brandow: *Old Saratoga and Schuylerville*, p. 42.

27. *Ibid.*, p. 43.

28. Butler: *Lake George and Lake Champlain*, p. 62.

new reinforcements reached St. Frederic, 30 Indians from Bécancour and 24 from St. François. December 1, M. de Gannes was detached to lead to the fort 60 Abenakis and Malecites; on the 20th, 18 Iroquois of the Sault went to join them. Governor Clinton wrote December 9, that 20 companies had been organized in the English colony to march against Crown Point in the spring; the force would consist of 1,000 men under Lieutenant Colonel Roberts.

To return for a moment to Father Alexis du Buron. During the three years of his service he made thirty-six entries in the register, which he did not cross out! The principal signatures of his time are the following: Rigauville, Montessont-Croizille, Hertel de Beaubassin, Chevigny, father and son, Louis-Adrien, Sieur du Sablé, Marie-Anne Lamothe, J. Barsalou, Marianne Texier (or Tessier), and J. B. de Montigny.

M. de Noyan was commandant at the beginning of 1747, Father Bonaventure Carpentier was chaplain. During his very short sojourn, there were four baptisms, the first, January 10, and the last, February 8. Among the witnesses is "Sieur Charles Lemoine de Longueuille, écuier, sieur officier." In his second baptismal entry the godfather was Sieur Herbin, officer at the fort; the godmother "was although absent Mademoiselle Catherine de Noyan," daughter of the commandant.

The Chevalier de Niverville, "having failed to take a fort,"[29] says Father Baudry, retired to Fort St. Frederic with his wounded. There he organized a new party with which he set out "toward Fleorie (sic!) where he burned five forts and about 100 houses."[30]

Sieur de Gannes returned from St. Frederic to Montreal, where he reported that, during the month of March, Lieutenant Herbin had set off toward Saratoga with 30 French and Indians. Near Fort Clinton he had encountered a party of 25 English en route to Albany; he killed six of them and took four prisoners; the rest fled. The prisoners told him that there were 12 cannon and 100 boats at Fort Clinton for the transport of the expedition against Fort St. Fred-

29. Fort No. 4 of the English, located at Charlestown, N. H., on the Connecticut, was established in 1743 and abandoned within a few years. In 1747 Captain Stevens was sent to command the garrison. He arrived March 26, and successfully resisted an attack a few days later by the French under "Debeline." See Crockett, Hall, and Robinson, already quoted; Wells: *History of Newbury*, gives "de Niverville" as commander.

30. "Fleorie" is a place which I have not identified; doubtless it is an English name phonetically transcribed by some French writer.

eric. Sieur Herbin brought letters seized at Saratoga in which this expedition was discussed.

In the *Collection des Documents relatifs à la Nouvelle-France*, Vol. 3, p. 335, we read: "We learn by courier from Montreal that in the latter part of April a party of Mohawks and English fell upon 21 French scouts near Fort St. Frederic of whom they killed five men who were scalped. Sieur Laplante officer was badly treated, having been wounded by seven shots; this unfortunate blow fell through too great confidence on the part of the French who were surprised." This occurrence occasioned the first entry of the new chaplain at the fort, Father Hippolyte Collet: "The year one thousand seven hundred forty-seven April 29 were buried in the cemetery of fort Saint-Frederic, the bodies of M. de la Haye, merchant of Montreal and officer of militia; of Jean Poitevin, resident on the Chambly River, Antoine Durand of the parish of St. Ours, Joseph Lajeunesse of the parish of the Assumption, Clarimont soldier of the company of du Plessis and native of Laon, all assassinated the evening before half a league from the fort in the Bay . . ."

In May, it was learned that the English were definitely preparing to attack St. Frederic by way of the Great Carrying Place and Wood Creek; consequently, the governor gave orders for the raising of 500 or 600 men at Montreal and of 100 militiamen and 30 or 40 Indians at Three Rivers. This detachment was placed in command of M. Rigaud de Vaudreuil, Major of Three Rivers.

As soon as he arrived at Fort St. Frederic, M. Rigaud sent M. de Lacorne de St. Luc[31] with 200 men[32] to attack Saratoga. With its leaders, Sieurs de St. Lac, de Carqueville, and de St. Ours, this party left St. Frederic at midnight of June 23. On June 30, after considerable scouting in the vicinity they attacked. In spite of the new defenses of Fort Clinton, twice as large as the fort destroyed by Marin in 1745, the French quickly gained the upper hand and returned to St. Frederic with 40 prisoners including Lieutenant Chews, the English commander. Quite a few English were drowned trying to escape by swimming.[33] Among the captives was a certain Joseph Grays, native of "Georgia in New England," says the register. He

---

31. ". . . notorious for brutal inhumanity"—Winsor: *Narrative and Critical History of America*, VI, Part I, p. 294.

32. "20 French and 200 Indians"—Butler, p. 55; cf. Brandow, pp. 45-53.

33. Brandow: *Old Saratoga and Schuylerville*, p. 53. See also Sylvester: *Historical Sketches*, "Saratoga."

abjured July 15, received the last sacraments, and died about midnight August 4. M. Celoron de Blainville, the new commander, was present at his abjuration.

M. Rigaud and the rest of his troops followed Sieur de St. Luc's detachment. The Indians left M. Rigaud, who withdrew into "Grande Baie" (South Bay), where he would be within range to protect St. Frederic. After M. de St. Luc's return, M. Rigaud went to Montreal, sending back to St. Frederic the Sieur de Langy, "Le brave Langis," with 50 to 60 French and about 30 Indians to get in wood for the garrison.

July 16 found Sieur de "Mery" (de Muy) at Grande Baie with 450 French and Indians, scouting and cutting trees on both banks of Wood Creek, casting the trunks into the water to prevent navigation.[34]

In August M. de St. Luc's Indians went toward Albany and returned with a few scalps. M. de Repentigny with 26 Abenakis scouting near Fort Clinton attacked a cart-load of slate for the construction of a chimney. At the very gates of the fort he killed four men and took four prisoners.[35]

The report came in October that the English were ready to attack. Live cattle "were sent to supply the garrison at Fort St. Frederic—whom it is necessary to treat well." Ensign de Léry returned to Montreal with 35 prisoners "by the coasts of New England"; he reported that Lydius was to start out with 1,500 men to attack Canada. The governor sent M. de Sabrevois to take command at Fort St. Frederic urging him to carry on active scouting.

Because of the attacks so often repeated and always disastrous, the English burned Fort Clinton October 5, 1747, declaring that it was impossible either to defend or maintain it. October 24, M. de Repentigny fell upon a convoy of munitions and provisions on the road between Albany and Saratoga, two of the English being killed.

In Canada the Chevalier de Longueuil announced in November that the English expedition was getting ready and "that the enterprise against Fort St. Frederic will take place unless the English be interrupted." The discovery of the desired interruption was soon made. Toward the end of November Sieur de Villiers with 70 French and Indians visited Saratoga; he found Fort Clinton in ruins, burned by

34. Butler: *Lake George and Lake Champlain*, pp. 54-55.
35. *Doc. Col. Hist. N. Y.*, X, p. 35. Butler: *Lake George and Lake Champlain*, p. 54.

the English, a fort "133 feet by 150 with a score of houses within the enclosure." M. de Villiers sent the governor his report, which arrived December 15. Because of the abandonment of Fort Clinton the Iroquois allowed their friendship for the English to cool a little; it seemed to them that the English were fleeing before the French attacks.

During this year of war, which saw three commandants and two chaplains at Fort St. Frederic, Father Collet officiated at eleven burials and a single baptism. Life at the fort must have been full of action; the arrival and departure of numerous expeditions and the presence of enemy scouts in the neighborhood could not fail to upset the peaceful existence of the inhabitants. It is said that, apart from the great military movements, twenty-seven small fighting units were sent out from Fort St. Frederic in 1747.[36]

The chronicle of the post in 1748 concerns only minor happenings; the commandant and chaplain have not been changed. January 4, the burial record of Jean Beaudin contains this phrase: "Dead yesterday by accident having been killed instantly by his gun upon which he had leaned being on duty in the woods. . . ." This excerpt leads one to presume that the militiamen of those days, while knowing how to fight like heroes, were not expert in handling their guns. In fact this same year in the burial record of Jean-Baptiste Charpentier on July 24, we find "dead yesterday at nine o'clock in the evening, after having received the Sacrament of penitence and extreme-unction, having received a shot from his own gun in the abdomen."

In May, M. de Sabrevois reported to his superiors that Sieur Hertel de Beaubassin with 11 Abenakis and 3 Canadians had burned thirty houses near Orange on the first day of the month, had ruined three little forts (blockhouses) and one mill, all abandoned, but had not had the opportunity to take any prisoners.[37] On May 30, the Sieur de St. Blain, cadet, 2 Canadians and 9 Indians set out toward the south, returning June 19, with five scalps taken within a few leagues of St. Frederic; this is the affair which the English call the Londonderry skirmish. On June 11, M. de St. Blain had met the party of Captain Eleazer Melvin scouting with 18 men from Fort Dummer; they were on the banks of the West River thirty-three miles from the

36. Butler: *Lake George and Lake Champlain*, p. 57.
37. Butler: *Lake George and Lake Champlain*, p. 63.

English outpost; five of the English were killed and one mortally wounded; the rest reached Fort Dummer safely.[38]

The Sieur Mouette ("Manet" in the English chronicles) with 30 Indians made an attack near Fort Dummer in the month of May; the same Captain Melvin led the English. On his return journey to St. Frederic the Sieur Mouette was surprised five or six leagues from the fort by an enemy force of superior strength and was forced to retreat.[39]

July 14, 1748, a party of French and Indians met 18 English at Fort Hinsdale on the Connecticut, only half a mile from Fort Dummer. During the ensuing skirmish four Englishmen were killed; the French, although losing six men killed and wounded, captured six of the English.[40] After the encounter, they traveled up the Connecticut, then the West River, and to the source of Otter Creek which they followed to Lake Champlain and St. Frederic, whence the captives were sent to Canada.[41]

The register of St. Frederic for 1748 contains eight burials and four baptisms. The most important occurrence was the arrival, in August, of M. de Niverville, who brought to the commandant a copy of the order to suspend hostilities; the treaty of Aix-la-Chapelle had been signed in April.

Governor Shirley of Massachusetts wrote the governor of New France May 9, 1749, to protest against the establishment of French settlers about Fort St. Frederic, since he considered the fort an encroachment on the territory of the King of England. In reply the Marquis de la Galissonnière sent M. Celoron de Blainville with 300 soldiers, regulars and Canadians, to place lead plaques graven with the arms of France along the frontier; some of these were found much later as far west as the banks of the Ohio River.[42]

Peter Kalm, the eminent Swedish traveler, visited St. Frederic, July 2, 1749, on his journey from Albany to Quebec. June 29, after building a boat at the site of Fort Anne, Kalm and his companions embarked on Wood Creek; just before nightfall they met a French sergeant and six soldiers sent by the commandant of Fort St.

38. Crockett: *History of Vermont*, I, pp. 105-106. Cabot: *Annals of Brattleboro*, p. 19.
39. Cabot: *Annals of Brattleboro*, p. 18.
40. B. H. Hall: *History of Eastern Vermont*, p. 48.
41. Crockett: *History of Vermont*, I, p. 108.
42. *Voyage de Pierre Kalm* (W. Marchand, traducteur), II, p. 28.

Frederic to conduct three Englishmen to Saratoga and to protect
them from a band of Indians who were seeking to take vengeance on
the English for the death of a relative. The French spent the night
with Kalm's party, and the sergeant advised Kalm to accompany him
to the nearest English settlement and then to return under his escort
to Fort St. Frederic, because of the danger if Kalm should happen to
encounter those Indians. Kalm refused, giving his boat to the
French, for "we could not make any further use of it, on account of
the number of trees which the French had thrown across the river
during the last war, to prevent the attacks of the English on
Canada."[43] In exchange Kalm was to take one of the French boats
left farther down the river toward Lake Champlain, which he did;
after mistaking his way[44] and suffering from lack of food he finally
reached the fort.

"This fortress (Fort St. Frederic) is built upon a rock of black
calcareous schist; its form is almost quadrangular; its walls, thick
and high, are built of this same stone, of which there is a quarry
about half a mile from the fort. A high and very strong tower,
bomb-proof and supplied with cannons from top to bottom, defends
the eastern part; there resides the governor. The enclosure of the
fort has within it a pretty little church and stone houses for the officers and men."[45] In a note to the French edition of Kalm's works,
M. Marchand speaks of a broad deep ditch, cut into the rock by im-
mense labor, and he says that the walls, of logs and earth, were 22
feet thick and 16 feet high.[46]

The register in 1749 contains eight entries by Father Collet,
whose last entry is August 16; there are four baptisms, one marriage,
and three deaths. The commandant (I do not find the date of his
appointment) is Paul-Louis Dazemard, Sieur de Lusignan.[47] Kalm
found him at the fort July 2; "M. de Lusignan the governor, received
us very politely. He is a man of about 50 years of age, well versed
in literature and who, thanks to the numerous journeys which he has
made in this country, has formed definite opinions on many useful
and interesting subjects."[48] Again, speaking of his departure he says:

43. Kalm: *Travels into North America*, II, p. 142.
44. He had gone up the Poultney River for some distance.
45. *Voyage de Pierre Kalm* (translation by W. Marchand), II, p. 3.
46. *Ibid.*, II, p. 34.
47. Proprietor of the seigneurie de Lusignan on Missisquoi Bay. See p. 219.
48. *Voyage de Pierre Kalm* (translation by W. Marchand), II, p. 3.

"Our stay in this place was marked by many attentions, especially on the part of the governor of the fort, M. de Lusignan, a man of learning as well as of exquisite courtesy, to whom we are much indebted; he treated us with the same regard as though we had been his own relatives. Finally he overwhelmed us with more attentions than we could have expected from a compatriot, and the officers were also more than courteous."[49]

At dinner July 5, they were disturbed by shouting several times repeated, coming from some distance up Wood Creek.[50] M. de Lusignan told Kalm that this shout was not of good omen, for he concluded from it that the Indians, those whom Kalm had just escaped meeting near Fort Anne, had accomplished their plan of vengeance on the English.

Kalm informs us concerning the garrison and its life at the fort: "Each soldier receives a new coat every two years, and annually a waist-coat, a cap, a hat, a pair of breeches, a stock, two pair of socks, two pair of shoes, and wood as much as is needed in the winter. Their pay is five sous a day and amounts to thirty sous when they have some special duty to perform for the King's service . . . If a soldier falls ill, he is taken to the hospital where the King furnishes him a bed, nourishment, medicines, nurses and servants . . . the soldiers respect and honor the governor and their officers, and nevertheless officers and soldiers often talk together as good friends without ceremony, but with a freedom which remains within the bounds of propriety."[51]

Professor Kalm left the fort about eleven o'clock in the morning, July 19, after having waited for several days for the arrival of the schooner which plied regularly between St. Frederic and St. Jean during the summer. The captain of it was French, born in this country, and he had constructed the schooner himself.

M. de Lusignan must have been absent for some time in 1750, Sieur Herbin acting as commandant. The major of the post was M. Lefournier du Vivier; the storekeeper, M. Coulonges; the surgeon, Louis Landriau; and Captain Joseph Payan commanded the "navy," which consisted of the schooner St. Frederic.

49. *Ibid.*, II, p. 30.

50. Kalm calls thus that part of Lake Champlain between Fort St. Frederic and Whitehall—this is the "Grand Marais" of most French writers of the time.

51. *Voyage de Pierre Kalm* (translation by W. Marchand), II, p. 14.

Captain Stoddard, sent to examine Fort St. Frederic, made his report to Governor Clinton July 30, 1750: "32 leagues south of St. Johns, on the Lake Champlain, is the Fort Saint Frederick (called by us Crown Point) where a bay and a small river to the eastward forms a point on which the fort stands. This fort is built of stone, the walls are of a considerable height and thickness, and has some 20 pieces of cannon and swivels, mounted on the ramparts and bastions, the largest of which are six-pounders, and but a few of them. I observed the wall cracked from top to bottom in several places. At the entrance to the fort is a dry ditch, 18 or 20 feet square and a draw-bridge; there is a subterraneous passage under this draw-bridge to the lake which I apprehend is to be made use of in time of need to bring water to the fort, as the well they have in it affords them but very little. In the northwest corner of the fort stands the citadel; it is a stone building eight feet square (*sic!*) four story high each turned with arches, mounts twenty pieces of cannon and swivels, the largest six pounders, four of which are in the first story and are useless until the walls of the fort are beat down. The walls of the citadel are about ten foot thick the roof high and very taut covered with shingles.

"At the entrance of the citadel is a draw-bridge and ditch of the same dimensions as that to the entrance to the fort. . . . The land near the fort is level and good, also on each side of the lake which they are settling, and since the peace there are 14 farms on it, and great encouragement given by the King for that purpose, and I was informed that by the next fall, several more families were coming here to settle."[52]

In the year 1750 the register records twelve baptisms, two marriages and six deaths. Father Hippolyte Collet gives a few records interesting from the point of view of exactness. Here is a burial record which is very precise; the date November 10, "a savagess," and for all information the words "died suddenly"; again, "the year 1750, the *thirty-first* of June, burial of Pierre Lusignan"; September 27, was buried "the body of henry called Chevalier, native of Metz, soldier of Sabrevois' company found dead by accident in the woods at the end of four days."

The year 1751 began with M. Herbin commandant; M. de Lusignan reappears about August 4. Peace was established throughout the country, and the only information about life in the fort comes from the register. Father Collet records 19 baptisms, 5 marriages

52. New York State Historical Society, *Proceedings*, X, pp. 108-113.

and 7 deaths. With the exception of 1755 this year of 1751 records the greatest number of baptisms; seven of the number were Indians. October 5, the good Father omitted to sign the marriage record of Louis Larrivée and Marguerite Deny. In 1752 the same commandant and the same chaplain served the fort.

Sieur Franquet, colonel, inspector of fortifications, in spite of what he had not done at Louisburg, was assigned to examine the outposts. He came to St. Frederic, and according to a plan annexed to his report, it is evident that the wooden stockade had been replaced by more scientifically planned defenses. However, Franquet did not find them sufficiently strong and proposed the construction of a lunette, an impractical addition of which he made a very pretty drawing.[53]

There was a cloud over the fort; Franquet says that Madame de Lusignan[54] had caused misunderstandings between the commandant, her husband, and his officers because she wished to arrogate to herself the exclusive privilege of buying and selling everything, and that she paid in brandy; on the other hand, the *Memoirs* attributed to Vauclin say that M. de Lusignan was primarily interested in his own fortune. It is the period of the Bigot régime, under which each officer, with rare exceptions, hastened to enrich himself at the expense of the colony, following the example clearly set by the intendant.

Those same memoirs say that Fort St. Frederic "was dominated by the very eminences on which it should have been constructed,"[55] and that it had greater reputation among the English than its strength merited since it could neither protect navigation on the lake nor prevent attack on New France by that route, objectives which seem to have determined the location of this fort. Kalm had commented in a similar way in 1749.[56] It is true, however, that the route from Albany to Fort St. Frederic was heavily wooded and several mountains intervened, which made approach difficult for an attacking army, especially when equipped with artillery. To remedy the defects of location, the Marquis de Vaudreuil "sent" M. de Lotbinière to Carillon,[57] five leagues from St. Frederic, to build there a square

53. Bibliothèque Nationale in Paris has a copy of this report.
54. She was Marie-Marguerite Bouat, sister-in-law of François Daine, Seigneur de Boisfranc et de Pancalon, and of Jean-Baptiste de Gannes.
55. The same criticism is made later of the location of Fort Carillon.
56. Kalm: *Travels into North America*, II, p. 209.
57. It is possible that M. de Vaudreuil had this site surveyed in 1752; he did not become governor until 1755. The construction of Fort Carillon was

wooden fort with four bastions to cover the approach to Fort St. Frederic.

In this year Father Collet records in the register fifteen baptisms, four marriages, and only one death; in 1753, sixteen baptisms and two deaths. Father Collet in his eagerness for exactitude went to the point of recording the very hour when he performed the functions of the Church, and as a result some rather curious entries were made. As he sometimes does not mention the day and the month, the information given, detailed though it be, is not always complete; for example, "The year 1753, at four o'clock in the evening, baptism of Françoise Marchand alias Barbézieux," "The year 1753 at three o'clock in the morning, baptism of Marie-Catherine Tiriac." Still another entry excites our interest: On December 7, 1753, the baptismal record of Marie-Louise, daughter of Michel Boileau, reads: ". . . the godfather, godmother, and father of the child declared they did not know how to sign." Now Michel Boileau, the father, had signed many times, the twenty-first of the preceding February, only two pages before that on which appeared this declaration, being the latest instance; was it a refusal or an accident which moves him to make such a declaration?

The good Father Collet records in 1754, seventeen baptisms, one marriage, and two burials. In addition we find on March 3, a copy of the abjuration of Joseph Baudin; the original document, signed by M. de Lusignan, Landriaux, Foucher and others was sent to Mgr. the Bishop of Quebec: "We declare the present writing to be in conformity with its original." Again a burial record shows the unusual qualities of precision manifested by the parish priest: "The year 1754 at four o'clock in the evening the burial of Jérôme 8abenaqui of Saint-Francis."

The last record by Father Hippolyte Collet is dated August 11, 1754. He had been at the fort since April 29, 1747; he had seen as commandants MM. de Noyan, de Lusignan, Herbin, and again de Lusignan. Some very famous people signed his register as witnesses: Du Vivier, Coulonges, Lafon, Etienne Hertel, Hertel de Beaubassin, Lusignan, Musseaux, Lanoue, Sarrobert, Herbin, Landriaux, de Cesne, de Niverville Herbin, Damours Louvière du Vivier, Celoron de Blainville, Joseph Payant, Varennes, Herbin the younger, de Muy, Lepailleur, Laforce, "gille victore Lusignan, écuier," Bouat de

completed in 1756. Perhaps the wooden fort was only temporary, later replaced by stone construction.

Lusignan, Limoge Laforce, Marion Coulon de Villiers Douville, Marie-Louise Douville, Surville, Geneviève Lambert Porlier, etc.

August 30, 1754, a party of French and Indians attacked Fort No. 4 where they took as prisoners James Johnson, his wife and three children, Miriam Willard, sister of Mrs. Johnson, Ebenezer Farnsworth and Peter Labaree. Mrs. Johnson was about to become a mother; at the junction of Knapp's Brook and Black River (Reading, Vermont) her daughter was born and christened Captive.[58] The commandant of Fort No. 4, in his report to the General Court of Massachusetts, speaks of ten assaults on the fort, by the enemy, in two years.[59]

Father Didace Cliche came to Fort St. Frederic about November 1, and before the end of the year had recorded two baptisms, using a rather original form of entry: "Has been baptised John Doe born October 14, of the present year with the ordinary ceremonies of legitimate marriage . . .," etc.

June 29, July 1, and July 16, Father Didace was at St. Jean where he officiated at baptisms. He recorded them there, but in order not to lose the memory of them, he recorded them also at St. Frederic.

Again war threatened New France. The English, especially those of New York, had never abandoned the plan to destroy Fort St. Frederic, regarded as a constant challenge to their power. In 1754, they had communicated with the King of England and had organized, with his approval, four expeditions for 1755: 1. against Fort Duquesne; 2. against Fort Niagara; 3. against Acadia; 4. against Fort St. Frederic. Without formal declaration of war King George II sent two regiments of English regulars under command of General Braddock to assist in these expeditions. General Braddock embarked in January, meeting defeat and death in the disastrous skirmish near Fort Duquesne. Sieur Daniel-Hyacinthe Liénard de Beaujeu planned the ambush in which he also lost his life. Governor Shirley failed before Niagara; Winslow took possession of Acadia; General William Johnson was named commander of the fourth expedition.[60]

58. After her ransom, Captive Johnson married George Kimball of Cavendish, Vermont.

59. Hall: *History of Eastern Vermont*, pp. 64-68.

60. For the story of this expedition see Hill: *Old Fort Edward*, pp. 68-99. Parkman: *Montcalm and Wolf*, I, pp. 294-363. Fiske: *New France and New England*, pp. 294, *et seq. Doc. Col. Hist. N. Y.*, X, "Journal de Pouchot."

May 3, 1755, Baron de Dieskau, a general of German birth formerly serving under Marshal de Saxe, set sail from Brest to place himself under the orders of Marquis de Vaudreuil, governor of New France. Letters of General Braddock, found on the battlefield and sent to M. de Vaudreuil, informed him of the English plans against Fort St. Frederic. August 15, he sent Baron de Dieskau with an army of 3,573 men to the fort; in September the King's approval arrived, and the order was given to advance.

September 4, Dieskau left 1,800 men at Carillon where M. de Vaudreuil had ordered construction of a post to cover approach to St. Frederic and left with the rest of his troops for Fort Lydius (Fort Edward, N. Y.). The result is well known; Dieskau changed his mind and on September 7 attacked Johnson at Lake St. Sacrement, where, seriously wounded, he fell into the hands of the English. The French army, now commanded by M. de Montreuil, fell back to St. Frederic, arriving on September 11, not having tasted food for four days.

M. de Vaudreuil withdrew the Battalion of Béarn from Fort Frontenac to reinforce the army at St. Frederic. He actively pushed forward the new fortifications at Carillon, encouraged by the report of M. de Lotbinière. In January, 1756, he wrote that he had had 2,000 men at Carillon since May, that he had sent 12 cannon and 8 other pieces of artillery to the new post, and that he had transferred to it the munitions previously stored at St. Frederic. He announced also that he had seized the Little Carrying Place between Carillon and Lake St. Sacrement and had fortified it by a redoubt with two bastions garrisoned by 670 soldiers. This was called Fort Vaudreuil.

The English continued scouting in the vicinity of Carillon and St. Frederic, and we find on November 4 the following record, written by Father Didace but signed by Brother Elzéar Maugé:

By me undersigned chaplain of the King at the Royal fort of Carillon was buried with the ordinary ceremonies in the new cemetery of this fort The body of a certain Jean Chartier, resident of Beaumont, killed by the English on a scout, aged twenty-six years or thereabouts, having been given the Sacrament of The extreme unction. In testimony of which I have signed at fort Saint-Frederic the day and year above.

This record shows that a new cemetery had been opened at St. Frederic. Days were coming when the wisdom of this precaution would be shown.

The register in 1755 shows 22 baptisms, 2 marriages and 21 burials.

M. de Lusignan was still commandant in 1756 and was until the end of French occupation. The chaplain was still Father Didace who had not lost the faculty of inventing strange phrases. March 22, he recorded the burial in the cemetery of Carillon of "François Saquin alias Jolibois, a native of Voïcourt, jurisdiction of Neufchâteau in Lorraine, sergeant of the d'Hébécourt company of the regiment of La Reine, assassinated cruelly by the mohawks near fort Carillon, with the Sacraments of Penitence and of extreme unction, aged twenty-four years or Thereabouts."

Louis-Joseph Gozon de Véran, Marquis de Montcalm, was appointed lieutenant general of the troops in New France, January 25, 1756. The history of the great campaigns of the French and Indian War is well known; it is not necessary to retell it here. The English expeditions of Generals Abercrombie and Amherst, the capture of Fort William Henry by Montcalm, even the remarkable failure of M. Rigaud de Vaudreuil before this same fort, have been many times related. What concerns us is the chronicle of the French settlements in the valley of Lake Champlain. Therefore, I shall not even give a résumé of the thrilling story of those campaigns but shall limit myself to the chronicle of deeds little heeded until now.

Colonel Fitch wrote from Albany to John Winslow, leader of the English colonial troops, saying, "Friday, 1 oclock; Sir, about half an hour since, a party of near 50 French and Indians had the impudence to come down to the river opposite this city and captivate two men."[61] The register of 1756 is in keeping with this disastrous period: 10 baptisms, 3 marriages, and 75 burials. Almost all of the dead are soldiers or militiamen, the latter coming from almost everywhere in New France.

January 15, 1757, Captain Robert Rogers and Lieutenant John Stark left Fort Edward with a detachment of 80 men to scout in the vicinity of Lake Champlain. Between Carillon and St. Frederic, at the mouth of the "Rivière à la Barbue"[62] Rogers undertook to stop the French convoys of men and supplies. His ambushed Rangers fell upon a convoy January 21, seized several sledges and captured seven men. The others returned to St. Frederic to give the alarm. M. de Lusignan sent out 100 men with MM. de Basserade and de

61. Letter quoted in Parkman: *Montcalm and Wolfe*, I, p. 401.
62. Smith: *History of Essex County, N. Y.*, p. 77.

Lagrandville to cut off the retreat of the English. The struggle lasted from three o'clock in the afternoon until midnight. The English left 42 men on the field, the French losses being 9 dead and 18 wounded, among the latter M. de Basserade. His wounds were soon healed by the cross of Saint-Louis bestowed upon him in recognition of his distinguished services.

After the capture of Fort William Henry by Montcalm, in August, English and French parties roamed the forest constantly, each trying to discover the plans of the other; rarely are conflicts noted between these hostile groups. In October, Fort Carillon was still unfinished; it is said that most of the batteries were only temporary construction. This year Father Didace records 8 baptisms, 1 marriage, and 11 burials, 8 of which were of soldiers.

During the winter of 1757-1758, Captain d'Hébécourt of the battalion of La Reine was commandant at Carillon and M. de Lusignan at St. Frederic. The English often made their presence known, but the winter was comparatively calm. MM. de Langis, de Montigny, and de la Durantaye were often out on scouting trips. Abercrombie in July attacked Fort Carillon, valiantly defended by Montcalm. At twilight on the eighth the English beat an ignominious retreat; six assaults against the French entrenchments had cost them 551 dead, 1,356 wounded, and 37 missing. Montcalm's forces suffered the loss of only 377 dead and wounded. In August, General Abercrombie was recalled to England; Jeffrey Amherst, famous as leader at the capture of Louisburg, replaced him.

Montcalm, early in the fall, feared that the French would be driven from their posts on Lake Champlain. He suggested that the forts be blown up at the last moment and that a stand be made at the north end of the lake. Governor de Vaudreuil, jealous of Montcalm's popularity, secretly worked against him. Montcalm quotes in his correspondence these verses of Corneille in reference to the frequent differences between him and the governor:

> *Mon crime véritable est d'avoir aujourd'hui*
> *Plus de nom que (Vaudreuil), plus de vertus que lui,*
> *Et c'est de là que part cette secrète haine*
> *Que le temps ne rendra que plus forte et plus pleine.*
>
> *My real crime is to have today*
> *More renown than Vaudreuil, more virtue than he,*

And that is the source of his secret hate
Which time will but render more strong and more complete.

At Fort St. Frederic Father Didace records his last entry June 17, 1758; there were this year 6 baptisms, 4 marriages and 2 burials. There is an interesting record under date of April 11 evidently concerning prisoners of war: "Baptised with the usual ceremonies Marie-Marguerite, born near fort Dummer in New England, daughter of Benjamin Moores, deceased, native of Lancaster in old England and of Marguerite Moores native of Boston . . . the child appears to be four months old according to the testimony of its mother," etc.

The following signatures appear in the register which, except for interlineations, is well written and neatly kept: Thérèse Blainville; Denys Thibaudière; Landriaux; Louise du Sablé; Bécancourt; Bouat de Lusignan; Lusignan; Duvigneaux; Laguerre de Monville; and "Chr degannes Falaise."

I have said that Father Didace wrote well and that his register was neatly kept; his successor may boast, as Molière, "of having changed all that." Father Antoine Deperet wrote badly, made blots and spilled ink. He began his service about July 23, the date of his first record, and in the course of the year recorded 9 baptisms, 1 marriage and 5 burials. October 21, Father Denis Baron came to St. Frederic from Fort St. Jean; he officiated at two more burials "in place of Father Antoine Deperet." (He always wrote "le sacrement dex tremonction" in the register of St. Frederic as in other registers he kept.) A few days later we read;

Lan 1758, 6 9bre par-moy [crossed out]. Je soussigne ptre aumonier au fort Saint-Frederic soussigne [crossed out] Certifie que le reverend pere denis baron, aumonier de ce fort (en mon abcense) est decede est qu'il a Ete enterre dans le cymetiere de ce poste a St frederic ce 6 9bre 1758 en foy de quoi iai signe. Fr. Antoine Deperet.

The year 1758, November 6, I the undersigned priest chaplain at fort Saint-Frederic certify that the Reverend Father Denis Baron, chaplain of this fort (in my absence) died and was buried in the cemetery of this post at Saint-Frederic . . .

December 22, the chaplain is again preoccupied by the military threat of English aggression. I find this record: "Bapitaire" of a daughter born that day to François Varlet and Marie-Josette Durbois; fortunately written in the margin there is "Marie Varlet."

However, we cannot always trust the margin. The two records which follow bear respectively in the margin, "Bapt. de marianne jeanpetiot" and "Bapt. Deradegonde jeanpetiot"; and, upon reading the text, we see that it concerns twin daughters of Raymond Lacombe and Jeanne Lavergne!

Montcalm, the greatest military leader sent to New France, clearly sensed, long before the final campaign, the imminent loss of the colony if France did not adequately meet the crying need of food, munitions, and men. The tragic outcome became more clear to him as time passed, and in the spring of 1759 he wrote: "If the war continues, Canada will belong to England, perhaps this campaign or the next. We want provisions; we want powder; and France should send 10,000 men to preserve our colony." The one thought in Montcalm's mind was the preservation of New France with no selfish desire to profit from his brilliant military exploits. The French officials in Canada, on the other hand, were constantly engaged in jealous wrangles, and Governor de Vaudreuil even accused Montcalm of insubordination, neglect to follow instructions, and lack of adaptability to command in Canada. Referring to these petty quarrels, Montcalm wrote: "If there be peace, the colony is lost unless the entire government is changed." His repeated requests for recall, eagerly endorsed by M. de Vaudreuil, were unheeded in France by the Crown and military authorities who appreciated his genius. "You must not expect to receive any military reinforcements; we will convey all the provisions and ammunition possible; the rest depends upon your wisdom and courage and the bravery of your troops." Wisdom, courage and bravery were unavailing before the power of the English advance. In discouragement, Montcalm wrote to a friend in France: "There are situations when nothing remains for a general but to die with honor."[63] Prophetic words! Seemingly forgotten by his Mother-Country, his proud spirit remained faithful to his love for New France. Events moved swiftly; and mortally wounded on the Plains of Abraham, he was told that he could live but a few hours; quickly came his reply: "So much the better, I shall not live to see the surrender of Quebec."[64]

The English army under Amherst reached Lake St. Sacrement

63. O'Callaghan: *Documentary History of New York*, pp. 90-91.

64. Barnes: *A Brief History of the United States*, p. 89. Campbell: *Concise School History of the United States*, p. 68. The incident is recorded in many other accounts of the fall of Quebec.

June 21, 1759, and embarked for Carillon, July 22. The entrenchments so gloriously defended by Montcalm in 1758 were abandoned by the French this time after a trifling skirmish; Montcalm was not in command. Doriel and Bougainville were in France vainly seeking aid from the King, who was too harassed by European conditions to send additional forces to New France.

M. de Bourlamaque abandoned Fort Carillon, leaving with the main body of his troops July 23, before Amherst had set up his batteries. Until the evening of July 26 Captain d'Hébécourt kept his 400 men constantly firing on the English. Amherst was unaware, because of this ruse, that M. de Bourlamaque had withdrawn. About ten in the evening d'Hébécourt and his men abandoned Carillon, leaving a lighted fuse in the powder magazine. It blew up at eleven o'clock, destroying one bastion and setting fire to all the wooden buildings.

D'Hébécourt rejoined M. de Bourlamaque and his troops at St. Frederic. July 31, the French blew up Fort St. Frederic, withdrawing toward Isle aux Noix in the Richelieu River. Amherst reached St. Frederic, August 3. He prepared to restore the fort according to his custom but found it was impossible because Fort St. Frederic was in ruins! He then began, with a grandiose plan, the construction of the Amherst Fort, situated a few hundred yards inland; its walls, crumbled by time and weather, stand to-day upon the heights of Crown Point.

August 16, 1759, Major General Amherst received definite knowledge concerning the French forces in the valley from a deserter of the Regiment of Languedoc, who "came in from 4 vessels which lay below les Isles au Quatre Vent"; M. de Bourlamaque had 3,500 men in camp at Isle aux Noix with 100 cannon, "the same Troops which were at Ticonderoga." The fleet consisted of four vessels, *La Vigilante,* a schooner of 10 guns, 6 and 4 pounders with swivels mounted along the rails; "A sloop called *Masquelonguy*" of 8 guns (2 brass 12 pounders and 6 iron 6 pounders); *La Brochette* and *L'Esturgeon,* sloops of 8 guns (6 and 4 pounders); "all have swivels mounted." Three of the vessels were built in 1759; one was an old one and another was being repaired. M. de la Bras ("Delabarats," according to other authorities), "a Captain of Man of War," was in command, with M. Rigal "and other Sea officers." The vessels were all manned by men from the battalions of Languedoc, Béarn and La Sarre.

Upon the receipt of this intelligence, Amherst sent for Captain Loring, "who is building a brigantine at Ticonderoga." In order to have an adequate naval force to oppose the French fleet, Amherst and Loring decided to build a "radeau to carry Guns." For six weeks Amherst's advance down the Lake is postponed because the vessels are not ready. Scouts continued to report that the French fleet remained at anchor "in the same spot," near the Isles aux Quatre Vents.

September 1, 1759, prisoners taken opposite the Isle aux Noix reported that a new French vessel of sixteen guns was being launched. Amherst immediately urged Captain Loring to build a second vessel (already planned), "if it can be done without retarding the others." At the same time Amherst said, "I may try" to burn the new French vessel, if possible, before it is put into commission.

Captain Loring came to Crown Point September 3, and it was decided to build a sixteen-gun sloop in the endeavor to preserve naval parity. The unusually bad weather and the "Saw Mill being continually out of order retards us much." September 4, at night, General Amherst sent out Sergeant Hopkins with twelve men, "some of the best swimmers I could find, furnished with fire-darts and hand carcasses to burn the sloop at the Isle au Noix." Ten days later Sergeant Hopkins and his party returned. His report is best given in General Amherst's own words. "He attempted to burn the Vessell the 11th. at ten at night, had got the combustibles to the bow and had near accomplished the design, but I presume made some noise as a man on board discovered them and alarmed the Guard and the whole Camp from whence all the Guards fired, but the men got off unhurt, left the combustibles at the bow and two blankets on the shore. If they had more punctually obeyed my orders which were to do it at two in the morning, they probably had succeeded."

Amherst constantly urged the completion of the vessels. At last, on September 23, Captain Loring "thinks he shall have His Vessels ready in eight days." The 29th, the *Radeau* was launched, 84 feet in length, 20 feet in breadth, "to carry six 24 pounders," and the "Brig and Sloop" were promised for the next week. Fair weather and favorable winds for some days made General Amherst eager to begin his naval campaign against the French fleet, which while it remained in the vicinity of Crown Point would be a constant threat to British supremacy. It was October 10, when the brigantine *Duke of Cumberland* reached Crown Point; she carried six 6 pounders, twelve 4 pounders and 20 swivels, and had on board 70 seamen and 60 marines. The next day, the sloop *Boscawen* arrived, carrying four 6 pounders, twelve 4 pounders, and 22 swivels, with 60 seamen and 50 marines on board commanded by Lieutenant Grant of "Montgomery's." At four o'clock, October 11, the little fleet sailed north "with a fair wind and the troops followed (in bateaux) in four columns with a light hoisted in the night on board the Radeau." A detailed account of the engagement between the opposing fleets is given by General Amherst: "October 12, at daybreak heard some guns. Major Gladwin of Gage's sent me word he saw the vessels engaged but soon after found his mistake, and Major Reid returning with some batteaux of the R. Highland Regt reported the Sloops had fired on him, he had lost the columns in the night, followed the light of the Brig for the Radeau and at daybreak found himself amongst the Enemy's Sloops at les Isles au quatre Vent. they fired several Guns and I suppose struck one batteau as they took one with Lt. McKay one Serjeant one Corporal and Eighteen men. soon after I saw the Enemy's Sloops make all the sail they could. towards night bad weather came on and I ordered the troops into a bay on the western shore to be covered from the wind which began to blow hard. sent the men on shore to boil the Pots and rest themselves by walking about. I ordered the Rangers on an Island and Gages advanced on the shore.

"October 13, it blew a storm and quite contrary wind, continued so all day.

"October 14, I had letters from Captain Loring and Captain Abercrombie that on the 12th. at daybreak when they judged they were 45 miles down the Lake they saw the Schooner gave chase and unfortunately ran the Brig: and Sloop aground, but both got off again and then saw the Enemy's Sloops, which they had passed in the night, between them and the Army and chased to bring them to action, drove them into a bay on the western shore and anchored so as to prevent their getting away, the next day (October 13) went into the bay in search of them and found they (the French) had sunk two of them in five fathom water and run the third on Ground, and that the crews were Escaped, that he had ordered Capt. Grant with the Sloop to try to save the Vessel with the Stores, Guns, and Rigging and that he would go to his station and hoped to get between the Schooner and Isle au Noix, the men who brought me the letter said

Capt. Loring was about thirty miles off and that it was impossible for a boat to go back while the wind continued."

After several days of contrary winds, which prevented further progress northward, October 18 brought a favoring breeze from the south and General Amherst proceeded down the Lake to "where the French sloops are: one is so far repaired that she is sailed this day with the (English) Brigantine and Sloop." Two hundred men in whale boats were detached to aid Captain Loring in his search for the schooner *La Vigilante*, which had escaped toward Isle aux Noix.

The evidence of approaching winter convinced General Amherst that he should abandon, for this year, his attempt to force the French from their position at the Isle aux Noix. He returned to Crown Point without delay, arriving at 2 o'clock, October 21, and proceeded to do what he could toward completing his new fort there before winter set in. "I imagine Captain Loring will weigh up the two (French) sloops which are sunk; I have directed him to do as he Judges best."[65]

In 1759, Fort St. Frederic played a secondary military rôle; the post at Carillon became of first importance. Father Antoine was still chaplain, although it appears that he sometimes made long absences: "I the undersigned . . ., having been called to the aid of the sick at fort Carillon certify that during my absence were buried Pierre de Cormier alias Saint-Pierre or Bacallat, died at the hospital November 29, 1758, and Jacques des Payant alias Delorier, soldier of M. de Courtemanche's company of the Marine, March 29, 1759. In testimony of which I have signed the present certificate at Saint-Frederic this thirtieth of March 1759." On April 21, there is the baptism of Marianne Durant, "The father of the aforesaid is prisoner with the English." Fighting was still going on as is shown by the burial record of François Varlet alias La Vertu, "Died at the hospital of wounds received from the English . . . this third of June 1759."

The register is the sole source of information concerning the date when the settlers of the region about St. Frederic abandoned their homes. "The year 1759 July 15, by me undersigned priest chaplain certify I have buried the daughter of Charles Girard and of Catherine Arnaud named Marie-Louise Girard in the cemetery of

65. The account of General Amherst's campaign against the French fleet on Lake Champlain is based on a manuscript letter from General Amherst to the Honorable William Pitt, October 22, 1759. (Photostat copy in the Crown Point Museum.)

Fort St. Frederic, not having recorded it at Fort St. Frederic by reason of the evacuation. Done at Fort Chambly November 11, 1759. Fr. Antoine Deperet." Worried by the news from Carillon and Lake St. Sacrement, and still more perhaps by the orders of the Sieur de Bourlamaque to abandon the fort at the approach of the English, the settlers prepared themselves to leave their homes and their lands shortly after July 15. The record of the burial of young Marie-Louise Girard marks also the tragic passing of the settlement of St. Frederic.

The settlers went to Fort Chambly, where they remained for several months before merging their identity in the neighboring settlements. On October 6, 1759, Brother Antoine Deperet signed himself "Chaplain at Fort Chambly"; this was for the baptism of Madeleine Courtine; the godfather was Sieur Jacques Arnoux du Buisson, "surgeon with the French troops," and Madelon Arnoux, his daughter, was godmother. The baptismal record of Alexis Girard, October 20, notes that the parents are inhabitants "of St. Frederic passing through Chambly."

After the record of November 11, quoted above, Father Deperet disappears from the register; in this fatal year there were five baptisms and seven burials. In his time, when the importance of Fort St. Frederic diminished and that of Carillon increased, the signatures include the names of Blondeau, Gambet, Dalvo, DuBuisson, Madeleine Arnoux, "marianne tessié," Campan, and "barbe prudomme."

The next entry in the register records a baptism performed by Father Carpentier, curate of Chambly; they are not "our people" of St. Frederic although the record is found in "our" register; the names are entirely new to us.

At the beginning of 1760 the army was still in retreat. The register was carried to St. Jean where an entry was made by Father de Berey, who was there January 6 and 16, but once again the names do not belong to the parish of St. Frederic; neither are they of St. Jean. The old witness of "our days of combat, of glory and of misfortune," the old register, is silent.

In May, 1760, Amherst detached a party of 275 rangers and 25 soldiers, in command of Robert Rogers, with orders to attack the French posts of St. Jean and Chambly. Rogers landed at Rouses Point with 200 men June 4; the remainder of his force with Captain Grant camped at Isle La Motte. June 6, Rogers was surprised by the Sieur La Force with 350 French coming from Isle aux Noix.

Rogers succeeded in repulsing the French, killing 40 and wounding a number, including La Force himself. Withdrawing to Isle La Motte, Rogers remained there until June 9; on that day, landing at the mouth of the Chazy River, he passed unperceived through the woods around Isle aux Noix, destroyed Fort Chambly, took 25 prisoners, and withdrew to Crown Point.[66]

The three English expeditions of 1760 joined finally before Montreal, which surrendered September 8. Then came the fall of Quebec and the war in America came to an end. The Treaty of Paris, signed February 10, 1763, marked the definite cession of Canada to England and the end of French occupation in the valley of Lake Champlain.

Let us briefly consider the statistics concerning the post at St. Frederic. When the fort was finished in October 1731, the Sieur Hertel de Moncours became the first commandant; in November the first chaplain, Father Jean-Baptiste La Jus, entered upon his duties. The chronicle of St. Frederic naturally falls into three periods, of approximately ten years each. From 1731 to 1741, seven commandants and five priests are on duty; the register contains 40 baptisms and 14 deaths; from 1741 to 1751 there are again seven commandants and four priests; the records show 93 baptisms, 15 marriages, and 55 deaths; from 1751 until the end of the occupation in 1759 we have but one commandant and five priests (counting the two substitutes); the parish record shows 110 baptisms, 16 marriages, and 129 burials; 75 of the burials were during the terrible year of 1756. To sum up, during the 28 years of its existence, the post of St. Frederic saw 13 commandants and 13 parish priests. (Was 13 its unlucky number?) The parish register records totals of 243 baptisms, 31 marriages, and 198 deaths.

When it comes to evaluating the importance of the post, we have a problem to consider; the documents, with the exception of the register, inform us only of the military importance of Fort St. Frederic, very briefly or not at all of the population of the villages on both shores of the lake. The parish register gives no sort of census, only statistics of baptisms, marriages, and deaths; it does mention, however, two cemeteries in which we know there were 198 interments, concrete evidence that the settlers considered this their permanent home. The land grants in the neighborhood are of little aid, for

66. Crockett: *History of Lake Champlain*, pp. 105-106.

only too often we cannot discover whether or not the proprietor settled on his land. We must then search elsewhere, among the journals of travelers, who saw the post on friendly visits, or among the private papers of military leaders.

Kalm, the Swedish savant, did not arrive until 1749. This is unfortunate for us, as his inquiring mind would have secured and given us precious information concerning the early years of the post. According to his *Journal* both shores of the lake near the fort supported a good number of settlers, and they expected 50 additional families that fall; Captain Stoddard agrees with Kalm on this point, writing in 1750. The famous Robert Rogers speaks constantly of barns and houses in the vicinity, and of villages on both shores of the lake; of fields under cultivation extending some distance both north and south. Without fear of contradiction we may state that this region had a considerable population.

We have, however, other sources of information in the findings of the American historians who studied, in the early nineteenth century, the mute evidence of abandoned homes. Their investigations were made before all physical traces of settlement had been obliterated by time and the elements, if not by vandals. They were able to consult survivors, who held in memory the life of the settlements and the struggle which ended their existence. From their studies it is clear that there were several locations where traces of French occupation were still to be seen: Isle La Motte, St. Frederic, Chimney Point, Pointe du Détour, Rouses Point, the mouths of the Chazy and Missisquoi Rivers and Otter Creek, Carillon, Colchester Point, and Malletts Bay. Carillon had only a military existence, in reality very short, from 1755 to 1759; there was no village.

St. Frederic and Chimney Point[67]

Governor Tryon of New York wrote to Lord Dartmouth: "When the French, on the approach of Sir Jeffrey Amherst in 1759, abandoned Crown Point, there were found no ancient possessions, nor any improvements worthy of consideration, on either side of the lake. The chief were in the environs of the fort, and seemed intended for the accomodation of the garrisons."[68] The French had burned their houses before leaving; as for "ancient possessions," the settlement was only twenty-eight years old.

67. See pages 232-235 of this study.
68. Swift: *History of Middlebury and Addison County*, pp. 44-50.

Peter Kalm notes that in 1749 "the country is inhabited within a French mile of the fort."[69] Captain Stevens speaks of eighteen houses, "some on each side of the water."[70] Captain Stoddard in 1750 tells us that "since the peace there are fourteen farms . . ., and I was informed that by the next fall, several more families were coming here to settle."[71] Reverend Mr. Norton, an English chaplain, observes that during his imprisonment at St. Frederic "his lodging was in a house on the opposite side of the lake from the fort."[72]

Three of the stones forming the arched roof of the covered way at Fort St. Frederic (the first, the second, and the keystone), are owned by the Hon. Millard F. Barnes of Chimney Point. His grandfather made use of the ruined fort in veneering with brick the old tavern on Chimney Point built on the site of the "Fort de Pieux" of 1730. (See the De Lery Map.) It seems that Fort St. Frederic was the third fort constructed in this region: the "little stone fort" of Captain Jacobus De Warm (1690), the "Fort de Pieux" on Chimney Point (1730), and Fort St. Frederic on Crown Point (1731). The "Fort de Pieux" was apparently built on the site of De Warm's stone fort, as a stone wall two feet thick (incorporated in the home of Judge Barnes) joins at right angles another wall five feet in front of the front wall of the house; this seems to form one of the corners of De Warm's fort. The present stairway leading from the ground floor to the second floor was built by Judge Barnes' grandfather, who told his grandson that originally access to the upper floor was by ladder, which was drawn up afterward for protection; from the second to the third floor evidence of a stairway may be seen. During the eighteenth century in the Champlain valley, the French did not construct homes of more than one floor; only fortresses were raised to such a height. Timothy Dwight and Isaac Weld visited the Tavern and spoke of the very old building (about 1790-1795).

There are many cellar-holes of French homes still to be seen on and near Chimney Point,—two on the Strong farm north of the Point, three or four on the Vallance farm (still farther north), and a dozen or more on the Barnes estate. The mill stood where the east pier of the Lake Champlain Bridge was placed; the mill-wheel is to be seen at the foot of the slope in front of the Barnes home,

69. Kalm: *Travels into North America*, II, p. 208.
70. Crockett: *History of Vermont*, I, p. 130.
71. *Proceedings*, New York State Historical Society, X, pp. 108-113.
72. Parkman: *Half Century of Conflict*, II, p. 268.

near the wall of the old store-building. In excavating for the Lake Champlain Bridge, the floor of an old French home was unearthed, the fireplace and foundation stones being uncovered; there was a cemetery just north of the Bridge.[73]

"Proofs of a populous and continuous occupation are not wanting. The shores of Bulwagga Bay (called by the French 'Baie Saint-Frédéric') for many rods were graded and artificially sloped to the water. Signs of very old fences and enclosures, such as gardens and dooryards, are still to be seen (in 1889). In some enclosures, aged fruit trees were standing within the memory of the present owners. A street made of broken stone, like a macadamized road, can be traced. Ruins of cellars on each side of this street are also visible, in such proximity to each other as to indicate close settlement; while the narrowness of the street strongly suggests similar avenues in ancient French-Canadian villages. Sidewalks of flagging considerably worn and two large graveyards are found. The cemeteries of Fort St. Frederic were located on the Nadeau farm, just over the knoll from the present entrance gates of the Amherst Fort, and on a site three miles south. Settlers after the Revolution found a large tract, miles in extent, with evidence of a high type of cultivation; in these same fields now overgrown by forests, may be seen asparagus, herbs and bushes of man's cultivation."[74]

As for the population of the villages, I believe that the most reasonable figure is that of 800 persons, men, women and children, settled in the three villages dependent on Fort St. Frederic, namely, the one in the immediate vicinity of the post, and the two on the eastern shore of the lake.[75]

---

73. Invaluable data concerning these settlements have been furnished by the Hon. Millard F. Barnes of Chimney Point, whose recollections of conversations with his grandfather (a resident here about 1785) and his father were given to me in personal interviews. Judge Barnes preserves in his home many priceless relics of the French occupation of the region.

74. Murray: *Lake Champlain and Its Shores*, pp. 90-92.

75. Murray speaks of "5000 souls"; doubtless he refers to the time when Montcalm's army was stationed at the fort. Reid: *Lake George and Lake Champlain*, pp. 224-227, exaggerates in my opinion, in giving "1500 to 3000 persons." Hemenway: *Vermont Historical Gazetteer*, I, p. 660, gives the most reasonable estimate, that of 800 persons.

EVIDENCE points to French occupation of Colchester Point at the time of the construction of Fort Sainte-Anne in 1666. Captain John Schuyler, returning from La Prairie de la Madeleine, spent the night of August 25, 1690, at the point, then called "Pointe au Sable."[1]

Colchester Point was included in the grant to René Boucher de la Perrière, July 6, 1734. The grantee was a member of the little army of sons of Pierre Boucher, Seigneur de Grosbois and de la Boucherville, and his wife, Jeanne Crevier de la Meslé: Pierre de Boucherville, Lambert de Grand-Pré, Joachim de Montarville, Ignace de Grosbois, René-Jean de Montburn, Jean-Baptiste de Niverville and Charles de Grosbois; there were also Philippe and Nicolas, priests, and five daughters among his children who lived. René Boucher de la Perrière (1668-1742) served as officer of the colonial troops from about 1700 until his retirement on account of age; as ensign he joined in the leadership of the expedition of 1708 against Haverhill and Deerfield, went on a special mission to Albany in 1710, and became commandant of Fort St. Frederic in 1732. By his wife, Françoise Malhiot, he left two children, a daughter and a son, both of whom married children of François-Antoine Pécaudy de Contrecoeur.

At least three houses were built on the Point during the French occupation. The first English settler, Benjamin Boardman, on his arrival in 1789, found the remains of stone fortifications and other defensive works, three chimney bottoms (one on the Porter place, the others on the Spear farm located on the south side of the extreme point) and remains of walls near them. On these sites have been found leaden bullets, Indian arrowheads, rusted iron utensils, and pieces of silver and copper coin; two skeletons were washed out of the earth near-by in 1867. Gardens with red and white currant bushes of great age, planted in rows, were also found, and extensive clearings were seen in several places.

It is not improbable that the French occupied Colchester Point when they extended their fortifications toward the south in 1666. It would have been in keeping with their plan to make the lake a safe highway from New France to Alburgh. The Point was one day's journey south from Fort Sainte-Anne, and commanded an extensive

1. *Doc. Col. Hist. N. Y.*, II, p. 288.

view over the lake, making a surprise attack impossible. The first English map of the lake, published after the close of the war, indicated both the point in West Alburgh and Colchester Point as "Windmill Point." It is difficult to see any reason for the name unless from the fact that a mill stood there either then or formerly. Dr. E. Tudor, native of East Windsor, Connecticut, was surgeon with the 43rd Regiment of Foot, 1759, serving with Wolfe at Quebec. He told his grandchildren (Hon. John W. Strong and Mrs. Emeline Hard of Ferrisburg) that there was a French blockhouse fort on Colchester Point at the time of the English invasion of Canada, 1759.[2]

The mouth of the Winooski River just south of Colchester Point was the Champlain terminus of the great "French Road" to the Connecticut River and eastern Massachusetts settlements; from the beginning of the eighteenth century to the end of the French régime, the French Road was constantly in use; the name itself, given by the English, indicates the frequency of travel by this route. A fortified camp at the end of the arduous journey from the Connecticut River is quite in keeping with the French mode of travel. Soon the homes of a few settlers grew up near these defenses, the colonists acting as garrison in time of need. When the military forces left the Champlain valley in the summer of 1759, the settlers of Colchester Point joined their compatriots from Carillon and St. Frederic in the retreat to the Richelieu River.

A short distance north of Colchester Point, another vestige of French settlement is found at the head of Malletts Bay. Here was the home of Captain [?] Mallet, of whom little is known; a Frenchman, he had probably settled there under a French grant many years before the Revolution; he was known to be there from 1774 until his death in 1790. Captain Mallet (whose name probably should be written "Maillet" or "Malet") was apparently a man of considerable independence of spirit; he feared no one and acknowledged allegiance neither to the English King nor to the American colonies. It seems that he never accepted the Treaty of Peace which gave control over his lands to the English; his sympathies were on the side of rebellion, for he welcomed spies and smugglers into his home all through the Revolutionary period.[3]

2. Hemenway: *Vermont Historical Gazetteer*, I, pp. 754-756; article by the Hon. David Read.

3. Hemenway: *Vermont Historical Gazetteer*, I, p. 761. Crockett: *History of Vermont*, I, p. 241.

The proximity of Captain Mallet's tavern-home to the ruined defenses at Colchester Point would seem to indicate that he had been connected with the settlers of that hamlet in some capacity. Surveys were not too accurately made in those troubled times, but it is reasonably certain that Captain Mallet's home was also included within the limits of the seigniory of La Perrière.

CHAPTER XIV. *Conclusion*

FROM the arrival of Samuel de Champlain in 1609 until the conquest by the English in 1759 the only permanent inhabitants of the valley of Lake Champlain were French. It is true that the Iroquois exercised a sort of indeterminate sovereignty over this valley for some centuries; they did not, however, have permanent villages because of the ease of attack by way of the lake; for them it was only a hunting-ground. The vestiges of Indian occupation prove that it was a favorite hunting-ground but never a continuous home of the tribe. After 1650 when the Algonquins were driven out of New England and began to look for a new home, Vermont became a no-man's land in which neither Iroquois nor Algonquins wished to remain as the highway of the lake rendered the establishment of villages too dangerous. The Algonquins withdrew into New France where they were welcomed by the French governors and the Church; the Iroquois were content to remain in their vast territories along the Mohawk River and on the shores of Lake Ontario.

By right of discovery and exploration by Champlain the valley of the lake belonged to France and formed an integral part of New France. After the expeditions of MM. de Tracy and de Courcelles in 1666, the French learned much from traders and official couriers concerning the geography of this region and became aware of its value in the expansion of the colony. Beginning in 1684 the cartographers indicated the frontier of New France by a line drawn east and west through the southern end of Lake Champlain. Plans for the development of this territory were suggested in rapid succession toward the end of the century but remained indefinite during times of war.

From the vague ideas of the pioneers, by the beginning of the eighteenth century something concrete began to take shape. A vast and important province was to be established in the region south of the St. Lawrence River, bordered on the east by the Connecticut River, and on the west by Lake Ontario; on the north the St. Lawrence would form a natural frontier, but on the south would be only the English. It was decided, therefore, to push the frontier toward the south as far as possible, leaving to the English only what it would be impossible to hold. The capital and metropolis of this rich province would be located on that point where Champlain had defeated the Iroquois, that cape which juts into the lake; it was admirably situated for fortification and control of travel through the valley; a fort built on that point would protect the growing settlements of the whole valley and the inhabitants could develop their farms without fear, protected by the garrison of the fort. The only obstacle to this project for colonization was the determination of the English to expand into the same territory as soon as the threat of French domination became evident. The French were the first to settle in the valley of Lake Champlain, claiming title by right of discovery, but after long years of struggle they were driven out by the English in 1759.

A question is involved, the discussion of which has no part in this chronicle, a question which has puzzled diplomats and statesmen through the ages: the old, old question of justice between the rights of discovery and priority of occupation and those of conquest and superior power.

When the French soldiers and settlers departed, they left no physical traces of their one hundred and fifty years of occupation other than the mute and deserted ruins of their homes and military posts, surrounded by the cultivated fields which represent civilization. They did leave, however, reminders of their life in this region which have endured even to our own day. The names of La Moelle, Valcour, Grand Isle, Isle La Motte, and many others ring in our ears, permanent traces of French occupation. In written history Montcalm, Lusignan, Contrecoeur, Marin, Hertel, Saint-Pierre, Celoron de Blainville, de Tracy, de Courcelles, and many other names famous in the chronicles of Canada, belong also to the history of Lake Champlain, of New York, and of Vermont, especially of Vermont whose very name is French.

A civilization cannot entirely disappear; it is cherished in the memory of those who come after its apparent extermination. The English, it is true, drove the French from the Champlain valley; then came the war of the Revolution. After the Treaty of 1783,

Appendix A. *French Routes Through Vermont*

I. Iroquois Route—Albany Route (18th century).
Richelieu River and Lake Champlain:

A. "The Kayadrosseras Trail": from Carillon through Lake George; portage of a few miles to the Hudson River at Glens Falls; through the villages of Moreau, Wilton, and Galway, reaching the Mohawk River near Amsterdam.

B. "Saratoga Trail": from Whitehall by Wood Creek to Fort Sainte-Anne; portage of ten miles to Fort Edward; then by the Hudson River to Schuylerville.

    1. By Fish Creek, Saratoga Lake, Kayadrosseras River and the Mourningkill to Ballston Lake; then by Eel Creek to the Mohawk River near Amsterdam.

    2. By continuing along the Hudson River to Albany, center of English activity against New France.

II. Route to the English settlements of the Connecticut River.
Richelieu River and Lake Champlain:

A. "French Road" or "Trunk Line" (so called by the English of Massachusetts): by the Winooski River to the Forks in the town of Washington.

    1. By Stevens Branch; portage to the sources of the White River and thence to the Connecticut.

    2. By the Winooski to the village of Plainfield; portage to the sources of the Wells River and thence to the Connecticut.

B. From Fort Saint-Frederic:

    1. By Otter Creek and Mill River to its source; portage to the sources of the Black River and thence to the Connecticut at Fort No. 4.

    2. By Otter Creek to its source; portage to the West River in Londonderry, and thence to the Connecticut at Fort Dummer (Brattleboro).

    3. By Lake Champlain to Whitehall, then by the Poultney River to its source; portage to the sources of the West River and thence to the Connecticut.

III. Route to the English settlements of New Hampshire and Boston.
St. Lawrence River by the Saint-François River and the Magog to Lake Memphremagog:

A. By the Clyde River to Island Pond; portage to the sources of the Nulhegan River and thence to the Connecticut; then by the Ammonoosuc and Androscoggin Rivers to the villages on the Penobscot.

B. By the Barton River to Crystal Lake; portage to the Sutton Lakes, down the Passumpsic River to the Connecticut, from which several trails led to the sources of the Merrimack River which led to Dover, Haverhill, and Boston.

Year of Appointment	Name and Title
1608	Champlain, Samuel de
1635	Châteaufort, Marc-Antoine de Bras-de-Fer, sieur de
1636	Montmagny, Charles-Jacques Huault, sieur de
1648	D'Ailleboust de Coulonge, Louis
1651	Lauzon, Jean de
1656	Lauzon, Charles de, sieur de Charny
1657	D'Ailleboust de Coulonge, Louis
1658	Argenson, Pierre de Voyer, vicomte d'
1661	Avaugour, Pierre du Bois, baron d'
1663	Saffray, Augustin de Mézy, sieur de
1665	Courcelles, Daniel de Rémy, sieur de
1672	Frontenac, Louis de Buade de Pallnau, vicomte de
1682	La Barre, Joseph-Antoine Lefebvre, sieur de
1685	Denonville, Jacques de Brisay, marquis de
1689	Frontenac, Louis de Buade de Pallnau, vicomte de
1698	Callières de Bonnevue, Louis-Hector de
1703	Vaudreuil, Philippe de Rigaud, marquis de (administrator)
1705	Vaudreuil, Phillipe de Rigaud, marquis de
1725	Longueuil, Charles Le Moyne, baron de (administrator)
1726	Beauharnois, Charles, marquis de
1745	La Jonquière, Jacques-Pierre Taffanel, marquis de (prisoner in London, 1746-1748)
1747	La Galissonnière, Roland-Michel Barrin, comte de
1749	La Jonquière, Jacques-Pierre Taffanel, marquis de
1752	Longueuil, Charles Le Moyne, 2d baron de (administrator)
1752	DuQuesne de Menneville, Michel-Ange, marquis
1755	Vaudreuil, Pierre-François de Rigaud, marquis de Cavagnal

INTENDANTS

1663	Robert, Louis	Daughter married nephew of Colbert
1665	Talon, Jean-Baptiste	Cousin of Louis Phélypeaux de Pont-chartrain, father of the chancellor
1668	Bouteroue, Claude de	Friend of the Minister Colbert
1670	Talon, Jean-Baptiste	
1675	Du Chesneau, Jacques	Aunt married M. Voyer d'Argenson
1683	Meulles, Jacques de	Married Mlle. Bégon, sister-in-law of Colbert; uncle of Intendant Bégon
1686	Bochart de Champigny, Jean	Nephew of the Duc de Choiseul
1702	Beauharnois, François de	Cousin of the Chancellor Phélypeaux de Pontchartrain; relative of the governor
1705	Raudot, Jacques	Mother was Mlle. Talon
	Raudot, Antoine-Denis	Son of the preceding; co-intendant

1712	Bégon, Michel	Nephew of Colbert; married the sister of the Intendant de Beauharnois
1724	Robert, Edmé-Nicolas	Nephew of the Intendant Robert
1725	Chazelles, Guillaume de	
1726	Du Puy, Claude-Thomas	Relative of the Comte Voyer d'Argenson
1729	Hocquart, Gilles	Relative of the Colberts and Talons
1748	Bigot, François	Cousin of the Marquis de Puysieux and of the Marshal d'Estrées

APPENDIX C. *Commandants and Chaplains at Fort St. Frederic*

COMMANDANTS

Date	Name
1731, October	Pierre Hertel, sieur de Moncours
1732, November	René Boucher, seigneur de la Perrière
1733	Claude Hertel, sieur de Beaulac
1734	Daniel Migeon de Bransac, seigneur de la Gauchetière
1736	Pierre de St. Ours, sieur de St. Ours
1739	Paul-Joseph Le Moyne, chevalier de Longueuil et de Soulanges
1739	François Lefebvre, sieur Duplessis-Fabert
1741, July (also 1734-1736)	François-Antoine Pécaudy de Contrecoeur, seigneur de Pancalon
1743, July	Joseph-Michel Le Gardeur de Repentigny, sieur de Montesson-Croisille
1746	Pierre-Jacques Payen de Chavois, seigneur de Noyan
1747	Pierre-Joseph Celoron, sieur de Blainville
1747, October	Charles de Sabrevois de Bleury, seigneur de Sabrevois
1749	Paul-Louis Dazemard, seigneur de Lusignan
1750	Frederic-Louis Herbin
1751, August	Paul-Louis Dazemard, seigneur de Lusignan

CHAPLAINS

1732, November	Jean-Baptiste La Jus
1733	Pierre-Baptiste Resche
1735, March	Bernardin de Gannes
1735, November	Emmanuel Crespel
1736, October	Pierre Verquaillié
1741, May	Daniel Normandin
1743, November	Alexis du Buron
1746	Bonaventure Carpentier
1747, April	Hippolyte Collet
1754, November	Didace Cliche
(Nov. 4, 1755	Elzéar Maugé)
1758, July	Antoine Deperet
(October, 1758	Denis Baron)

BIOGRAPHICAL INDEX

to

The French Occupation of the Champlain Valley from 1609 to 1759

BIOGRAPHICAL INDEX

Bécancour, Pierre Robineau, sieur de—Officer: son of René Robineau de Portneuf, baron de Bécancour, and Marguerite-Philippe Daneau de Muy: bapt., Montreal, Aug. 19, 1708: married, Montreal, Apr. 22, 1748, Marie-Louise Dandonneau Du Sablé (q.v.)

Bedout, Jean-Antoine—Royal Councillor and physician: son of Jean Bedout and Marie Begury of St. Rémy: married, Quebec, Feb. 10, 1744, Marie-Françoise (bapt., Quebec, Apr. 20, 1724), daughter of Claude Barolet and Françoise Dumontier

Belestre, Pierre Picoté de—Resident of Montreal: married Marie Pars (born, 1638: buried, Montreal, Nov. 3, 1684): buried, Montreal, Jan. 30, 1679

Belestre, François-Marie Picoté de—Son of the preceding: officer, chevalier, captain: bapt., Montreal, Feb. 5, 1677: married (1), Montreal, Aug. 24, 1709, Anne-Françoise Bouthier (1689–1710): (2), Montreal, May 27, 1714, Marie-Catherine (born, 1676: married [1], Batiscan, May 3, 1696, Jean Cuillerier: buried, Lachine, Feb. 26, 1731), daughter of Antoine Trotier des Ruisseaux and Catherine Lefebvre: buried, Detroit, Oct. 9, 1729.

Berthier, Alexandre—Captain in the regiment of Carignan-Salières: son of Pierre Berthier and Marguerite Bariac of St. Jacques de Bergerac, Périgueux: born, 1638: abjuration, Quebec, Oct. 8, 1665: commandant at Fort St. Jean, 1666: seigneur de Berthier and de Bellechasse, 1672/3: married, Quebec, Oct. 11, 1672, Marie, daughter of Charles Le Gardeur de Tilly and Catherine Juchereau: chief of militia, 1687: died before 1709

Blainville, Jean-Baptiste Celoron, sieur de—Lieutenant of the marine: son of Antoine Celoron and Marie Rémy of St. Sauveur, Paris: born, 1644: married (1), Lachine, Nov. 29, 1686, Hélène (born, 1656: married [1], Montreal, Aug. 23, 1676, Antoine de la Fresnaye de Brucy: buried, Montreal, Nov. 23, 1701), daughter of Pierre Picoté de Belestre and Marie Pars: (2), Montreal, Jan. 14, 1703, Geneviève Damours des Chaufours (1673-1703): (3), Montreal, Sept. 25, 1704, Geneviève-Gertrude Le Gardeur de Tilly (1666-1750): chevalier de St. Louis: buried, Montreal, June 6, 1735

Blainville, Pierre-Joseph Celoron, sieur de—Son of the preceding: chevalier and major of Detroit: bapt., Montreal, Dec. 29, 1693: married (1), Montreal, Dec. 30, 1724, Marie-Madeleine (bapt., Montreal, Dec. 18, 1704), daughter of Maurice Blondeau and Suzanne Charbonnier: (2), Montreal, Oct. 13, 1743, Catherine (1722-1797), daughter of François Eury de la Perelle and Charlotte Aubert de la Chenaye: died, after 1755

married, Montreal, Jan. 21, 1737, Jeanne-Charlotte (born, 1715), daughter of François-Antoine Pécaudy de Contrecoeur and Jeanne de St. Ours

Boucher, Jean-Baptiste—Sieur de Niverville: son of Jean-Baptiste Boucher de Niverville and Marguerite-Thérèse Hertel de Cournoyer: born, 1716: married, Montreal, Sept. 7, 1745, Marguerite (born, 1717), daughter of Frédéric-Louis Herbin and Louise-Françoise Lambert-Dumont: (2), Montreal, Apr. 23, 1755, Marie-Anne (bapt., Montreal, Dec. 8, 1729), daughter of Raymond Baby and Thérèse Lecompte-Dupré

Boucher de Niverville, Louis-Pierre—Sieur de Montizambert: brother of the preceding: bapt., Boucherville, Apr. 30, 1722: married, Detroit, about 1758, Elizabeth-Caroline Hate (Kate): officer: cadet in garrison at Fort St. Frederic, 1742

Boucher de Niverville, Marie-Anne—Sister of the preceding: bapt., Boucherville, 1719: married, 1741, Louis Herbin, captain at Fort St. Frederic

Boucher, Joseph, chevalier de Niverville—Brother of the preceding: born, Chambly, Sept. 22, 1715: bapt., Chambly, Jan. 25, 1716: married, Three Rivers, Oct. 5, 1757, Marie-Joseph, daughter of François Châtelain 143

Bougainville, Louis-Antoine, chevalier de—Son of a notary: advocate at the Parlement de Paris: captain and aide of the Marquis de Montcalm: chevalier de St. Louis: born, Paris, about 1729: in Canada, 1756-1760: commandant at Isle aux Noix, 1760: distinguished naval officer during the American Revolution: governor of Brest, 1790: died, Aug. 31, 1811

Bourbon, Jean, sieur—Son of Jean Bourbon and Antoinette Poivre of St. Etienne, Clermont: born, 1653: married, Boucherville, Feb. 27, 1680, Marie Benoît: killed by the Iroquois: buried, La Prairie, Dec. 5, 1690

Bourdet, Marguerite—Daughter of Nicolas Bourdet and Marianne Jacoti-Beausoleil: born, about 1723: married, St. Frederic, Nov. 14, 1741, Antoine Breilly 137

Bourdon, Jean—Sieur de St. François: engineer and attorney for the King: arrived with Father Le Sueur de St. Sauveur, Quebec, Aug. 8, 1634: obtained seigniories of Dombourg and Neuville, 1637 and 1639: drew first map of Canada, 1641: man of high reputation, honesty and intelligence: married (1), Quebec, Sept. 9, 1635, Jacqueline Potel (buried, Quebec, Sept. 11, 1654): (2), Quebec, Aug. 21, 1655, Anne

Douville, Michel Dagneau, sieur—Ensign and cadet in the company of M. Mine: married, Sorel, May 18, 1688, Marie (bapt., Quebec, Aug. 24, 1670), daughter of Isaac Lamy and Marie-Madeleine de Cheuraineville: buried, Montreal, Mar. 24, 1753

Douville, Alexandre Dagneau, sieur—Son of the preceding: bapt., Sorel, May 13, 1698: married (1), Montreal, Aug. 7, 1730, Marie-Anne, daughter of Nicolas-Antoine Coulon de Villiers and Angélique Jarret de Verchères: (2), about 1740, Marie (born, 1691), daughter of Antoine Courtemanche and Marguerite Vaudry

Douville, Marie-Louise Dagneau—Daughter of the preceding: bapt., Montreal, Feb. 16, 1734: married, Montreal, Apr. 23, 1759, Pierre-Philippe d'Aubrespy:

Douville, Marie-Claire Dagneau—Aunt of the preceding: bapt., Isle Dupas, Aug. 12, 1706: married, Montreal, June 23, 1736, Pierre de St. Ours: buried, Montreal, June 5, 1743:

Du Bois-d'Esgriselles, Jean Baptiste—Chaplain of the regiment of Carignan-Salières: still in New France, 1671

Dufresne, Jean-Baptiste Janvrin—Royal notary and official surveyor: son of Nicolas Janvrin-Dufresne and Marie-Madeleine Berson-Châtillon: bapt., Montreal, Aug. 2, 1695: married (1), Quebec, Oct. 16, 1722, Marie-Anne (1704-1739), daughter of Charles Damours de Louvières and Marie-Anne-Louise Thibaudeau: (2), Montreal, Nov. 24, 1744, Anne-Françoise (1706-1745), daughter of Jean-Baptiste Crevier-Duvernay and Charlotte Chorel de St. Romain: (3), 1745/6, Angélique Boisseau: buried, Pointe aux Trembles, Montreal, Oct. 14, 1750:

Dumesnil, Marie-Elisabeth—Daughter of Pierre Dumesnil and Marguerite Duchesnay: bapt., Quebec, July 9, 1723: married, St. Frederic, Nov. 14, 1741, François Moquier:

Duplessis, Antoine Lubet—Storekeeper at Fort St. Frederic: born, 1701:

Duplessis-Fabert, François Lefebvre, sieur—Captain: son of François Lefebvre Duplessis-Fabert and Marie-Madeleine Chorel de St. Romain: bapt., Champlain, Nov. 11, 1689: married, Montreal, Dec. 31, 1713, Catherine-Geneviève (born, 1689), daughter of Jean-François-Xavier Le Pelletier and Geneviève Le Tendre

chois: in France, 1757: honorary member of the Superior Council, Feb. 1, 1758

Forestier, Antoine—Surgeon: son of Jean Forestier and Françoise Ricard of Severac-le-Château, Rhodez: born, 1646: married, Montreal, Nov. 25, 1670, Marie-Madeleine (1656-1719), daughter of Robert Cavelier Deslauriers and Adrienne Duvivier: buried, Montreal, Nov. 7, 1717

Foucault, François—King's storekeeper and Councillor: son of Eusèbe Foucault and Catherine Catelan of Bayonne: born, 1689: married, Quebec, June 3, 1718, Catherine (1689-1731), daughter of Denis Sabourin-Chauniers and Catherine Nafrechon

"Frappe d'abord"—Soldier in the company of M. de la Perrière: buried,

Frémin, Jacques—Jesuit: Missionary to the Iroquois: at Fort Ste. Anne,

Frontenac, Louis de Buade de Pallnau, comte de—Governor of New

Gabriel ("Bosoleille"), Jean—Soldier in the company of "St. George de

Gannes, Louis-François de—Sieur de Falaise: lieutenant: chevalier de St. Louis: son of Louis de Gannes, sieur de Falaise et de Rosne, and Marie-Françoise Le Bloy of Buxeuil, Poitiers: born, 1666: married (1), about 1688, Barbe Denys de la Trinité, widow of Antoine Pécaudy de Contrecoeur: (2), Montreal, July 12, 1695, Louise Le Gardeur de Tilly: (3), about 1700, Marguerite (1680-1760), daughter of Michel Le Neuf de la Vallière and Françoise Denys de la Trinité: major of Acadia

Gannes, Charles-Thomas de—Chevalier de Falaise: lieutenant: major at Fort St. Frederic, 1743: son of the preceding: born, 1714: married, Three Rivers, Oct. 23, 1749, Angélique (born, 1726), daughter of Nicolas-Antoine Coulon de Villiers and Angélique Jarret de Verchères: at

Gâtineau, Jean-Baptiste, sieur de—Captain of militia: son of Nicolas

Hertel, Zacharie-François—Sieur de la Fresnière: son of the preceding: chevalier: reserve lieutenant: captain in the marine: wounded at the capture of Sementile: born, 1665: married, Three Rivers, Jan. 17, 1695, Marie-Charlotte (born, 1677: buried, Nov. 29, 1756), daughter of Michel Godefroy de Linctot and Perrine Picoté de Belestre: buried, Montreal, June 20, 1752

Hertel, Jacques—Sieur de Cournoyer: brother of the preceding: captain in the marine: bapt., Three Rivers, Mar. 19, 1667: married, Three Rivers, Marguerite-Thérèse (1667-1739), daughter of Michel Godefroy de Linctot and Perrine Picoté de Belestre: buried, Three Rivers, Sept. 4, 1648

Hertel, Jean-Baptiste—Sieur de Rouville: brother of the preceding: captain and commandant at Fort de Toulouse, Cape Breton, 1720: lieutenant in the marine: chevalier de St. Louis: bapt., Three Rivers, Oct. 26, 1668: married (1), Three Rivers, Nov. 23, 1698, Jeanne (1683-1700), daughter of Jacques Dubois and Jeanne Auber: (2), Quebec, Feb. 6, 1708, Marie-Anne (1685-1745), daughter of Gervais Beaudoin and Anne Aubert: died, after 1720

Hertel, Louis—Sieur de St. Louis: brother of the preceding: bapt., Three Rivers, May 14, 1673: married, Montreal, Aug. 21, 1730, Marie-Catherine (bapt., Montreal, Sept. 1, 1692), daughter of Jean-Baptiste d'Ailleboust des Musseaux and Anne Le Picard: buried, St. Antoine de Chambly, Oct. 14, 1757

Hertel, René—Sieur de Chambly: brother of the preceding: bapt., Three Rivers, Mar. 26, 1675: killed by the English, Haverhill, Aug. 29, 1708

Hertel, Claude—Sieur de Beaulac: brother of the preceding: bapt., Three Rivers, Jan. 2, 1682: married, Geneviève (bapt., Quebec, June 7, 1707), daughter of Etienne Miranbeau and Jeanne Levasseur

Hertel, Pierre—Sieur de Moncours: brother of the preceding: bapt., Three Rivers, Mar. 19, 1687: officer: married, Montreal, Nov. 17, 1721, Thérèse-Judith (1702-1738), daughter of Paul d'Ailleboust de

brother of the preceding: born, 1711/2: married (1), Montreal, Dec.
10, 1742, Marie-Anne (buried, Montreal, Jan. 3, 1753), daughter of
Jean-Baptiste Hervieux: (2), Montreal, Sept. 3, 1757, Marie-Josette
(bapt., Montreal, Nov. 18, 1714: married [1], Jacques Le Gardeur de
St. Pierre), daughter of Charles Guillimin and Françoise Lemaître-
Lamorille: (3), Montreal, Apr. 9, 1774, Marie-Marguerite, daughter
of Pierre Boucher de Boucherville and Marguerite Raimbault: one of
the seven survivors of the wreck of the *Auguste*, 1761: at Longueuil,
Mar. 28, 1762: commandant of the Canadians with Gen. Burgoyne,
1778: member, Legislative Council of Quebec, 1775-1784

La Durantaye, Olivier Morel de—Ensign: lieutenant: captain in the regiment of Carignan-Salières: son of Thomas Morel de la Durantaye and
Alliesse du Houssay de la Lande-Carbissaye: born, 1644: in France,
1667-1670: married, Quebec, Sept. 14, 1670, Françoise (buried, Quebec,
Sept. 15, 1719), daughter of Denis Duquet de la Chenaye and Catherine Gautier: seigneur de Bellechasse, de la Durantaye and de Kamouraska: officer with the Iroquois expeditions, 1684 and 1687: reserve
captain, 1689: commander of a battalion of militia, 1696: partisan of
Vaudreuil against Callières, 1698-1699: member of Council of Quebec, 1703: died, about 1727

La Durantaye, Charles-Alexandre Morel de—Chevalier de la Durantaye:
grandson of the preceding: son of Louis-Joseph Morel de la Durantaye and Elisabeth Rasné-Béquard: born, about 1700: married (1),
Beaumont, Feb. 21, 1724, Marie (bapt., Beaumont, Nov. 23, 1697:
buried, Kamouraska, Nov. 2, 1745), daughter of Charles Couillard
de Beaumont and Louise Couture: (2), Kamouraska, Apr. 26, 1746,
Marthe (widow of Pierre Hayot: buried, Beaumont, Nov. 4, 1748),
daughter of Barthélemi Normandin-Lajoie and Marie-Françoise Du-
pille: (3), after 1748, Marie-Anne Ouimet: buried, St. Thomas, Mar.
31, 1774

Lafleur—see Poupart

Lafon (Lafond), Simon—Soldier and surgeon: son of Jean Lafond and
Pétronille Chailla of St. Martin du Bois, Bordeaux: born, 1710: married, Montreal, Jan. 7, 1738, Marie-Anne (bapt., Montreal, Nov. 22,
1716), daughter of Pierre Lamotte and Marie-Anne St. Yves: resident
at St. Frederic, 1742 152

LaFontaine, Jacques de—Sieur de Belcour: secretary to the governor: son
of Jean de la Fontaine and Bernardine Jouin of Versailles: married (1),
Quebec, Oct. 24, 1728, Charlotte (bapt., Quebec, Apr. 30, 1704: buried,
Quebec, Nov. 22, 1749), daughter of François-Joseph Bissot de la
Rivière and Marie Lambert-Dumont: (2), Lévis, Aug. 7, 1751, Gene-
viève (bapt., Quebec, Oct. 22, 1723: buried, Quebec, Jan. 10, 1756),

and Marie Nolan-Lechevalier: lieutenant, 1687: in Acadia, 1691: lieutenant, 1693: with Villebon, 1700: captain, 1706: chevalier de St. Louis, 1712: of extraordinary valor, wounded 40 times: buried, Montreal, July 10, 1737

Lambert, Françoise-Geneviève—Daughter of René-Louis Lambert and Elisabeth Pinguet de Targis: bapt., Quebec, Sept. 29, 1732: married, Quebec, Sept. 25, 1752, Charles Porlier de Vincennes

Lamothe, Marie-Anne—Daughter of Pierre Lamothe and Marie-Anne St. Yves: bapt., Montreal, Nov. 22, 1716: married, Montreal, Jan. 7, 1738, Simon Lafond

La Motte-Lussière, Pierre de St. Paul, sieur de—Captain in the regiment of Carignan-Salières: son of Jean de la Motte and Clémence Badon: born, about 1635: came to New France with M. de Tracy, 1665: built Fort Ste. Anne at Isle La Motte, 1666: commandant at Fort Ste. Anne, 1666-1669: at Montreal, 1669-1670: returned to France, 1670

Landriaux, Louis—Surgeon in the company of M. de Lusignan: son of Louis Landriaux and Marie-Louise Bouroud of Luçon, Poitou: married, St. Frederic, June 8, 1756, Marie-Anne (bapt., Montreal, Nov. 30, 1739), daughter of Jean-Baptiste Prud'homme and Marie-Anne Tessier

Langy, Jacques-Joseph Levraux, sieur de—Officer: son of Léon-Joseph 157 Levraux de Langy and Marguerite Trotier: bapt., Batiscan, June 19, 1708: married, before 1743, Marie-Anne (bapt., Champlain, May 29, 1717: buried, Batiscan, Jan. 30, 1755), daughter of Jean-François Chorel d'Orvilliers and Marie Couillard-Desprès: buried, Batiscan, Apr. 30, 1777

Langy (Langis), Jean-Baptiste Levraux, sieur de—Ensign: distinguished officer: half-brother of the preceding: son of Léon-Joseph Levraux de Langy and Marguerite-Gabrielle Jarret de Verchères: bapt., Batiscan, Oct. 11, 1723: married, Verchères, Feb. 14, 1756, Marie-Madeleine (bapt., Montreal, Apr. 20, 1703: married [1], Montreal, Nov. 24, 1721, Jean Jarret de Verchères), daughter of Nicolas d'Ailleboust de Mantet and Françoise-Jeanne Denys de la Ronde: "Canadian officer, active, vigilant, and always ready for the march or for distinguished action: sent to Orange to watch the English Army and found it encamped a league from the city: returned with full and important infor-

born, 1632: married, Quebec, July 11, 1656, Marguerite (1642-1722),
daughter of Jean Nicolet and Marguerite Couillard: buried, Montreal,
Sept. 8, 1709

Le Gardeur, Jean-Baptiste-René—Sieur de Repentigny: lieutenant of infantry: grandson of the preceding: son of Pierre Le Gardeur de Repentigny and Agathe de St. Per: bapt., Montreal, June 15, 1695:
married, Montreal, July 24, 1718, Catherine (bapt., Montreal, Sept.
23, 1693: buried, Montreal, Aug. 12, 1727), daughter of Charles
Juchereau de St. Denis and Denise-Thérèse Migeon de Bransac: entrusted with the discovery of the western sea, 1750: commander of the
Indians with Dieskau at Lake St. Sacrement, 1755: killed in battle,
July 8, 1755

Le Gardeur de Repentigny, Alexandre—Sieur de Montesson: lieutenant:
uncle of the preceding: son of Jean-Baptiste Le Gardeur de Repentigny
and Marguerite Nicolet de Belleborne: bapt., Quebec, Jan. 15, 1666:
killed by the Iroquois: buried, Montreal, July 22, 1692

Le Gardeur de Repentigny, Joseph-Michel—Sieur de Montesson-Croisille:
nephew of the preceding: son of Charles Le Gardeur de Croisille-Bécan-
court and Marie-Anne Robineau de Bécancour: officer: bapt., Boucherville, Dec. 30, 1716: married, Quebec, Oct. 25, 1745, Claire-Françoise
(born, 1705: married [1], Jean-Baptiste Pommereau), daughter of
Pierre Boucher de Boucherville and Charlotte Denys de la Ronde

Le Gardeur, François—Sieur de Courtemanche: brother of the preceding:
born, 1711: married, Montreal, Aug. 26, 1737, Marie-Louise (bapt.,
Montreal, Nov. 8, 1715), daughter of Pierre de St. Ours and Hélène-
Françoise Celoron de Blainville

Le Gardeur, Augustin—Sieur de Courtemanche: son of Charles Le Gardeur de Tilly and Geneviève Juchereau de Maure: bapt., Quebec, Oct.
15, 1663: married (1), Montreal, Nov. 8, 1688, Marguerite, daughter of Jacques Vaudry and Jeanne Renault: (2), Lévis, July 20, 1697,
Marie-Charlotte, daughter of Etienne Charets and Catherine Bissot de
la Rivière

Le Gardeur, Pierre-Noël—Sieur de Tilly: brother of the preceding: bapt.,
Sillery, Dec. 24, 1652: married (1), 1675, Marie-Marguerite (bapt.,
Three Rivers, Nov. 25, 1659), daughter of Claude Volant de St.
Claude and Françoise Radisson: (2), Boucherville, Nov. 24, 1680,

Marie-Madeleine (1661-1739), daughter of Pierre Boucher de Boucherville and Jeanne Crevier de la Meslé: buried, St. Antoine de Tilly, Aug. 13, 1720

Le Gardeur de Tilly, René—Sieur de Beauvais: chevalier: captain in the marine: brother of the preceding: bapt., Quebec, Oct. 3, 1660: married (1), Montreal, Sept. 19, 1694, Marie-Barbe (1670-1705), daughter of Pierre de St. Ours and Marie Mulois: (2), Montreal, Oct. 6, 1715, Madeleine (1660-1722), daughter of Jacques Marchand and Françoise Capel: (3), Montreal, Dec. 23, 1725, Louise (1682-1764), daughter of Isaac Lamy and Marie-Madeleine de Cheuraineville: buried, Montreal, Dec. 26, 1742

Le Gardeur de Tilly, Philippe-René—Sieur de Beauvais: son of the preceding: bapt., Montreal, Dec. 31, 1700

Le Gardeur de Repentigny, Jacques—Sieur de St. Pierre: officer: son of Jean-Paul Le Gardeur de St. Pierre and Marie-Josette Le Neuf de la Vallière: grandson of Jean-Baptiste Le Gardeur de Repentigny and Marguerite Nicolet de Belleborne: bapt., Montreal, Oct. 24, 1701: married, Quebec, Oct. 27, 1738, Marie-Josette (bapt., Montreal, Nov. 28, 1714: married [2], Montreal, Sept. 3, 1757, Louis-Luc de la Corne), daughter of Charles Guillimin and Françoise Lemaître-Lamorille: commanded a party of Indians with Dieskau, 1755: killed, Lake George, Sept. 8, 1755

Le Mercier, François-Joseph—Jesuit: born, Paris, Oct. 4, 1604: novitiate, 1622: came to New France, 1635: Huron Mission from 1636 until its end: Iroquois and Onondaga Missions, June 1656 and 1657: Superior of Canadian Missions, 1653-1658 and 1665-1670: vicar of Quebec, 1660: in France, 1673: Superior in Martinique: died, June 12, 1690 ..

Le Moyne, Charles—Sieur de Longueuil and de Châteaugay: son of Pierre Le Moyne and Judith Duchesne: born, 1624: arrived in Quebec, 1641: married, Montreal, May 28, 1654, Catherine "Primot" (born, 1641: adopted daughter of Antoine Primot), daughter of Guillaume Tierry and Elisabeth Messier: ennobled, July 10, 1676

Le Moyne, Jacques—Sieur de Ste. Hélène: son of the preceding: bapt., Montreal, Apr. 16, 1659: married, Montreal, Feb. 7, 1684, Philippe-Jeanne (bapt., Montreal, Sept. 19, 1672: married [2], Montreal, Dec. 13, 1691, Joseph de Monic), daughter of Philippe Carion du Fresnoy and Pétronille Maurel des Hèvres: lieutenant: buried, Quebec, Dec. 4, 1690

Le Moyne, François—Sieur de Bienville: bapt., Montreal, Mar. 10, 1666: killed by the Iroquois near Repentigny: buried, Quebec, June 7, 1691

Le Moyne, Pierre—Sieur d'Iberville: brother of the preceding: bapt., Montreal, July 20, 1661: married, Quebec, Oct. 8, 1693, Marie-Thérèse Pollet de la Combe-Pocatière: captain of frigate: governor of Louisiana, 1704: buried, Havana, July 9, 1706

Le Moyne, Paul-Joseph—Chevalier de Longueuil: nephew of the preceding: son of Charles Le Moyne, baron de Longueuil, and Claude-Elisabeth Souart d'Audoncourt: captain: governor of Three Rivers: chevalier de St. Louis: bapt., Longueuil, Sept. 19, 1701: married, Quebec, Oct. 19, 1728, Marie-Geneviève (1703-1766), daughter of Pierre-Jacques Joybert de Marsan, sieur de Soulanges, and Marie-Anne Béquart de Grandville: buried, Tours, France, May 12, 1778

Le Moyne, Charles-Jacques—3rd baron de Longueuil: officer: nephew of the preceding: son of Charles Le Moyne, 2nd baron de Longueuil, and Catherine-Charlotte Le Goüès de Gray: bapt., Longueuil, July 26, 1724: married, Montreal, Jan. 7, 1754, Catherine (bapt., Montreal, Aug. 7, 1740: married [2], Montreal, Sept. 11, 1770, William Grant), daughter of Joseph Fleury d'Eschembault and Catherine Véron de Grandménil: with Dieskau, July 1755: killed at the Great Carrying Place, Sept. 8, 1758

Le Moyne, Simon—Jesuit: born, 1604: novitiate, Rouen, Dec. 10, 1622: instructor, Collège de Rouen, 1627-1632 and 1636-1637: came to New France, 1638: Huron Mission, 1638-1649: Iroquois Mission, 1653-1658 and 1661: died, Cap de la Magdeleine, Nov. 24, 1665 ....

Le Pelletier, Catherine-Geneviève—Daughter of Jean-François-Xavier Le Pelletier and Geneviève Le Tendre: born, 1689: married, Montreal, Dec. 31, 1713, François Lefebvre Duplessis-Fabert: resident at St. Frederic, 1740

L'Epervanche (L'Evervanche), Charles-François de Mézières, sieur de—Ensign, officer, chevalier: son of Henri de Mézières and Marie Tracet: married, Detroit, Dec. 17, 1725, Marie-Louise-Suzanne (bapt., Montreal, Oct. 29, 1702: buried, Montreal, Dec. 26, 1782), daughter of Jean-Baptiste Nolan-Le Chevalier and Marie-Anne de la Marque

L'Epinart, Antoine—Traveler through the Champlain Valley, 1686 ....

Lerolle, Louis de Canchy, sieur de—Nephew of Marquis de Tracy: officer at Fort Ste. Anne, 1666: captured at the Chazy River by Iroquois, May 1666

Léry, Gaspard Chaussegros de—Engineer, pupil of Vauban: son of Gaspard Chaussegros de Léry and Anne de Vidal of Toulon: born, France, 1682: in New France, 1716: supervised the fortification of Quebec and Montreal: married, Quebec, Oct. 13, 1717, Marie-Renée (1697-1743), daughter of René Le Gardeur de Beauvais and Marie-Barbe de St.

Ours: chevalier de St. Louis: died, Quebec, Mar. 23, 1756

Léry, Gaspard-Joseph Chaussegros de—Sieur de Léry: military engineer: lieutenant in the marine: son of the preceding: bapt., Quebec, July 21, 1721: married, Quebec, Sept. 24, 1753, Louise-Madeleine (bapt., Quebec, July 13, 1738), daughter of François Martel de Brouague and Louise-Madeleine Mariauchau d'Esglis: leader of expedition against Forts William and Bull: emigrated, 1761: returned to Canada: "Grand Voyer" of the Province of Quebec, 1768: member of Legislative Council of Quebec, 1778: member of the Council of Lower Canada, 1792: chevalier de St. Louis: died, Dec. 11, 1797

Le Tendre, Geneviève—Daughter of Pierre Le Tendre-Laliberté and Charlotte Maurice: born, about 1668: married (1), Sorel, May 7, 1685, Jean-François-Xavier Le Pelletier (killed by the Iroquois, 1692): (2), Sorel, Dec. 9, 1693, Etienne Volant de Radisson: died, St. Frederic, Dec. 28, 1740

Levasseur, René-Nicolas—Naval constructor: sent to New France, 1739: born, 1707: Chief of Construction, 1749: inspector of Timber and Forests, 1752: visited Lake Champlain (Missisquoi, Saranac and Au-Sable Rivers), 1744 and 1745: naval engineer in chief, Charlesbourg, May 22, 1754: returned to France with M. de Vaudreuil, 1760: sold his property in New France, 1763: married, Marie-Angélique Just (born, 1712)

L'Evervanche—see L'Epervanche

Limoge (Limoges), Agathe—Daughter of Pierre Limoges (Arnaud-Joli-coeur) and Catherine Grenier: bapt., St. François, Isle Jésus, Nov. 12, 1712: married, Terrebonne, Nov. 25, 1744, Michel Pépin-Laforce

L'Invilliers, sieur de—Volunteer with expedition against the Iroquois,

Lorimier, Jeanne de—Daughter of Guillaume de Lorimier and Marguerite Chorel de St. Romain: bapt., Lachine, Sept. 10, 1702: married, about 1735, Joachim de Sacquespée: buried, Lachine, May 13, 1765

Lotbinière, René-Louis Chartier de—King's Councillor: lieutenant-general (civil and criminal): son of Louis-Théandre Chartier de Lotbinière and Marie-Elisabeth Damours: born, 1642: married (1), Quebec, Jan. 24, 1678, Marie-Madeleine (bapt., Quebec, May 11, 1662: buried, Quebec, Nov. 15, 1695), daughter of Eustache Lambert and Marie Laurence:

Ramezay, Claude de—Lieutenant, 1685: with Marquis de Denonville, 1686: at Quebec, 1690: governor of Three Rivers, June 1, 1690: commandant of the Royal troops in New France, May 28, 1699: chevalier de St. Louis, June, 1703: administrator of New France, 1714-1716: son of Timothée de Ramezay and Catherine Tribouillard of La Gesse, diocese of Langres: born, 1657: married, Quebec, Nov. 8, 1690, Marie-Charlotte (1668-1742), daughter of Pierre Denys de la Ronde and Catherine Le Neuf de la Poterie: seigneur de Monnoir, Mar. 25, 1708: buried, Montreal, Aug. 1, 1724

Ramezay, Marie-Françoise-Louise de—Daughter of the preceding: bapt., Montreal, July 8, 1705
Resche, Pierre-Baptiste—Recollect: chaplain at Fort St. Frederic, 1733-
Rigal, sieur—Naval officer with M. de la Bras (Delabarats), Aug.-Oct.
Rigaud, Philippe de—Marquis de Vaudreuil: governor of New France, 1704-1725: chevalier: commandant of the Royal troops: son of Jean-Louis de Rigaud and Marie de Castel-Verdun of Vaudreuil, diocese of St. Papoul: born, 1643: married, Quebec, Nov. 21, 1690, Louise-Elisabeth (born, 1675), daughter of Pierre Joybert de Marsan and Marie-Françoise Chartier de Lotbinière: buried, Quebec, Oct. 13, 1725
Rigaud, Pierre-François de—Marquis de Cavagnal-Vaudreuil: governor of New France, 1755-1763: son of the preceding: bapt., Quebec, Nov. 22, 1698: married, Quebec, May 2, 1733, Louise (born, 1713), daughter of Joseph de Fleury d'Eschembault and Claire Joliet d'Anticosti: chevalier de St. Louis: governor and major of Three Rivers, 1742: buried, Quebec, Nov. 16, 1793
Rigaud de Vaudreuil, Philippe-Arnaud de—Chevalier and marquis de Vaudreuil: brother of the preceding: bapt., Quebec, Feb. 9, 1705: married, Antoinette Colombel
Rigauville, Jean-Marie des Bergères, sieur de—Officer: son of Nicolas des Bergères de Bellechasse and Marie-Françoise Pachot: bapt., Berthier, Oct. 28, 1720: married, Lac des Deux Montagnes, Nov. 9, 1751, Louise-Suzanne (born, 1739), daughter of Louis-Jean-Baptiste Celoron de Blainville and Suzanne Piot de l'Angloiserie: officer at Detroit, Feb. 9, 1755

Note: In the collection of biographical data, I have largely used the invaluable "Dictionnaire Généalogique des Familles Canadiennes" by Cyprien Tanguay (Quebec, 7 volumes, Quebec, 1871-1890), the "Dictionary of Canadian Biography" (Toronto, 1926), and the manuscript "Register of Fort St. Frederic."

Other Champlain Valley Classics
Published by Purple Mountain Press

Sails and Steam in the Mountains: A Maritime and Military History of Lake George and Lake Champlain

by Russell P. Bellico

"Bellico fully traces the roles played by Lake George and Lake Champlain in the French and Indian War, the American Revolution, and the War of 1812, then moves beyond to the canal boats and steamships that plied them in more peaceful pursuits during the nineteenth and twentieth centuries." ----*American History*

"What makes Bellico's work stand out from the literature in the subject is his extensive use of original diaries and journals of the soldiers who fought the battles at the lakes. At points it achieves the narrative flow and high drama of the new hit movie *The Last of the Mohicans*." ----*Times Union*, Albany

"Attractively illustrated, handsomely printed and bound, this new history of maritime and military affairs on Lake Champlain and Lake George gives a thorough review of the exploration and early, crucially important military history of the Champlain Valley." ----*Sea History Magazine*

"Bellico's book meticulously traces the history of these two lakes. In all of this material Bellico presents much primary data as well as a complex synthesis of events. . .the volume also offers copious textual and citation footnotes and additional page-end comments. . .Exquisite photographs provide a counterpoint to the historical illustrations in the text." ----*American Neptune: A Quarterly Journal of Maritime History*

400 pages, over 200 illustrations, 7 x 10, paperback and hardcover

Chronicles of Lake George:
Journeys in War and Peace

by Russell P. Bellico

"In this anthology we hear firsthand reports of soldiers and travelers on Lake George during the past 250 years. Professor Bellico has scouted out vivid accounts from dozens of obscure sources. He introduces us to each of his travelers and carefully sets the stage for their journeys on this historic lake. Through the eyes of Bellico's witnesses, we watch the lake change, providing ever-new experiences for generation after generation of those drawn to its deep, clear waters." ----Nicholas Westbrook, Director, Fort Ticonderoga Museum

"*Chronicles of Lake George*, built around nineteen journals and publications of travelers, provides a stunning account of the lake. . .both useful to historians and fascinating to general readers. The central role of Lake George in both military and social history emerges in the words of eyewitnesses, and Bellico's extended introductions to each chronicle provide the best compact history of the lake to date. . . . This volume deserves wide readership." ----Robert Foulke, Professor Emeritus at Skidmore College, and Patricia Foulke, authors of *Colonial America*

"Drawn by the circumstance of history, enthralled by its breathtaking beauty, writers have long chronicled their travels in the Lake George region. By placing original accounts in historical context, Professor Bellico succeeds admirably in weaving the threads of the history of Lake George into a lucid and engaging whole." ----Charles E. Vandrei, Historic Preservation Officer, State of New York

415 pages, over 200 illustrations, 7 x 10, paperback and hardcover

Chronicles of Lake Champlain:
Journeys in War and Peace

by Russell P. Bellico

"Russ Bellico has been a student and teacher of the Lake Champlain-Lake George corridor for more than three decades. He loves the region, recognizes its contributions to our present-day society and is eager to share it with new generations. In *Chronicles of Lake Champlain*, Bellico evokes the voices of people who recorded their observations at various moments in time. Through the use of journalists' personal experiences, Bellico captures the texture of each period.

"These are exciting times for America and for the region. As the nation moves into the next millennium, where will it find the touchstones of its origin and character? Where can we locate a more accessible chronology of the evolution from the world of Native Americans, military contests, canals and commerce? The Lake Champlain chronology leads us to our recreational present and challenges us to be caretakers of the environmental and cultural legacy of this special place. What better laboratory for a new generation of citizens to gain a perspective on the interrelationship of history, archaeology, economics, art, and the environment?

"Russ Bellico's *Chronicles of Lake Champlain* combines the best of historical source material to bring this special place to the reader and visitor and, in so doing, reminds us why Lake Champlain is historically the nations first Great Lake." ----Arthur B. Cohn, Director, Lake Champlain Maritime Museum

415 pages, over 200 illustrations, 7 x 10, paperback and hardcover

Lake George Reflections:
Island History and Lore

by Frank Leonbruno

"The Lake George islands and all public lands in the Adirondack Park are protected as forever wild by the New York State constitution. But even wild lands require loving stewardship. Frank Leonbruno provided that for over four decades. He cared for our public property as though it were his own. His work enriched the lives of thousands of folk who learned to share his view that Lake George is one of the most beautiful bodies of water on earth." ----Peter A. A. Berle, Director and host of *The Environment Show* on National Public Radio; past president of the National Audubon Society

"This very interesting book will fill a niche that has not been extensively covered by other writers. By focusing on the islands, the author has a topic that should be of keen interest to Lake George enthusiasts, and because of his 42-year career as an islands ranger, Frank Leonbruno is in a unique position to record this story." ----Russell P. Bellico, Author of *Sails and Steam in the Mountains*, *Chronicles of Lake George*, and *Chronicles of Lake Champlain*

"When I am asked why my wife, Pat, and I work for Lake George through our involvement with the Lake George Association, the answer is easy: Frank Leonbruno's influence on all 'his kids' on the islands instilled a respect for and love of this place. Each chapter of his book is part of my childhood memories----memories that would have been different if Frank had not been there caring for the lake and for us. This is an important book for everyone who knows and loves Lake George and a wonderful introduction for all others." ----Dick Swire, Executive Vice President, Lake George Association

236 pages, illustrated, 6 x 9, paperback

History of Lake Champlain
1609-1814

by Peter S. Palmer

No inland body of water has played as decisive a role in the history of the Western Hemisphere as has Lake Champlain, and it holds a special position in American naval history as the birthplace of the United States Navy. Within a short span of 65 years three wars were fought on its shores and waters, each leaving an indelible mark on the destiny of North America: the French and Indian War, which decided whether the continent was to be ruled by the French or the English; the War for American Independence, which settled the question of British or American dominion; and the War of 1812, the last gasp in the struggle between the British and the the Americans—decided once and for all in the Battle of Plattsburgh. It was the last battle fought between fleets of English-speaking nations and by some historians termed crucial to the fate of the Union.

The author has concentrated largely on the military events of those three wars and chronicled them with such detail that his book has been a resource for students of Lake Champlain history for more than one hundred years. This paperback edition is reprinted from the fourth edition to which thirty illustrations and maps were added or improved.

Peter S. Palmer (1814-1890) was one of Plattsburgh's most prominent citizens in the nineteenth century. He was an attorney and a judge and held almost every possible civic position in his community. Besides this pioneer *History of Lake Champlain* he published a history of Plattsburgh, the memoirs of Peter Sailly, and numerous articles on Lake Champlain and Adirondack history.

250 pages, illustrated, 5.5 x 8.5, paperback

Purple Mountain Press, Ltd., founded in 1973, is a publishing company committed to producing the best original books of regional interest as well as bringing back into print significant older works. For a free catalog of hard-to-find books about New York State, write Purple Mountain Press, Ltd., P.O. Box E3, Fleischmanns, NY 12430-0378; or call 914-254-4062; or fax 914-254-4476; or e-mail Purple@catskill.net.

http://www.catskill.net/purple